THE PLAYWRIGHT AT WORK

THE PLAYWRIGHT AT WORK

CONVERSATIONS

Rosemarie Tichler
and Barry Jay Kaplan

NORTHWESTERN UNIVERSITY PRESS
EVANSTON, ILLINOIS

Northwestern University Press
www.nupress.northwestern.edu

Printed in the United States of America

10 9 8 7 6 5 4 3 2 1

LIBRARY OF CONGRESS CATALOGING-IN-PUBLICATION DATA

The playwright at work : conversations / Rosemarie Tichler and Barry Jay Kaplan.
    p. cm.
    ISBN 978-0-8101-2762-3 (pbk. : alk. paper)
    1. Dramatists, American—20th century—Interviews. 2. American drama—20th
century—History and criticism. 3. Playwriting. I. Tichler, Rosemarie, 1939– II. Kaplan,
Barry Jay.
    PS350.P57 2002
    812.5409—dc23

                                        2011043118

For Ellen and Theo, always.—RT

For Ron, for everything.—BJK

CONTENTS

FOREWORD

Marcia Gay Harden

In the beginning, there was the word. Enter: The playwright.

Playwrights *are* a kind of god . . . creating a universe with their words. The idea that the word *already* existed perhaps indicates that we have an innate need to give voice to the reality that is unique to each of us. Words that existed before there were words? What does this mean? Could this be likened to the blank sheet of white paper waiting patiently before the playwright? The blank computer screen humming, waiting, for words and ideas which already exist in the playwright's mind but aren't yet released as characters, as form and structure.

As Thornton Wilder writes in *The Skin of Our Teeth,* "Just like the hours and stars go by over our heads at night, in the same way the ideas and thoughts of the great men are in the air around us all the time and they're working on us, even when we don't know it."

And again from Thornton Wilder, in *Our Town:* "Everybody knows in their bones that *something* is eternal, and that something has to do with human beings . . . There's something way down deep that's eternal about every human being."

Words . . . just syllables and consonants and vowels. Words put together with pauses, and rhythm, making a kind of music. Words with emotion, words carrying thoughts, words with intention, words that fall on the ears of an audience, words in the mouths of characters, well-crafted words shaped into a play that can magically illuminate the human condition and invite a spiritual connection to the unique universe in which we celebrate life.

But . . . what words? How do playwrights choose their story, plot, characters, and words?

I have no idea how Tony Kushner could come up with a six-hour play about AIDS in the Reagan era and make it a comedy called *Angels in America*. No idea where Shakespeare's *Romeo and Juliet* came from, and I still can't believe he let them die! Or Sam Shepard's *A Lie of the Mind* . . . how could he have written this sad and violent American family so truthfully? It's best to leave the lonely scribbling or the hurried regurgitation of a cataclysmic event or the budding and nurturing of a small idea—in other words, the painstaking process of writing a play—to the playwrights.

The inspiration and the passion to reveal a particular story actually *are* a magical mystery to me. A play will often begin its life beyond the page with a read-through, a gathering of actors invited by the playwright or theater to sit around a coffee- and bagel-laden table and read the play in an emotionally connected way. This may be the first time the writer has actually heard the play. It is an invaluable tool, as what is on the page can be quite different than what is on the lips. The small audience gives feedback to the writer, and then both playwright and play disappear. The actors typically stay until the bagels and cream cheese are gone.

In the blank halls of rehearsal spaces, I have been blessed to participate (as a tiny spoke on the playwright's wheel) in the exciting process of bringing to life what has not yet been voiced. In this moment the playwright becomes a sort of mad scientist in the lab, throwing sentences out, rearranging scenes, furiously discussing with the director how to actor-proof the play, and listening, always listening, for the music of the words. It is a raw period in the development of a play. Each writer works differently, but the commonality I have witnessed, as the new material shudders in its insecure birth, is the playwright's great love of words. And not just the word itself, but the sounds of words, the way a particular word shapes your mouth, the way the vowel rolls through the air, the way a consonant can vibrate your lips. Like the word "love." If you hit the *v*, your bottom lip tingles. Try it: linger on the *v*, your lip will tingle. Tony Kushner once told me to make sure I hit the *z* sound in the word "lies." He pointed out that it would resonate to the back row, and the audience would cry. Astonishing. They did.

Words carry vibration. This vibration, the energy of the actor carried on the resonance of sound, physically enters the body of an audience member—evoking a gamut of emotion, from hilarity to great sadness.

The playwright knows the power of stop plosives like *k*'s and *t*'s and *p*'s, the snakelike possibilities of an *s*. These sounds can be used to machine-gun a thought to another character; they are very effective in an attack; they can be wonderful seducers. An actor is grateful for these gifts from the writer; they are clues, they absolutely support the emotional playing of a scene. Christopher Hampton translated Yasmina Reza's *God of Carnage* for its Broadway run. In Alan's final scene, when he berates Veronica, Christopher chose the word "category" over "group" for the line, "You're part of the same category of woman . . ." Thus Jeff Daniels, playing Alan, was able to fairly spit out the words "category . . . committed . . . custodians," hitting the *k* sounds hard, using the words as pellets. The playwright delights in the juxtaposition of opposing words to create an illusory image; the title of John Guare's *The House of Blue Leaves* and Nilo Cruz's title *Dancing on Her Knees* are both evocative images describing impossible situations.

The playwright recognizes the need for specificity of words. Again in *God of Carnage*, there was a huge discussion with Christopher Hampton as we tried to translate Yasmina's original French word "toilette" to the American "toilet"—or "loo" in the British version. For an American, whether a character says "bathroom," "toilet," or "restroom" may reveal quite a bit! Hampton had to make these choices in his translation. By using specificity of accent, dialect, psychology, and worldview, the writer ensures that the characters are individuals rather than homogeneous archetypes. After all, no two of us are identical, but each is linked to the eternal by our place in the aching, triumphant gene pool of humanity.

During the rehearsal of the play itself, the playwright sits with a notepad, often not actually watching the scene, but with eyes closed and head cocked, just listening—scribbling sometimes (the sound of which has made me freeze many a time) but with an ever-ready ear, twitching, to hear the rhythm and beats of a scene. To hear, for instance, when there are too many words. The need to edit can send even the most seasoned playwright into a paralytic night at the computer. They are forced to amputate certain parts—of themselves!—so that the whole of the *play* works more efficiently. Sometimes, there are not *enough* words. This is the moment when many actors assume that they are in fact playwrights and will often write a monologue or scene to fill this void, only to experience great relief the next morning when the playwright brings in just the right missing moment, in beautifully crafted words, and removes the egg from the actor's face.

Sometimes the playwright can only hear when the rhythm is off but can't articulate how to make it work. Sam Shepard directed his play *Simpatico* at the Public Theater. During the first three weeks of a four-week rehearsal, I couldn't figure out my character—where she came from, what she was about, how did she talk? Sam kept asking, "How does it feel?" and I would rejoin, "Feelings are arbitrary . . . *Who* is she?" He wanted me to discover it; I am not sure he knew himself! Finally, as I was about to slit my wrists, a friend saved me by noting that the character was quite indiscreet and sounded like a chatty Kathy. Aha! The Midwest! Yes! The next day in rehearsal, Sam simply said, "Yes. Now you are in the groove." He is a drummer and heard the rhythm of sound and character meeting. His ears heard the flow, just as one hears the syncopated rhythm in a drummer's riff.

OK, so yes, in the beginning there was indeed "the word," and it is *just* this desire to communicate, this need to relate to those around us, that is perhaps that "something" way down deep and eternal about every human being. Alas, all this, and still no inkling as to what moves the playwright! For that bit of sleuth work, Rosemarie Tichler and Barry Jay Kaplan have combined their esteemed talents in a series of conversations with thirteen playwrights. Here you will learn firsthand about the plays that influenced some of our great writers; you will discover the moments of inspiration when the blank white sheet begins to fill with reams and reams of words. You will delight in the idiosyncrasies of process. You will share the despair of a bad review and will identify with the struggle of creation. Above all, you will begin your own personal relationship with the people, the words, and the ideas that are shaping our modern American theater.

PREFACE

These conversations with major writers for the theater cover the art and craft of playwriting, the uses of training, the pitfalls of development, the rehearsal process, the working relationships between playwrights and actors, directors and designers, and the playwrights' paths to work and to success. The interviews reveal how these playwrights got their early work seen, to what extent they use their own biographies in their work, and how they managed to carve out personal lives, if indeed they have, at the same time. What is unique about *The Playwright at Work* is that its focus is playwriting itself, as an art form, as a means of personal expression, and as a commercial venture. It is meant to stimulate, intrigue, and inspire, to take joy in the process and revel in the act of creation itself.

The challenge in writing this book was to select the playwrights. Our choices are not comprehensive or definitive. We greatly enjoy and value the work of everyone we've chosen.

The pleasure in these interviews—for us and for the reader—is that by definition playwrights understand language and the effect language has on the listener. Their answers in these conversations are apt to be shaped into a performance of some sort and that is a truth of another sort. Haven't their plays already told us everything? Why, after all, should they tell us anything more? Why, in fact, should they tell us anything at all about their process? How much of what they do is even known to them?

We asked them the questions we did so we could find out.

ACKNOWLEDGMENTS

We want to thank our agent, Emily Forland, and our editor, Mike Levine, for their help in bringing *The Playwright at Work* into being. This book, of course, would not exist without the participation of thirteen extraordinary playwrights. We want especially to thank each of them for their generosity, their patience, and their willingness to answer our questions and share their hard-won wisdom about the elusive art of playwriting. We are most grateful to the people who transcribed the interviews: Iris Chung, Jeremy Kamps, Chelsey Lora, Ricardo Perez-Gonzalez, A. Zell Williams, and Cate Yu.

THE PLAYWRIGHT AT WORK

JOHN GUARE

We bump into John Guare outside his apartment building as he is bringing in bags of groceries. He ushers us into the lobby, where he jokes with a very old man holding onto a wheelchair who, in his youth, John tells us later, took photos of a nude Tennessee Williams on the beach in Provincetown. John's apartment is maze-like, rooms leading into rooms leading past mirrored hallways, so that without him as a guide, we're not quite sure where we are. Books are everywhere, on floor-to-ceiling shelves, stacked on the floor and on tables. We follow John's voice, stepping over a pair of scampering plump black pugs, and gather around a dining room table in a room painted deep bloodred. John has spiky white hair and an air of loose-limbed affability. He is wearing jeans and a pale blue shirt. He is very tall. During our talk he jumps up from the table several times to read to us from one of his plays or to show us some treasured photos, of himself and the equally tall Arthur Miller flanking a very short Harold Pinter, another of him whitewater rafting in Alaska with Tony Kushner and Wallace Shawn. In contrast to his characters, who often seem to be speaking in a stream-of-consciousness style, John is a man of carefully considered words.

When you started, did you know you wanted to write plays?

Yes.

How did that come to you?

Because I saw plays as a kid and also I had two granduncles who toured from 1880 to 1917 in a dozen plays, twelve to sixteen plays. I have copies of them. They toured with their rep company, and that was part of the family lore. And so I knew that there were plays. My mother always wanted to go in. They wouldn't let her. And there was this touring rep company that did plays. Toured around the country. So I knew what a play was.

When did it become clear to you that someone wrote the words being said onstage?

I had seen the scripts of my granduncles' plays, and I think I have one of them here, and I had assumed, wrongly, it turns out, that they had written them. What they had were just the sides. They saw the play then bought the plays outright. And there were plays like *The Old Tall House* which began with the old man played by my granduncle, pacing up and down: "Here it is, twenty-five years ago this very night my son left taking the money he did not know was rightfully his. Oh, that I could see him again. Oh, thunder, lightning. Knock knock knock. Who can it be?" You know. So they were real melodrama. See, I knew about *these*. And I assumed they wrote them, but there's no author on any of them. And in those days you would buy—I learned later—you would buy a play outright. This was before the Dramatists Guild and one of the reasons the Dramatists Guild was formed.

You're from New York. Did your parents take you to the theater?

Yeah, for my birthdays and Christmas.

Were they theater lovers themselves?

Yeah.

So what did you see?

Annie Get Your Gun.

That was your first?

Sure.

With Ethel Merman?

Sure. I mean at the time, everybody had seen either Artaud or *Annie Get Your Gun*. I saw that. I saw *Where's Charley?* And *Gentlemen Prefer Blondes* and *The Lamp*. I just saw lots of things.

Did you see Arthur Miller or—?

Ne-ver. I had to see musicals. I had a choice to see *Waiting for Godot*—I only had enough money for one ticket—and should I see *Waiting for Godot* or *The Most Happy Fella*? No choice. But there was going to be a talkback after *Waiting for Godot*, with Tennessee Williams. So I thought I could get the most bang for my buck if I could go see *The Most Happy Fella* and then run over and see Tennessee Williams talking about *Waiting for Godot* with Bert Lahr and all onstage.

What did he say about it?

He didn't understand one word. It was just, you know—didn't understand anything about it. I had read it and didn't know what it was about, so I was clearly seeing *The Most Happy Fella*, because I was just ignorant. You didn't know that it was the future. I mean, you knew it was the future, but it didn't seem to have any room for you in it the way *The Most Happy Fella* did.

So why didn't you write musicals, or did you?

I did! I wrote songs, I wrote musicals. When I was in college, I wrote a musical of *The Great Gatsby,* and some of the songs in that ended up in *House of Blue Leaves*. I loved musicals. I still do.

When you were growing up, there was Tennessee Williams, William Inge—

I worked for him. I was his assistant on his last play.

What was it called?

It was called *Family Things, Etc.,* and it opened on Broadway as *Where's Daddy?* It was a ghastly experience. Something horrible happened to him, and he took to his bed. I had to drive him to a television show with Elliot Norton, Boston's leading critic, who did a nightmare thing. He said, "I want to read my review of your play." And he just decimated the play. "You should've done this, or that." And Inge said, "Oh, very good, thank you," and left. He went back and got into bed and never got out of bed again as far as I could tell. I have a letter, years later, xeroxed, I keep it here, a letter from William Inge, a little bit before his suicide.

> *Dear Jean Kerr: I never read the* New Yorker *but I'll always read any letter signed by Jean Kerr. I'm afraid I cannot contribute to the New Dramatists. I am no longer part of the New York theater. The best help I can think of to give aspiring new dramatists would be to find them some other livelihood that would give them a feeling of respect and human dignity. So I am flattered to be thought of so prosperous to make a donation at anything. Yours very truly, William Inge. P.S. Isn't helping new dramatists a little like helping people into hell?*

And then he died.

Oh my God.

When I was across the street from where I still lived, there was a man who I revered because he just had a play on Broadway. I was a little kid. I knew Glenn had a play on Broadway. He expected to be a big hit, and it ran nine performances. He took to bed after the opening. He never got out of bed again, for all intents and purposes, for the rest of his life. I learned from Glenn, I knew somebody who had written a play. And the fact it was a play that Oscar Hammerstein produced before *Oklahoma!* and that a play could kill. I realized then a play could not be your whole life. I learned this at a very early age, ten . . . nine, that those things could end up killing you as well.

Landscape of the Body *was done in Chicago, and it did very well. When it came to New York. was it Richard Eder at the* Times *who killed it? I remembered saying to you or someone that people are going to be walking on that review in the rain—that the review is going to be stepped on. You came back the next night to talk to the cast. Your director didn't.*

He never directed a play again, rightfully so.

He was broken by it. He never came back. You went back to buoy the actors. So you did learn that. You learned you were hurt but you could go on. You were strong enough.

That's too meager. It's not about being hurt—it's about being killed.

So one person can do that?

What do you mean?

Well, I saw it. I loved it. The audience I was with loved it. So if an audience loves it and a critic—

But you're being naive. That's the rules of the game.

But it's worth commenting on because some people are destroyed by it. You've mentioned two. How is it . . . is it DNA . . . how do you get through it and not be destroyed by it?

Ask Arthur Miller. Ask Edward Albee. Ask Keith Reddin, who is one of my favorite playwrights who has never had that one lucky production . . . and he still keeps writing. He writes because he writes. He's a writer. Gerry Ragni, who wrote *Hair,* wrote a musical, *Dude,* which had a great song in it: "You Can't Make Me Hate Myself." It's just like that. You should interview someone like Keith Reddin. He's a spectacular writer, whose body of work is so amazing. Had two plays in the last eight years that were all the rage, and they both barely got reviewed because Keith had been around too long.

Did you feel, when you got some obviously bad reviews in your early years—

Or later—

—but in later years you were more armored—

You're never . . . you're never more armored.

Never?

There's no such thing as armored.

But you survive and keep writing. Well, some people don't. Maybe I'm call-ing it armor to define whatever it is that makes you know you're going to go on—you're going to get through it.

My only rule is, with the rehearsal of the play, I know I have another play waiting. I have a play in preparation. So the morning after the reviews come out, I have something to go to. Because if the reviews are good, which rarely happens, I won't be distracted by, "Wow, they're great." Or else if the reviews are horrible, I can go, "Well I'm on to the next. I'm already in the middle . . ."

Did you ever have an experience that wasn't like that, where everything was riding on that one play?

I'll tell you. The opening night of the original production of *House of Blue Leaves,* which we'd been trying to get up for a long time, I hadn't any-thing else. And then opening night, Steve Sondheim, who was not Steve Sondheim yet but a friend, sent me a telegram that said, "Have a wonder-ful opening. Your entire future depends on it." And he was right.

It opened and everything opened.

For a while.

So how do you write? Do you have a particular routine?

Sure, I get up in the morning and write.

You write in this room?

No, I write next door.

You get up and you go to your desk. And you stay there for a number of hours?

Yeah.

Do you know when to stop?

When I'm hungry. About one or two o'clock.

That's a ritual that you do every day.

Yeah. I mean, I'm writing a preface to an Arthur Miller play. So writing an essay is just a nightmare. So I have to finish that. So I've been working on that. I feel good because I have two new plays that are unproduced.

Two? Besides A Free Man of Color? *Another one?*

Yeah. So we're going to do that at Princeton.

The other one?

Yeah. I got a Ford Fellowship.

What's the name of it . . . can you tell? Oh. You don't know yet. OK. Uh. Do you show your work to people while you are writing it?

Uh-uh.

So you write until you think it's ready to go into rehearsal?

No, until I'm ready to let somebody see it.

When you go into rehearsal, do you think, "This is just pretty much it"?

No.

With Rich and Famous *and* Marco Polo Sings a Solo, *you were writing all the time they were in previews. Do you still do that? Were you rewriting based on audience reaction? Based on discussions with the director?*

It was that something wasn't landing. Whenever there's a problem, it's never where the problem is, it was five or ten pages beforehand that the problem is. So you listen to people. Or you look at it, mainly to say, I can make this better. And sometimes you go too far. I love to rewrite. I love to be in a room with actors. It's very exhilarating. There was one play where I said I'm not going to do any rewrites, I'm just going to trust the play, and I'm sorry I didn't.

What play? Oh. You don't want to say. Do you ever write for an actor or does an actor ever inspire you—?

Well, *Free Man of Color* I wrote for Jeffrey Wright. I wrote it especially for him.

That was part of a commission.

George Wolfe came to me, he said Jeffrey Wright is one of America's finest actors.

I agree.

He's so brilliantly trained and there are no roles for him. I want you to write him a part that will show off his ability to do style and language that he's never been given before.

That was the only time? Six Degrees of Separation: *did you write it for Stockard Channing?*

No. Stockard was last minute. Stockard was great. She knows where the laughs are. She's so wonderful to work for. In *Free Man of Color*—which we're going to do at Lincoln Center, hurrah!—I had a very clear conception of how the part should be played, and I saw actors at auditions and nobody could get it. And one day Daniel Swee brought in the polar opposite of what I'd written, and the actor was brilliant. David Pittu. I don't know what the future will bring, but I love being surprised by actors. They're just thrilling.

So the way he did it changed your conception of the role?

I'd seen the character as very dithery and out of breath and overweight. And David came in and he is like an arrow. It was just a new way to do the part. Thrilling. It didn't change the writing of the part. I saw that I got the reactions that I wanted in a different way.

When you see different productions of, say, Bosoms and Neglect, *with two different casts, do you think, "Oh, that's it. And the other one isn't as it"?*

Sometimes you see a bad production. You don't judge anybody. You know. Sometimes you're lucky to see two different productions. You have a platonic idea in your head.

What about your directors? What do you like most in a director? What do you value?

I once asked Lanford Wilson how he chose a director, and he said very simply, "I give them a copy of my play, and when we meet I ask them to tell me the story of my play. And if the story that they tell me vaguely jibes with my intention of it, I know that we at least perhaps could be working together." I just came off a great experience with George Wolfe. I'll tell you something, I like the director who has that rarest of gifts, a narrative sense. Most directors work moment to moment with actors and it's all about moment to moment and they don't understand the narrative line of a play and how to hold that narrative in their heads. A director like George Wolfe, who has also been a playwright, has probably one of the most finely tuned senses of narrative, of what's happening in the play at that moment. He knows what that scene has to accomplish. You can't find the truth of a moment if you put it onstage and it's not at the right tempo or it's not at the right code.

That's great. I've never thought of that. And it's great for your work.

Well, no, it's not for my work. It's for any work. And that's what makes Verdi a great composer. His dramatic sense. What makes Puccini great. What makes Meryl Streep a great actor is that she has an unerring narrative sense of where she is in the text at that moment. And most actors and directors work just moment to moment.

They're used to working or are trained to work in kitchen sink plays, where you can work moment to moment.

But you have to know where you are in that kitchen sink narrative—

I think it's less necessary.

It's one of the evils of the Actors Studio that it gets to be a series of moments rather than seeing how those moments fit into a whole. In acting schools, you're doing scene work and no sense of story work, or what your purpose is in the role at that moment. I once read in a book about Actors Studio—it was the best acting thing I've ever read. It was by Shelley Winters, and they asked Shelley how she prepared her roles, and she said—I'm paraphrasing—"I see why I am needed to tell the story, I see what the story is, and then what I am needed in the telling of the story and how I must tell my part of the story."

That's unusual.

Yeah.

Estelle Parsons talked about this too—when she worked with Arthur Penn, this was the way he worked, each actor was part of the story, and for the first time she saw how she could be singular onstage and part of the story.

But they only worked together in a movie.

No, they worked before that in The Skin of Our Teeth *in the Berkshires. That's how they met.*

I see.

Do you talk to actors during the rehearsal?

Sure.

Your directors don't want you to filter your comments through them?

It's not a healthy rehearsal. I mean, it's like in movie directing, Louis Malle said the confident director wants the writer there all the time. Everybody gets excited. But certain times, you realize you can't countermand the director, it's a simple thing of etiquette. But sure, you have to talk to an actor. Sometimes a director will have given an actor a note and then the actor isn't taking it and you have to go back and remind the actor what he was told to do and is not doing.

I think the directors—not all of them—have taken over the process. It's crazy. The director has more control than the playwrights.

There are playwriting schools that shall be unnamed where they are told that the director will supply the meaning of the play. Well, that's OK for some people, but that's not my kind of theater.

Have you directed your work?

No, I'm not a director.

You've never been dissatisfied with the way things are going and thought, "I can do this."

No, because I don't have the patience to be a director. I directed a one-act play at Lincoln Center one time, and I don't have the patience because one actor might have got there already, and then this actress, oy oy oy, I have to work to get her up, but then I lose the first actor, he loses his performance, and I'm keeping all the plates spinning: I don't have the patience. And also I see playwright-directors working too slowly. I think you need the tension of two metronomes going.

Do you deal with the other personnel in the process, like designers . . . ?

Absolutely. It's im-per-ative. Your play can be made or broken by the set that they're in or what they're wearing.

Are you present when the director meets with the designers?

I hope, I try. Yeah. Why wouldn't you want to be there? The Dramatists Guild exists to say that everything that happens on that stage is playwriting. The playwright has the right to be involved. Nothing that is put on that stage is without the playwright's input. The playwright can forgo that right, but I really believe in . . . I love the joy in working with Tony Walton on the set of *Blue Leaves* or *Six Degrees*—it was a great experience. I love working with designers.

Your stage directions are very evocative.

I try to have no stage directions.

Well, I just read Blue Leaves, *and it seems to tell me what it would look like. I mean, I've read plays where it just says it's a living room.*

Let me read from the script: "The living room of a shabby apartment in Sunnyside, Queens. The room is filled with many lamps and pictures of movie stars and jungle animals . . . the bay window . . . the folding gate across the front . . . outside the window a fire escape . . . uh . . . it's late at night, the street light. The piano is covered with hundreds of pages of sheet music."

That's evocative.

But those are things that are important. They're not there to be evocative. They're there to tell that there are important things that the nuns are going to . . . the woman is going to try to jump out . . . it's important to know that the windows are barred and that the house is locked up. So that's important. It's not there to be evocative—it's to tell what is necessary. I mean Tennessee writes very evocatively, he's a poet. An evocative way to do it is, "The room is overshadowed by bars that give a feeling of imprisonment." My intention is to give information to the designer and to give basic information to the reader. To say what to look at. Tennessee is a poet, and so he loves to write beautiful stage directions, which are wonderful. But in the plays of the turn of the last century by George Bernard Shaw and Eugene O'Neill, the stage directions were very very detailed. I think even in *Strange Interlude*: "Anita leaves, her green eyes are aslant." But what they were doing, in that time in history in the culture, plays were read, so the playwright was encouraged for the published version to write novelistic stage directions that would aid the reader in imagining the play. But right now in my stage directions I only write what is necessary for the designer and actor to know.

Let's go back to writing. In terms of how you start.

It's different with every play.

Do you have a plot or an image or a character or a song in your head . . . ?

If I knew, I'd go back to that way every time.

Do the people in your life ever think rightly or wrongly that they're in your plays?

Well, I remember in *House of Blue Leaves,* my mother, who was blind, couldn't see the play, so I taped the play for her to listen to, and she said, "Oh, that actor! Oh, he's wonderful! That's Eddie! That's Eddie! That's Eddie!" And for the part that was modeled on her, she said, "Oh, what a good actress!" More often, I've had the experience of people assuming that something was modeled on them and either being angry or happy about that. People want to be in your play.

In terms of writing a play, are some easier or . . .

Each play has its own hurdles. You look to write to the part where you can gallop. That's what you're writing for—to make the place where you can get into the gallop, really feel that you can cut free.

Is there some point where you know where it's going? Or do you always know where it's going? Or do you sometimes know where it's going?

Everything's different.

At the point where you suddenly know where it's going, does that make you feel confident?

Yeah. Sure. That's what you write for. That's one of the highs. "Ah-ha!" When you find your footing.

Have you found, at some point, when you've entertained some sort of solid success, that it made you feel more confident when you wrote or more challenged or more scared?

Neither. It was just writing.

So you weren't affected by your success.

After *Two Gentlemen* opened in 1971, I was offered a lot of musicals. And it gave me the confidence, finally when it was over, when it opened in London, instead of coming back to do the musical I was offered—and a very prestigious one—instead, I went to Nantucket and started a theater. It gave me the confidence to surprise myself. To put myself in hot water. To put myself in a place where I didn't know where I'd be, because I had the luxury. For the first time in my life, I had some money and I had the confidence and the ability to say, "Oh, good, I don't have to worry. There are a lot of things I don't have to worry about . . . like staying alive, like eating." I had money in my pocket, and that gave me the confidence. I realized that I did not want the money from *Two Gentlemen* to give me a lifestyle that I would then have to do stuff I didn't want to do in order to support it. When I was having a play done at the Caffe Cino, my father came down. He saw my play down there once and he was shocked. Because at the end of the play, the actors and the playwright pass a hat among the audience, and my father was horrified that I was passing the hat. And he said, "I see how much you like working at this place. What I wish you would do is write a hit musical so you could make a lot of money and then you could come back to the Cino and you wouldn't have to pass the hat." And I went, "Oh, that's ridiculous." Then it was, when *Two Gentlemen* opened, and I suddenly had money, that it came back to me that it was my obligation to find my own Caffe Cino—which was now long since gone—and to go on and do what it was I wanted to do. So it's just writing. It's to keep that pleasure and anxiety going.

That was a great thing that your father said. Was that the kind of encouragement that you always got?

Yeah. He said, "Never get a job." He hated his life. He said, "I don't care what you do, just never get a job. Don't end up like me." So I didn't. They were very happy when they knew I was going to be a writer. They always encouraged it. When I was twelve years old they gave me a typewriter to write plays, which I used until I got my computer. They didn't understand it, but they never stood in the way of it.

Do you feel that your work is . . . apprehended, appreciated in the way that you think it should be? Do you feel people get it, your audiences?

All you want is enough energy to get on to do the next play. I don't care about that. If I write a play and at the end of the play I can't wait to write another one, then it's been a success and I mean that. That's about the past, the perception. All you want to get out of that is enough oxygen to move on to the next one. I've known people who've had successes. People, playwrights that you know, that have had successes and have been paralyzed by it. Successes that were applauded on every level, critically, commercially, and they were paralyzed. They couldn't work for many years, if ever. All I want to do is get on to the next play.

You have a wonderful career.

Let me see, fifty years ago, I was nineteen. I went to Georgetown and I saw this thing on a tree announcing the first Georgetown masque and ball playwriting contest. First annual, I think it said. They never had one before, and I felt like I was looking at my future. I wrote that play and I came in second because comedy always had to come in second and the serious play had to come first, but I've been writing plays since '57.

In terms of the New York theater scene, I guess it was '69.

'68.

The theater scene has changed since, but it always does. Is it easier now? I know it's never easy.

It's just that the rules keep changing all the time. People can think of any reason not to do a play at any time in history.

You've had a few homes, for a while. You had The Public as a home for a while.

As a home I had to leave. I never felt completely at home there.

And Lincoln Center?

It's wonderful. I mean I'm not dependent. I feel I have a home at Lincoln Center and the Signature. The Signature came along at a very important time in my life. I've written two or three plays expressly for them. I've had about five or six plays down there at Signature, which I love. So I felt that was a terrific home. There's a theater I loved out there in Chicago. Academy Festival Theatre. It was alive for a couple years. That's where *Landscape of the Body* was first done. And I felt very much at home there. *Two Gentlemen* allowed the Public to move into another gear. What I was most proud of was that the Beaumont had been given one last chance to come alive and *Blue Leaves* did it: that was thrilling. I feel a great inclusion in the life of Lincoln Center in the way I never did with the Public.

That was major. They were foundering and they could have closed.

Well, they needed space for parking. I liked working at the Public. I did *Rich and Famous* and *Marco Polo* and *Landscape of the Body*. And then I was going to do *Bosoms and Neglect* there, and I went in to Joe one day and Gregory Mosher asked me to come to Chicago. He was going to start a new theater; David Mamet and I were going to be the artistic directors. And it seemed to be so terrific. And I just could see the life at the Public. It's the opening week and mixed reviews and closing it and doing battle with Joe. And it seemed to be exciting to go to a new theater out at the Goodman and build something new. So I did that. I'm not sure if the new theater was going to start then, but I wanted to find out a new way of doing plays, so I met Gregory Mosher at the Goodman. I liked what they were doing, what his plans were for the future. So I left . . . I remember I went in to Joe and said I was taking the play away, and it was a horrible scene.

But then it was done at Lincoln Center. Was it done at the Goodman first?

It was done at the Goodman first and then Broadway. I liked working in Chicago. I felt that there was a time in the seventies where like a Chinese restaurant or Indian restaurant, the magic in the kitchen moves around: "Oh, forget Luck Village, go to Hunan Paradise." The energy just moves. It was thrilling being in Chicago because Steppenwolf was brand new, and they were doing things in a new way and so it was just fun to be part of that. I liked Chicago. I liked the tempo, I liked the tenor of the time out there. It reminded me of ten years before in off-off-Broadway, that things were beginning, that things were not starting to get institutionalized.

So you became an artistic director?

Gregory was going to run it. And then what happened is that in the middle of all this, Gregory was offered Lincoln Center and so left the Goodman. He brought back that impulse. The first play was David Mamet's, the second play was mine. He was trying to have that, you know, that popular theater, all seats for ten dollars. Popular prices. You felt that he was starting something brand new, which was what he was trying to do and keep something alive. In Chicago, a variation happened. And that was exciting.

And maybe that's also what is with Signature now.

The Signature was going to do an Arthur Miller season, and the Public—I think it was the Public—said they needed the space, and it was May or June and they were out on the street, no place to go, and somebody said there is a bodega on Forty-Second Street and Eleventh Avenue that I want you to see. They went into this bodega, and they decided they could make a theater out of this and it opened in September. I mean, they raised this money and built a theater out of this supermarket. And I love that seat-of-the-pants moment.

Do you still teach playwriting?

I do.

You started the program at Juilliard.

Terrence McNally and I did. I just did that a year. And then I stopped because I was working in other things. I only did it one year. And then I taught over at NYU sometimes, I taught at Harvard, but then I wasn't seriously teaching. About six or seven years ago, when James Bundy took over Yale, he asked me if I would teach a playwriting course, so I made up a course which I loved.

What's the course?

I don't like New Haven—I don't like to get involved in academia—so I said I would teach if they would come to me in New York. The course is to demystify New York, to demystify theater. So the students come to me at the Dramatists Guild from two to five. And then we have supper with somebody like Christopher Shinn or Steve Sondheim and then see a play and then meet the cast and playwright and director and producer after. So it goes from two to eleven. They take the 11:20 train back to New Haven. And it's an exhilarating plan.

How is it to go back and forth between your own writing and what you teach?

Oh, I love it because you can only teach the problems you're going through. There's no other way to teach playwriting. When you teach playwriting, all you can do is hope they have a voice that you can help locate. And selfishly, I use the class to work on problems that I'm going through. Narrative problems or character problems. Finding the curtain, what the curtain of the play is. How to begin the play. Exposition. Focus in on that to help me to work through something.

Do you use the plays they're working on as well?

Yeah. If I can find their problem. You have to examine what it is that they like and learn what it is that they can and can't say. You have all these words to say, "Oh, it's a piece of shit, don't bother, it makes me sick," but you have very few words to say, "I loved it." And what do we do when we love something? How do we make that part of us? It's imperative. How do we make that which we love a part of ourselves?

Are you also saying that they have more of a vocabulary for ways to be critical of something?

They have no vocabulary. You have to teach them not to write plays by David Mamet or Harold Pinter. They're talented so they write with recognizable voices, so you have to get them to write in their own voice. You have to give them the vocabulary. It's about developing a critical vocabulary. The kids at Yale have a level of confidence and daring that is picked up nowhere else. It's the life in New Haven. I think part of it is this paradise of Yale being in this hell of New Haven. The tension between the two is thrilling. When they come to New York in my class, they're being given this entrée. They learn that everyone is just working. You know, they saw *Impressionism* with Jeremy Irons, directed by Jack O'Brien, and it was awful, but to see Jack, to see what they liked, what went wrong. You learn success is just so generous. You say, "Wow." You learn more from something that didn't work, so we try to take things apart and ask, "Why didn't it work? How would you do it?"

This must be very different from what you did when you were a student at Yale.

Happily, John Gassner went away my second year. It was wonderful, he took a sabbatical. A man named Edwin Wilson came, who became a critic for the *Wall Street Journal,* came up and taught and all Ed did was say, "Well, you just have to see your work," and we all got productions and everything and it was just exhilarating. And he also pointed out what was good in your work and what he didn't like, what you could build something on. He would say, "This is where your play works. Right here. These four lines." For me he was brilliant. And then Gassner came back and said he was shocked that we were all having productions. He felt we weren't ready, but we were ready for it. It was all learning by doing. I found the playwriting classes at Yale very tedious, and I was the first one, I believe, to ask if I could take set design with Donald Oenslager, and costume design and lighting design. Because even though I couldn't do any of those things, I wanted to know how they worked. And I learned more about plays by the great designer Donald Oenslager—about how to set a play, how to read a play, and the production of a play.

You didn't do acting or directing?

Acting was always terrifying to me. No directing.

Why were the classes tedious?

John Gassner at that time said every play was basically Ibsen, and anything he liked, he said, "We'll see what you're doing . . ."—it's *The Zoo Story,* for example—"you may think it's avant-garde, but it's pure Ibsen." And maybe Ibsen was great, but it was the kind of playwriting that I try not to do now, which is that it was reduced to formula. Ibsen was well-made. Formulaic.

It has always seemed to me that you just broke down doors and buildings and worked in a way that made it possible for Chris Durang and for Harry Kondoleon.

Harry was one of my students. Yes, I loved Harry. I miss him very much. Well, I mean I've had a number of wonderful students but two memorable ones: Harry Kondoleon and Tarell McCraney. Tarell is someone who just came fully formed and to get *The Brothers Size* in your class is holy crap. You had to teach Tarell how to value himself because certain things came so easy for him he didn't appreciate how rare they were.

Did you have mentors—somebody who told you something like that? Or playwrights who changed your thinking?

Yes. I mean, every play I read. I would see plays all the time. I mean, yes. Edward Albee. Tennessee Williams. I mean, my mentors were the people who thrilled me. I remember hearing about this guy Harold Pinter. I went up to Boston to see the *The Caretaker*. I couldn't wait for it to come to New York. I was sitting in the last row of the second balcony. People were fleeing the theater. By the end of the play I was sitting in the front row of the orchestra. I mean, those were my mentors—I didn't know what I would learn. I saw *The Visit* with the Lunts, the Dürrenmatt play. I'd never seen anything like that. I knew I was seeing something. It was overwhelming. Those were my mentors. Plays have always been my mentors. Whether it's *The Visit* or *The Zoo Story*. A play by Anouilh, *Time Remembered,* I saw it fourteen times. And I just sneaked in, missed the first act, but I saw the second and third acts, and I saw it and it was just perfect. It was a play that had a full orchestra, which Vernon Duke had written a full score to, and the music played through the entire play. It was thrilling. I'd never seen anything like that. It was Richard Burton and Susan Strasberg. And I learned a lesson at that play because Helen Hayes was out of this world. She was great. And I said, "Oh, she is a great actress. I see." Then the play went to Boston. It got OK reviews, and then it opened in New York. The play got so-so reviews, but Helen Hayes got magnificent reviews so I went back to see it again. And the play was just flat. Helen Hayes was unbearably awful.

What happened?

The audience loved her. I read an interview with her, and they asked her, "How are you giving this great performance in *Time Remembered*?" She said, "In Washington"—where I was when I saw it—"I have never been so terrified in my life, I didn't know what I was doing in this play and every night I went out on that stage in complete chaos and fear. And it wasn't until I got to Boston, saying how I am going to get to continue in this play, that I was in my dressing room not knowing how I was going to get a performance and I had the radio on and they played a Bach fugue on a harpsichord and I said 'Oh, that's my performance.'" And I saw that she had drained all the life out of it. I saw the value of what I was appreciating on that stage was her terror and her chaos. And that was a mentoring. So you say, OK, how do you get an actor onstage to convey that terror, that life and exhilaration, onstage? And I saw actors like Ron Leibman and Linda Lavin who had that desire to get lost onstage.

But that's wonderful because that's your writing too. And underneath the wildness and humor is terror. And actors can go inside that.

So I guess I'm grateful to Helen Hayes.

You have Helen Hayes to thank.

In England they say "Helenaise. That's what American actors put on ham."

What do you do the night a play opens? Where are you?

The theater. Where else would I be?

Where in the theater?

The back. Just checking on it. Hovering around. Sometimes you're in the theater and you can't get in, they don't have any back room. Sit in the last row. I want to know the performances that they're reviewing, and I want to see the performances that my friends are seeing.

I just wanted to ask about Landscape of the Body. *What were the hurdles in that play and how did you deal with them?*

It was so mysterious a play. I wrote it . . . it was just . . . I have to think . . . It was one of those rare times that the hurdles were casting, finding the right people for it. It seemed to be an easy play, although I did not solve the first act curtain until we did it at Signature. I realized I never wrote the first act curtain. And I realized it when we were in rehearsal. When we did it at Williamstown, I said, "The scene that opens the second act is the first act curtain scene." And so I moved that. The boys sing and in the text it ends. It ended too abruptly, this first act. So that was a hurdle that took me thirty years to solve, finding the right first act curtain. The hurdle in that play is always casting, finding the people who can play the music of the scene. Now here's an example. When we did that play, Jonathan Fried, an actor I like very much personally, wanted to play this role of Durwood Peach, my Good Humor man, and I'd always seen the man as being a very handsome Southern gentleman who just might be a good bet for her to run away with. Why wouldn't she? And I had seen the play and cast it like that. You know: Rex Robbins. I was seeing really stately people playing the part and then it was revealed he was crazy. Well Jonathan Fried said he wanted to play it, so he did it up in Williamstown. And he played it in an entirely different way that was absolutely right. His need was terrifying from the beginning. He came in covered with it, the costume emphasized his sweat. His need, his need was so naked that it scared me. And when she ran off with him you just went, "Oh my God, you just changed the stakes of the play." There's a case of an actor showing me something. So you just love actors. Actors are tubes of paint. So you think you may want cadmium yellow, but what you really want is ultramarine blue. Each actor is analogous to the tube of paint. But sometimes people will get too creative with it and ignore the basic intentions. The basic intentions, the parameters of the part. You just don't want to see something brand new for the hell of it. I've seen *Blue Leaves* where the actor playing Bananas will be so psychotic, you just say, "Put her away, lock her up, she's not playing the truth of it." You're playing a different truth, you're playing a naturalistic truth, you're not playing the truth of the play.

Are there particular actors who have tuned in to your writing?

Stockard and Swoosie Kurtz. Ron Leibman. People all through my life. I've been blessed with actors at a certain time . . . Kate Reid in *Bosoms and Neglect*. Sigourney Weaver was exhilarating. An actor like Bruce Norris who has now turned into a wonderful playwright . . . he's one of those ac-

tors I put in that category. Anne Meara. I was really grateful to Katherine
Helmond because we couldn't have cast that part in *Blue Leaves* without
her. I've been blessed also in my plays with actors like Sherie Rene Scott.
Or Beth Marvel. We just did a reading of *Blue Leaves* with Beth Marvel,
Sherie Rene Scott, and Paul Giamatti that was perfection. Whether that
will ever happen, I have no idea. We did a reading of *His Girl Friday,* an
adaptation I did at the National Theatre with Allison Janney and Alfred
Molina that was heartbreaking because it was perfect.

Are they going to do it?

No, because the Roundabout couldn't afford it and Alfred can't afford it.
You know, he's in five movies, an actor is working, same as Paul Giamatti.
But you see something and say, OK, well at least I know they're out there.
You asked before what response do you want. You want to know there are
actors out there. If I could never find anybody who could do my plays,
I'd say something's wrong. But I've also had actors who can know how to
take your work and ruuuuuuun with it. Have that sense of the speed. John
Mahoney. That revival cast with Chris Walken was staggering. And Ben
Stiller. I knew Ben Stiller. He had never acted before. I knew Ben Stiller
offstage because of my friendship with Anne Meara. And I called up
Anne, and she said, "Yes, have him come down and audition." He didn't
even have an Equity card. He came down and auditioned.

That was the first thing he ever did.

He was perfect. That's what you look for. That why I always liked working with you as a casting director, Rosemarie, because you understood
the needs, you listened to the text. That's what made you a great casting director. You listened *to* the text and always brought in challenging
choices. You understood.

*Did you write in one play that line that I always attribute to you but have
never seen, that "the terrible thing about life is that anything can happen"?*

Yes. It's in a play . . . it was originally called *Gardenia.* I rewrote the play
when we did it at Signature because there was something in the play I

never liked when we did it at Manhattan Theater Club. I could never find the title of the play, and I realized that I had been too cautious with the people at the end of the first act. The name of the play is now *Bullfinch's Mythology.* And so I changed what they do up in their island retreat. In the rewrite they're involved in how to change people's lives. Lydie says when she goes to visit her husband in prison that the terrible thing in life is that anything can happen. So you can attribute it to me.

I knew it was you. I just didn't know where in what play.

One thing you can talk about is the element of luck that takes place in anybody's career, and I've had some very key good luck, like the way we lost a certain actor in *Six Degrees* for reasons that are completely unknown to me and we were going to close the play and then luckily—for me—Neil Simon pulled the plug on a play Stockard was in and she was suddenly available. And she came in and opened with ten days' rehearsal. So you never know. I mean, the gods! The element of luck in anybody's career is awe-inspiring and humbling.

DAVID HENRY HWANG

We meet David Henry Hwang in the glass-enclosed conference room at the Public Theater—a fitting place since he had his first New York success just downstairs in the Shiva space with his play *FOB*. Shrugging off his down jacket, and wearing black jeans, boots, and a loose-fitting shirt, David is one of those people who seems to age in place: he hardly looks older than when he was a twenty-three-year-old who created a sensation in the New York theater with an insider's look at the Chinese American experience; only a few stray gray hairs give any sign of the middle-aged man he is. He's exactly on time and is patient with us as we set up our tape recorder—later too when we have to change batteries—and seems to relax when we explain how we're going to structure our questions; David admits to liking to see the destination as he begins a ride. As soon as he knows that the interview is going to proceed in a certain way, with a particular end in sight, he plunges right ahead, full of stories, self-deprecatory but not falsely modest, and extremely open about his methods. He doesn't like to teach, he tells us, because he feels that all he knows would be summed up in one class. If that's so, what a class that would be.

How did you come to write plays?

I started writing plays as an undergrad in college. I got to Stanford and I remember that in freshman year they had you fill out a form that said, "What do you want to do that you haven't done before?" And I remember writing "journalism and playwriting." At some point in my freshman year we went up to see shows at ACT. They would bus up the whole dorm. I think I saw *The Matchmaker* and Bill Ball's production of *The Winter's Tale*. And I started thinking, "Oh, I think I can do that," so I started writing plays in my spare time. There was a professor at Stanford named John L'Heureux. I was taking an introductory drama class from him and I wrote a play. I think it was something about God and death and a musician or something like that. I showed it to him, and he said it was bad, which it was. My problem was that I wanted to write plays, but I didn't actually know anything about the theater, so John then kind of became my independent study advisor. The first thing he had me read was *The Tooth of Crime*. Then I started reading a lot of plays and seeing as many plays as I could. And eventually we found a way to structure that into a playwriting major at Stanford in the creative writing department, because they didn't have a playwriting program and they still don't. Then, before the summer of my senior year in college, I was home in LA and I saw an ad in the *LA Times* that said, "Study Playwriting with Sam Shepard," so I thought, "Well, that's good." It was the first year of what eventually became known as The Padua Playwrights Festival, which for many subsequent years was a big event in Southern California. But this was the first year that they ever tried to do it. There were only two people that applied to be students, so we both got in. What happened to the other guy I don't know. I bumped into him in the theater district once but I don't think he's a playwright. Before I went there I kind of thought the way that you wrote a play was essentially like the way I write a movie now. You structure a bunch of scenes and then you execute them. Sam and Maria Irene Fornes and Murray Mednick, who founded the festival, began to teach us to write more from our unconscious. There were writing exercises, and as I did them, I found that a lot of the stuff that I ended up writing about started coming out and appearing on the page. I didn't know I was going to write about East/West stuff or Asian American stuff. I just wanted to be a playwright. But when this stuff started coming out, I realized, "Oh, some part of me is very interested in this and my conscious mind hasn't figured that out yet." And so from that, I began writing a play, went back to school, finished it, and decided to stage it in my dorm. That was *FOB*. And then . . . you know some of the ends of that story.

So this writing from your unconscious was the way you found your subject?

I think that was the way I found my voice and the way I found my subject, yeah. I think it's Irene's exercise that I now do in workshops. You
start writing a two-character scene. You go on for around twenty minutes, then everybody stops and you draw a line across the page. Then you
continue writing that same scene, but whoever is leading the workshop
starts throwing out random words or phrases. It's your job to incorporate
them into the dialogue and then you go on for another forty minutes.
And then everybody reads them. I've done this exercise over the years,
and I've found that most of the time the second half of the exercise is
more interesting than the first half. Because the second part, to some extent, recapitulates the process of when you're writing alone and some impulse comes into your head and you don't necessarily understand it but it
feels very strong. So even the kind of random impulses that are generated
by a teacher just saying a phrase turn out to make the work more alive
than when the writer is just kind of trying to do what he or she set out
to do.

*Were you then able to incorporate the way you first described how you plot
scenes?*

No. I think at that point I started realizing that I didn't want to structure
my plots too tightly when I was going into a first draft. *FOB* is kind of
special for me because it was the play that I wrote before I knew how to
write. So therefore there are some things in it that I don't really understand, but it has the kind of impulse and life to it that takes me back to
that time. It feels very special.

What did you write after that?

The summer after *FOB* got staged here at The Public, I went to the Bay
Area Playwrights Festival in San Francisco, and again Sam Shepard was
there. I started writing what became *Family Devotions* and got it done in
about three days. That took a while longer to get produced in New York.
The Dance and the Railroad, which was the second play to be produced
in New York, was actually a commission from the U.S. Department of

Education back in the days when they still commissioned plays. It was done through Henry Street Theater. They commissioned four ethnicities or something and everybody was supposed to write a children's play so they could bus in school kids. I had met John Lone and Tzi Ma on *FOB* and so I wrote *The Dance and the Railroad* for them. We did it for kids in the afternoons. In the last performance, Frank Rich came and gave it a very nice review in the *Times.* And then Joe Papp brought it here to the Public.

What's your writer's day like? Do you wake up and go right to your desk?

My process has changed over the years. I used to write as much as possible around sleep. So I would have a pad next to my bed and I'd write as I was falling asleep. Then I'd wake up in the morning, grab my pad and I'd write some more. I was trying to get as close as possible to the unconscious dream state. I think I've had some of my best ideas in the morning. Now they tend to be in the shower. So nowadays, I get the kids off to school, make breakfast, lunches, and at ten I go down to my little office. I've always worked at home. I write from ten to one-ish. Today I knocked off at 12:30 to get here at 1:30. The afternoon is for lunches and emails and that sort of thing.

Is it dark in your office?

Not particularly.

Do you look out the window?

No, as a matter of fact. We actually just moved. We bought a brownstone in Fort Greene so my office, which we still have to really build, is what they call the garden level in the brownstone. My wife had covered up the windows for Halloween with little things with spiderwebs on them, and I just kept them up because I don't like people looking in on me as I'm writing. I like getting a little sun. I don't know what we're going to do eventually.

You say you write every day . . . is it taking notes, is it structuring the play, is it just observations . . . ?

It varies but the only thing that really feels like writing to me is when I'm actually writing the dialogue. Some days I do that, some days I'm just structuring a story or doing a treatment for something, particularly when I do work for hire or work on other people's vision, but it's not the same as actually writing. Actually writing feels to me to be the real work. When I'm writing the dialogue, I'm writing the script, I'm writing the actual script.

And that varies.

For the last fifteen or twenty years, it's really trying to fit in, find time to do my own work because I do a lot of work for other people—and I like the work for other people—but I think particularly when we were doing *Yellow Face,* I realized, "Oh I kind of made a mistake in that I let ten years pass without having really written an original full-length play." And so, happily, I do have a new play. So I've really tried to carve out time to get back to doing my own work.

You do have a new play? Is it all written?

It's mostly written. We've already had a reading, and Oskar Eustis showed up. And there have been conversations going on. So.

Is there a certain moment when you say, OK, I've written as far as I can at a desk, now I have to show it to somebody?

Generally, I like to go through the whole first draft by myself. In this particular case—in my new play, which is called *Chinglish*—it's bilingual, it's in English and Mandarin. It's about an American trying to make a potential business deal in a potential city in contemporary China, and I don't think you can represent that experience without really dealing with language. I've never seen a play or movie that deals with it. Nobody deals with language well.

You do an interesting thing in FOB *with language. There is a difference when the character is speaking Chinese and when he is speaking English.*

I've thought of different ways to do it. *FOB* does that. In *Golden Child*, the English could stand in for Chinese; therefore, the British pastor speaks broken English. They're all different devices, but I'd never used the actual other language. At any rate, this is the first time I'd ever done a reading of something before it was completely done. We did it two weeks ago. I'm still not finished. I was working on it this morning. I'm about three-quarters of the way through. The reason I had the reading is because Leigh Silverman, who will direct it, and I have been talking for two years about doing this play. She said, "Schedule the workshop. If you schedule the workshop, you're gonna have to finish it." In fact, I got most of it done by the workshop. She scheduled another workshop for January twenty seventh. I have to get the whole draft out by January twenty fifth.

So did she read it before the workshop?

Oh, she read it before the workshop.

Who do you usually choose to show it to? Or does it vary?

It varies, but I would say Oskar has been consistently someone I show work to. We met in '93. He directed a one-act play of mine called *Bondage* at Louisville, and at one point I just decided that a dramaturg is a very personal relationship and Oskar was the best dramaturg for me, so when he was at Trinity, I would always send him things. We didn't do much together at Trinity, but he was like my best dramaturg.

Do you hear something in a reading that helps you finish it or change it?

In this particular reading, there were a couple things. I need to move some scenes around, but basically what I learned is trying out this notion of doing things in two languages and having something projected and what's that going to feel like and the fact that essentially, as the audience, you're reading whenever there's Chinese. So where the subtitles break becomes very important in terms of a long speech. But basically the device works. You can still have humor, and that was very good. There's a play there, and it's not in bad shape for an unfinished first draft.

In the past, with other plays, when you decide that they're done, do you go into rehearsal knowing that they're going to be changed?

I always expect to rewrite. Some plays take more rewriting than others. *Yellow Face* got rewritten a lot from the first draft. Sometimes they come out of the oven pretty much done and sometimes they come out still needing to find their shape. But I always expect to do some rewriting. There's a way in which playwriting is like, say, novel writing, in that it involves words and plots and characters. But in a deeper way, playwriting is like writing music. In the case of music, it's really about how it sounds. The notes on the staff are not, in themselves, important. Similarly, the words on the page are not important. At least that's how I view playwriting. It's really about how it sounds. I don't feel like I know what I've got until I hear it.

So you would differentiate language from words.

Yes. I would differentiate the experience of an interaction between live people because it depends to some extent on the words and also on a lot of other things. And to me the stage experience is about the interaction of live people onstage with live people in the audience and words go a way toward determining that, but they don't determine everything.

What about choosing a director? What qualities do you look for?

That's the toughest choice, because it's such an important one. If the playwright and director essentially see the same play, then it really just comes down to an infinite number of individual decisions. But if you don't see the same play, you're screwed. It won't get worked out. And how do you know? Usually, the artistic director or somebody suggests a director, you go out to lunch, and if the director is charming and facile you might decide to take the plunge and get married. But it's really hard to know. Having said that, I think the best technique that I've seen or experienced in that first meeting, for deciding whether you're going to get married, was with John Dexter. The producer Stuart Ostrow had suggested him for *M. Butterfly,* and I was really excited because *M. Butterfly* was, in a larger sense, structured as a Peter Shaffer play. It has that Peter Shaffer structure that you see in *Equus* and *Amadeus.* It's the guy at the end of his life, who in the play comes forward, talks to the audience, says, "I don't understand what quite happened . . . I'm still trying to figure it out," and then the play goes back in time sequentially with the guy playing himself in the earlier scenes, in the past, in the flashbacks.

Did you know that so clearly when you wrote the play?

Yeah. All my plays are kind of worked up from other plays structurally. And then with *M. Butterfly* I sort of did my own twist. So John obviously did *Amadeus,* and so I was very excited about that. I met him at some hotel bar and he said how much he loved the play, which always helps. John actually didn't like to talk about things, which is weird for a director. He just likes to handle things. He has a horrible reputation, as you probably know, for being like a tyrant and a bully. So John suggested that we read the play to each other. He took half the parts and I took half the parts. And that was a very visceral kind of simple workmanlike way to determine if we both saw the same play. It was fast. We ended up reading it in his room. I read all the Asians and he read all the white people, and it felt good and we decided we were going to do it. With Leigh on *Yellow Face,* Oskar put Leigh and me together. We met in his office and we actually did not have such a great first meeting. I thought there were a lot of things about it she didn't understand. And then I went home and thought some more and I thought, "Oh, the things that she doesn't understand are the things that are not yet clear." So that made me think, "Oh, she's really smart." And we had a great experience and we're doing another one now.

Do actors influence you once you're in rehearsal?

Oh, yes. I mean, again, because the words are not per se the most important things. In a funny way, I tend to be pretty open to actors who ask, "Well, can I say it this way?" Actors tend to do better when they own things. And to the extent that it's not a major change . . . if they want to contract something or they want to change syntax, most of the times it doesn't make a big difference to me. I mean, they have to ask me, and I have to agree, but I'm kind of open to that sort of thing. And I've written plays for actors, *The Dance and the Railroad* being the clearest example of that. I mean I specifically wrote for John Lone and Tzi Ma and named the characters Lone and Ma.

What do you do in situations where the director or the actor is just not getting it?

I would say that my experience with *Face Value* and Jerry Zaks was not . . . We were not ideally matched, and that was purely my fault because Stuart Ostrow really wanted to hire another kind of director, a classic British director, Lindsay Anderson, who was sort of not hot at that moment.

Ah, he's great.

But I had just seen *Six Degrees of Separation,* and I really wanted Jerry. It just didn't turn out to be the right fit. Maybe the play wouldn't have worked anyway. It didn't end up working, but when it was clear that there were more problems, Jerry's instinct was to go more conventional and my instinct was to go . . . Oh well, you know, we just couldn't make it work.

You saw the crash coming and couldn't avert it.

We closed it in previews. I was sort of OK with that, and Stuart was not really OK with that. It was Scott Rudin's idea.

Do you talk to the actors? Some directors like playwrights to be quiet.

I believe that the proper etiquette is that I should talk to the director, and the director should talk to the actors. Having said that, there are some directors who are OK with you talking to the actors. Leigh is fine with me talking to the actors. I really try to respect the fact that she has the primary relationship with the actors. So I usually talk to Leigh. Particularly if I'm going to contradict her. I don't want to . . . this may be very Chinese of me . . . but I don't believe I'm supposed to make her lose face in front of the actors, particularly if I disagree with her. Then I need to talk with her directly.

Do you attend all the rehearsals?

Yes. I mean, I don't know that I attend *all* the rehearsals. Sometimes I'm rewriting. In general, I like to attend rehearsals. I don't like to direct, for a variety of reasons. I just don't like having to show up at the same time every day. If you direct, you have to. As the playwright, you can kind of float in when you feel like it, you can go, "I like that, I don't like that," then you can leave.

Do you have a lot of input in terms of the design?

Design is one of those areas, because I don't consider myself particularly visual, that I don't feel like I have that much to bring to the table. For instance, Eiko Ishioka's design for *M. Butterfly.* Anyone who's seen the original production remembers that ramp. And when I read the play, I didn't know it was going to be done on a unit set. I think I can create blueprint situations onstage that someone who is visual can do something really interesting with, but I can't see it myself.

So when you write the play, what are you seeing?

I'm hearing mostly. I have good ears but bad eyes.

But when you go to auditions, do you have a strong sense of the scene?

I think I have a pretty good sense of auditions. I kind of depend on the director to understand actors better than I do, but I feel like I should get a vote. For instance, with Francis Jue for *Yellow Face.* Leigh really pushed for Francis, and I felt Francis was too young, because Francis was in *M. Butterfly,* and I guess I still remembered him as a twenty-seven-year–old, and obviously Leigh turned out to be very right.

What about the response to your work?

I want the work to be well received. Of course. Do I read reviews? My etiquette toward that has changed over the years. Jodi Long once told me that Kevin Kline told her that if you read the good ones, you have to read the bad ones, and I thought, "Oh, that makes sense." And then I started thinking, why do I have to be so catholic about it? If you're two people who are my friends and I know that you don't like the play, I'm not necessarily going to go up to you and say, "Tell me why you hated the play." Nowadays, I like to know what the reviews are because I like to know how the show is going to do, but I tend to only read the good ones.

I think Kevin probably said that because if you're going to believe the good ones, you better believe the bad ones.

I don't necessarily believe any of them. I believe what I believe about the play, but it's nice if people say nice things. Sometimes I think the people who say nice things may be wrong about certain things, but that's OK.

Do you have an ideal audience? An ideal audience member?

I don't think so. I think that the primary audience member is me and then after that, I hope someone else will be interested in what I'm interested in, and I don't really care who that person is.

Have you found there is an audience that particularly responds to your work?

Throughout most of this decade, my work has generally gone down better on the West Coast than it has in New York. Part of it has to do with the fact that it seems like Ben Brantley and I don't see eye to eye. But in terms of *Flower Drum Song* being a huge hit out there and not doing as well here and even *Yellow Face* getting pretty universally well received out there and getting mixed reviews over here . . .

Flower Drum Song *did well where?*

Flower Drum Song was a huge success at the Taper. It was like their biggest hit ever. I think there were a lot of political things that came into it in New York—critics kind of feeling that they needed to comment on what they saw as some sort of politically correct agenda about me rewriting Oscar Hammerstein, and I think that all came into it.

It seems like there is a big arc in your career so far, from FOB *to* M. Butterfly *and another arc from* M. Butterfly *to* Yellow Face, *in terms of the themes of Chinese identity and pop culture starting with* FOB *and exploding with* M. Butterfly *into a much bigger sense of identity.*

I think that's fair to say. After I discovered I was interested in kind of being Asian American, it coincided with the birth of an Asian American cultural movement within the broader aspiration of multiculturalism. In 1980, when we did *FOB,* the term "Asian American" hadn't really made its way into the culture. Multiculturalism was still a relatively new notion, and there were all those culture wars and dead white men battles and great books and all those things that happened in the nineties. So I feel that first impulse of writing which was basically the first three plays we did here at the Public with *FOB, Family Devotions,* and *The Dance and the Railroad* came at a time when I felt like the answer to the riddle of identity had something to do with ethnicity and I guess what eventually came to be called identity politics. But then, toward the end of that period, I began to wonder if I was creating kind of Orientalia for the intelligentsia—that is, repackaging the older kind of Oriental approach that was kind of more satisfying to the *New York Times* or whatever. And so that was one of the reasons that I ended up writing the plays that became *Sound and Beauty,* which are the two plays set in Japan, because I wanted to start to expand a bit. I did *Rich Relations* at Second Stage which was the first time I wrote a play with non-Asian characters, which was kind of a legitimate thing to do. I kind of wrote an autobiographical play about my family and just made them all white, so it lacked a certain authenticity. However, the experience of doing *Rich Relations,* and starting to feel more comfortable working with non-Asian actors and things, made *M. Butterfly* possible. *Butterfly* was, I guess, an attempt to take some of the themes that I had explored as an Asian American and see how they worked on an international stage with an international story. And then, following the big success, there's certainly for me this question of where do you go from here, and I think *Face Value* actually represents a journey that culminates in *Yellow Face.* And of course *Yellow Face* refers to *Face Value,* so the play is somewhat aware of its origins. It's not that it goes back to the Asian American stuff but tries now to understand it in the context of the broader society. What does multiculturalism mean and what are the flaws in the method? What are the good things about the method? And I guess strives toward something we now call postracialism. I don't think we were using that term in 1993, when I wrote *Face Value*. The basic idea was its being a farce on mistaken racial identity. It was written as a Feydeauesque or Ortonesque farce with this idea that we put on faces and we play our ethnic role, which is something that eventually ends up in *Yellow Face* being a farce on mistaken racial identity, but with a different structure, which is a *Laramie Project*/Anna Deavere Smith kind of staged documentary but turned into a stage mockumentary. It owes a lot to *The Laramie Project,* and it owes a lot to *Curb Your Enthusiasm.*

Did you feel that Butterfly *was an apotheosis of everything you'd done to that point?*

To that point, yeah.

Did it scare you about going further?

It didn't scare me thematically because it seems like I knew what I wanted to cover next thematically, because *Face Value* does end up being the play that introduces the themes that I then follow up in a number of different kinds of plays where people end up being different races. So you can take the line from *Face Value, Bondage, Trying to Find Chinatown* as leading up to *Yellow Face.* I think I knew what I wanted to write about. I think it was more the psychological/professional pressure of having a big hit and being afraid of not living up to expectations.

Didn't people know, walking into the theater to see M. Butterfly, *once the reviews came out and word got out, that the character was a man?*

There were a couple of different phenomena. Certainly, we tried to keep it quiet. It actually became *The Crying Game* model, and that's why we changed Brad Wong's name to B.D. and that kind of thing. Unlike us, people don't actually read reviews that closely. People vaguely get a notion: oh, there's something about this guy, honey, let's go see that. Most people, I think, who saw the original production did not know. But then you had a second wave of people who saw the production who had either seen it before or after *x* number of years and had kind of forgotten the plot. So then there were people who actually came up to me and said, "I've seen it before, but this time I forgot that it was a man." And to me, that exchange is a little more interesting, because ultimately that recapitulates what I feel that Gallimard, the Diplomat, goes through. I feel that Gallimard knows on some level that it is a man and chooses not to know. And when an audience member knows on some level that it's a man and chooses to suspend his or her disbelief, that feels to me to be more in sync with exactly what the story is about.

I just reread it, and I realized that for most of the play there was no way I would know it's a man and that I was completely engrossed in the plot. The play works on a plot level completely apart from the fact that Son is a man. And then the revelation is a shocker and takes the play to another level.

That's the whole experience of theater: the suspension of disbelief. You go in there and you know that even in a kitchen sink play you know it's not a real kitchen sink. Even when you see Cromer's production of *Our Town*, you go, "OK, that's real bacon I smell but that's not a real kitchen," and you suspend your disbelief and that works to the advantage of the play, I think.

I believe it's that way with casting. I mean, when the king says, "This is my son," and the actor playing the king is white, and the actor playing the son is black—

You go with it.

In Yellow Face, I wondered, would the play have worked if the character who was based on you was not so nakedly self-revealing and self-excoriating, if he had been the good guy.

I don't think so. I think part of the what makes the play work is there's a perverse thrill that the audience feels about the fact the author is either revealing the worst side of himself or sending himself up. I think it's true when we see *Curb Your Enthusiasm*. It's not fun to watch in a Larry Kramer play—it's not as funny, anyway—to be an authorial stand-in who's constantly justifying his or her existence and his or her actions. The fun of *Yellow Face* is that it does the opposite. Supposedly. I mean he's the biggest jerk onstage.

Did that give you some perverse pleasure?

Yes. It's fun. I think writing is naughty in some way—I've always felt that. And when I do my best work, I feel that I'm doing something I'm not supposed to be doing and the whole notion of putting myself, you know, in a porn shop and getting somebody off and create some porn, that's really fun.

Did you know when you were conceiving the work that it would involve this exposure of yourself?

I'd been thinking about *Face Value* ever since *Face Value* closed. How can I do a comedy of mistaken racial identity? And then there was a period around 2000, when a couple of Asian filmmakers put me in their movies playing myself. And one of them is a movie you can probably find on the Web called *Asian Pride Porn,* and I'm playing myself and I'm pitching politically correct Asian porn. It actually did pretty well on the Web. I thought that was really fun. So that to some extent was a feed. Also when I saw *I Am My Own Wife,* and Doug puts himself in the show, and I went, "Oh, that's how I could do it." I think there was always a notion that the David character in *Yellow Face* was going to be a humorous character.

What was your father's response to how you portrayed him in the play?

Well, actually the first act was written before my father passed away, and he read it. He liked the way he was portrayed, which shows a lot of how he is, who he was. But really, in the first draft the father wasn't as present as he ended up being, and I think the more I worked on it, the bigger presence he became in the play and kind of took over the play as he was wont to do in life. That was the other thing I learned going into the development process on *Yellow Face*: in the first draft, I wanted to make the play a little more fair in terms of divvying up the show between the DHH character and the Marcus character. In the first act you saw what happened to Marcus after he got fired after *Face Value* and how he ended up getting cast in *The King and I* and how he met Lea and all that stuff. The more we worked on it, the more I realized Marcus is only interesting as he affects David.

When you were a much younger man you said that being Chinese was on par with feeling like you had red hair. So what is it that makes you Chinese?

That's a really good question, and I think that's one of the things I'm trying to figure out in the work. There are times today that I feel like being Chinese is like having red hair. Because from being in my early twenties and feeling that knowing I'm Asian is the key to knowing my identity, to then realizing that, well, it's part of my identity, there are a lot of things that make up my identity and that's a part of it, and to now going, "There is no answer to the question of identity." If I figure out who I am, then I might as well just die, because there's nothing else to do down here. The significance of it, the meaning of that search really comes out of asking the question and asking that question at various points of your life and seeing how the answer changes. Hopefully you do change through life because otherwise . . .

Is it still a question in Chinglish*?*

It is a question in *Chinglish,* but *Chinglish* is not about the Asian American identity. Well it is about identity but it isn't about a sort of Asian American identity except in so far as by writing the play I'm trying to figure out what my relationship is to the root culture and more specifically how I feel about China nowadays. There are times when I feel like China is being demonized or sometimes I feel China deserves to be demonized. The whole rise of China has really shifted this dynamic and perception of Chinese Americans specifically, and Asian Americans in general. In the early eighties, the whole idea was, "Oh, we're not connected to root culture, we're Americans." They think of us as foreigners; accept us as Americans.

Who was saying this?

Asian Americans were saying this. Chinese Americans were saying this to the culture.

Were you saying that? Did you feel that?

Yes. I do feel like a lot of stereotypes around Asians have changed in my lifetime. When I was a kid, Asians were poor, illiterate, uneducated—manual laborers, cooks, waiters, laundrymen—that kind of thing. Then you fast-forward just forty years, and all of a sudden Asians are stereotyped to have too much money and we're too educated and we raise math scores. The thing that's happening—the thing that hasn't really shifted—is the notion of Asians as being perpetual foreigners, the way Americans argue about where are your loyalties. So that, I feel, has remained fairly constant. And then suddenly China became this huge glamour thing. And now we're going, "Well, we're half Chinese too." Chinese Americans are much more willing and interested in being associated with the root culture now than we were thirty years ago. Because the root culture is much more active now than it was thirty years ago. So, you know, what does that all mean? If there is likely to be some sort of conflict between the U.S. and China in the next decade, and the fact that we spent the first half of the twenty-first century saying, "Hey, we're really Chinese" . . . to what extent is that going to compromise us in the future? If, God forbid, the U.S. and China go to war, then we're kind of in deep shit. But *Chinglish* isn't about Chinese American identity except insofar as I'm trying to figure out my relationship to China and how I feel about China.

Did you feel along the way, and even now, that calling you a Chinese American playwright is reductive?

I've gone back and forth on that. At first I self-identified as an Asian American playwright, and I love the term Asian more than Chinese because Asian at that point felt to me more American. That is, Asians in Asia don't refer to themselves as Asians: they're Japanese, Chinese, etc. It's only in America that our experiences are sufficiently similar that we can begin to coalesce and feel that there is some commonality. So I thought of myself as Asian American and as an Asian American writer, and I was proud of that. And then I started to go, "Well, I feel like I've reached the top of this room. I've sort of hit a glass ceiling, in essence. Like, I'm a Chinese American playwright, but is my work considered universal in the same way that Tennessee Williams's is, although he writes about whites in the South?" It's a culturally specific experience but there's no, "Oh, his experience is only anthropological." So then I started to feel like the label is limiting. And then I started feeling that everyone gets labeled one way or another. If you think of a David Mamet play, you think of a particular type of play. He's not defined by his race, but it's just that everybody has a shorthand for writers. So my shorthand is that I'm an Asian American playwright, and I am Asian American and I am a playwright, so it's true. So it's OK. It's no worse than anybody else's label so long as I get to do what I want, which I feel I've pretty much gotten to do.

Do you feel when you write for hire, either because of the project you're offered or the project you choose, that you are able to bring some of your own feelings of identity into the project?

Yes. If I'm doing a good job on anything, I'm bringing a good part of who I am to it. A significant component of that has to do with my continuing interest in these questions of identity and the fact that I am Asian American. So I think I do bring part of that sensibility as part of the package of me to anything I work on.

You mentioned earlier that you don't think you're actually writing in terms of writing a screenplay or treatment. How is your approach different?

Doing a screenplay is a little different because the structuring and doing the treatment is a huge step toward doing the actual writing, because screenplays are not really about dialogue—screenplays are about structure. And that's why actors change dialogue and people get rewritten. So in that case, I would have to say structuring is legitimate work for the screenwriter.

And musicals too.

Musicals are about structure, largely. You know: where do you put the song?

In the musicals that you've done, is that part of your choice?

As the book writer, it's my job to go first. I feel like every form has one artist who has the full potential vision, and everybody else supports that. So if I'm doing a play, that's me. If I'm doing a movie, it's the director. If I'm doing an opera, it's the composer.

And musicals?

A musical is weird because a musical actually does not have one artist usually who holds the entire form. There are exceptions. In Michael Bennett's musicals, he was the primary artist, clearly. But most of the time, you do actually have to collaborate. You do actually have to find a shared vision together between the book writer, the lyricist, and the composer. And nowadays, the director too. And the producer. Or the producer could be the one with the primary vision.

And they really outline the way it should go?

No. No. In any case, I feel like it's my job to go first. So I'm going to toss out an outline. I'm going to put a song here and it's going to be called "Blueberry," and it's going to accomplish this, and then everybody can do their part. But somebody's got to go first, because you have to have something to really start in order to get your fingers dirty.

What else are you working on?

A couple of operas. That takes a while to get done. You have to keep on traveling. And a little movie I'm working on. And that's about it. You know what I would actually like to comment on is sort of my method for writing a play. Because I feel like there are three things I need in order to start writing a play. First of all, I need to have a question. I know that theoretically you're not supposed to write plays based on ideas; you're only supposed to write plays based on characters and situations. I do tend to write plays based on ideas, which I think is both a strength and sometimes a limitation. When I say it's based on an idea, it's not like I go, "Oh, I want to write a play about how all Asian men are affected by the West."

It's more like a question—something I don't understand. And I write the play in order to find out how I really feel about it in my unconscious. In the case of *Chinglish*, I'm trying to figure out, "How do I feel about China?" And so I need a question. As opposed to structuring things very tightly now, I don't. I tend to like to know where I'm starting and vaguely where I'm ending. So in the case of, say, *M. Butterfly*, I would start the play with the Frenchman fantasizing he was Pinkerton and that he catches Butterfly. And then at the end of play, the Frenchman realizes *he* was actually Butterfly and that he was deceived by love and the Chinese side had perpetrated that deceit upon the real Pinkerton, which, by the way, is also the *True West* structure. It's the two brothers who switch at the end of the play. So, on the one hand I like giving myself enough freedom to go wherever I want to go, but I also like to have the big notion of where I'm trying to end up eventually. In the case of *Yellow Face*, I knew I wanted to begin and end with two very big public events: the *Miss Saigon* episode and then the accusations against my father. And I felt there was some sort of relationship between the two and that I would figure out how to get there.

Do you just hold them in your head as you go?

It's kind of like taking a road trip. Right? I know I'm going to drive from New York to Boston but I don't know how I'm going to get there and the process of finding that road is the writing of the play. And the third thing that I need . . . I do model my plays on other plays. I feel like it's the structures, I suppose. Like *M. Butterfly* is a Shaffer play. *Yellow Face* is *The Laramie Project*.

Because your plays are fiction, they seem to comment on those plays at the same time.

Well, because *Yellow Face* is a mockumentary to some extent. I hadn't seen a staged mockumentary. I believe there's something which I've never seen called *The Plank Project*, which was done by one of the guys who did *Urinetown*, and he wrote kind of a send-up of *The Laramie Project*. But I've never seen it. By and large I haven't seen a lot of stage mockumentaries, and I like mockumentaries. I like *Spinal Tap*. A lot of writers will base characters on people they know. It's just kind of a way of jumpstarting the process. If you're writing well at all, you know that about a third of the way through that it's no longer your uncle Fred, and that character has become his own person. Similarly for me, thinking about another play helps jump-start my process. The weirdest one is that *Golden Child* is based on *Dancing at Lughnasa*. You can't see that at all, but the first draft of *Golden Child* had these long monologues by the contemporary character, and that was kind of the *Dancing at Lughnasa* model. It's just kind of a way to help me get going.

That is a great tip for young writers.

I think originality is overemphasized in our artistic culture.

CHRISTOPHER DURANG

We meet Chris Durang at the Juilliard School, where he has been teaching playwriting since 1994. He is casually dressed in a sport coat and slacks; his hair and neatly trimmed beard are whitish gray. We remark that since we last saw him, we have all become gray. He laughs then realizes he thought we said that we had all become great. Out of such mishearings are his comedy made. We follow him along the labyrinthine corridors of the school to the room he's booked for our interview. He worries aloud that there won't be a table for us, and as we walk down a corridor lined in vibraphones, we consider borrowing one. Luckily, the room is equipped with a table. Chris is initially rather shy. His manner is diffident, but once he warms up, he relishes talking and tells us everything we want to know; in fact, he often intuits our questions and answers them without our having to ask. He laughs easily, often comments on what he's saying, and makes connections that he had not thought of before. In this way, his conversation, circling back on events, relating incidents in his life to incidents in his work, gives us a clue to the way he mines the experiences of his own life, some of them painful, and transforms them into his work.

What's the first play you ever saw?

It may have been *Oklahoma!* My mother loved theater, and so she talked about theater a lot. I do remember the first Broadway show I saw, which was *Fiorello!*

Is that what drew you to the theater? Musicals?

I was really drawn to musicals. But when I was eight, I wrote a two-page play, which my second-grade class at Our Lady of Peace did. It was my first experience of people reading my words aloud.

What was the play?

It was my version of an *I Love Lucy* episode where they practice getting ready when Lucy's ready to go to the hospital to give birth. My mother had already lost two babies. And it's very odd that I chose this one, except it was totally funny and she found it funny too. I mean the episode of *Lucy*. My mother losing babies is also dealt with in *The Marriage of Bette and Boo*. It's sort of odd that I seemed so oblivious to the fact that I was writing about babies. And then after that I kept writing and each play became longer!

From a mere two pages, you didn't have far to go.

I sometimes would read in *TV Guide* a description of a movie. I remember it was *Dinner at Eight* with John Barrymore and Billie Burke, and all it said was, "A woman gets ready for a dinner party." I didn't see the movie, but I knew it was based on a play, so I wrote a twelve-page play about a dinner party.

You were an only child. Were you a solitary child?

I did have friends, but I was certainly solitary. I still believed in Santa Claus, and I had seen this Disney toy which was a proscenium stage made out of tin with painted curtains and stuff. And it was sold with little Donald Duck and Mickey Mouse and Snow White figures. My eyes lit up! When that was my Christmas gift, I couldn't believe how knowledgeable Santa Claus really was. I put the stage up in the attic on a little table and I put on plays for myself. And they got more and more elaborate. At one point I did *Bridge on the River Kwai*.

Who was your audience?

My cousin Peter would visit us sometimes. And I would put on shows for him, and he was actually quite patient. I would say the dialogue and move the things around. It was improvised dialogue, but I sort of knew what I was doing. And I did it until I was thirteen, and at that point I thought, "I think I'm a little too old to do this now." One of my friends from grammar school also loved musicals and so we wrote a show together called *Banned in Boston*.

Were there also playwrights that had an influence on you? That you either read or saw?

My mother's tastes were influential. She loved *Winnie-the-Pooh*. And she loved James Thurber. And I really, really grew to like his work. And she loved Noël Coward. I think her favorite was *Hay Fever*, which became my favorite. It's very freeform, not much plot, but funny. She had a reading of it in our living room. Isn't that interesting? She also loved *The Boy Friend*. Also I used to get those John Gassner books that had, like, twenty plays and I would read them.

Did you read them as if you were a playwright or as if you were a reader enjoying them?

I would say a reader enjoying as well as an audience person enjoying. You know, there are two things that I think have affected my style. One was *Oh Dad, Poor Dad...* Another was the musical *How to Succeed in Business* ... That kind of cartoonish exaggeration was something I felt drawn to. I liked to go to the bookstores and look at the theater books. I came across Joe Orton and I loved *Loot* and *The Ruffian on the Stair*. I remember my shock when I looked at the back of my Grove edition and it said, "He won this award, he won that award, he was murdered in 1967." I went, "WHAT!?"

By the time you went to Harvard, did you say to yourself, "I'm going to do this. I'm going to be a playwright"?

When I went to Harvard, I lost my self-confidence and I started to question whether I was meant to write and whether I was any good. And I sort of went into a depression and a sophomore slump and all of that. A nice teacher reached out to me, and I said, "You know, I've been skipping a lot of classes. Do you think I should go to the health services?" And he said, "Well, you know it couldn't hurt." You had to have a preliminary interview from a social worker to decide if you needed therapy. And, as I like to say, I passed! I told her about going home for Thanksgiving and my father was no longer living with us, and my mother fought with her family all the time. And they were very crazy. And I was sleeping a lot and going to movies all the time, and I wasn't doing my work, and she said, "Well, you're depressed." And I thought, "Oh! I am!" But I needed somebody to name it. My roommate was very unsympathetic and was doing very well in school, and he said, "Oh well, life's hard. What do you expect?" And the other thing this psychologist said was, "Do you realize you laugh at inappropriate times?" And no one had ever said that to me before. That could be said of Joe Orton's writing. It's sort of said of mine.

Where were you with your writing at that time?

One summer, I started to write a musical version of the gospels called *The Greatest Musical Ever Sung*. It had songs like *Everything's Coming Up Moses* and *You Can't Get a Man with a Prayer* that Mary Magdalene sang. I did this just to amuse myself, and then when I was at Harvard and eating in Dunster House I would sing songs, not loudly, but at the table. And someone or other went to the drama club at Dunster and said that they should do my play. I wouldn't have had the gumption myself because it was very silly. And I was also afraid because I had been so depressed the previous year, and I thought, "What if I get depressed in the middle of it and I don't follow through?" And then I decided, "No no no. I'll do it. I'll do it." So I directed it and I played the narrator, who sang occasionally. And it went really, really well. It was really fun. We had a poster that someone had made for us that said *The Greatest Musical Ever Sung* and it showed a pregnant Blessed Mother and in the foreground was a dove winking. And the show got a really good review in the *Harvard Crimson,* which in the small world of Harvard is a good thing. And then there was this letter to the editor from the Catholic chaplain saying that Harvard should not be making fun of religion. He got some of the professors to sign it, including my favorite one, William Alfred, who wrote *Hogan's Goat.* Six months later he accepted me in his playwriting seminar, the first time he had given it in my whole time at Harvard. And I had given him my play *The Nature and the Purpose of the Universe,* where the pope gets killed by this crazy nun. And I thought, "William Alfred's going to think I'm this psychotic anti-Catholic." But he quite liked it. At some point, I said, "Did you realize I wrote the play that you signed a letter against?" His answer was, "Yes, you're very mischievous," which made me laugh and laugh. He also said, "You may make people mad in the world sometimes." I still remain surprised at that.

How do you write? Do you sequester yourself in a dark room from eight A.M. to four P.M.?

No. I always wrote, and still do, with some exceptions, by impulse. I've sometimes given myself a schedule when I have a long period of not writing. My junior year, I got a job tutoring. This one day, nobody was there to be tutored, but I had to be there for two hours. And I started writing something called *Better Dead Than Sorry* that Sigourney later was to do in the Yale cabaret. I just had an impulse and I just started writing and I actually wrote the whole thing in one sitting. And then, like, two weeks later the same thing happened and I wrote *Nature and the Purpose of the Universe.* I can tell you what triggered me for that play. You know, I was in college '67 to '71. And in my junior year, there was a threatened takeover of some building. It was exhausting, those years, trying to figure out what was right and what was wrong. Someone put this pamphlet underneath my door, and I thought it said, "The Nature and Purpose of the Universe." And then I looked and it actually said, "The Nature and Purpose of the University"! But I got tickled by the idea that someone might write something called "The Nature and Purpose of the Universe." So I started really with the title. And I went to see the movie *Woodstock,* and there was this one woman character who was just talking about how much she didn't want the kids to come and she didn't like young people. And I thought, "That doesn't seem like a real woman. That seems like Elaine May pretending to be someone." So, with *The Nature and Purpose of the Universe*, I was telling a story about this housewife whose life was utter, utter hell. And God sends down an angel to make her life worse and worse and worse until she wants to kill herself. And the angel's name is Elaine May Allcot. While another angel, who's the narrator, comes and he's the Fuller Brush Man who's going to save her. At the same time, this abused friend of my mother asked the priest if she could use birth control in case her husband raped her. And he thought about it and said no.

It seems like there's an extraordinary amount of rage that's transformed into humor.

My worldview got dark, but funny. That's one of the things I was so excited by when I read Joe Orton. Because unlike Noël Coward, who doesn't really have a dark viewpoint, Joe Orton's view is very dark. I truthfully wasn't angry writing *Nature and Purpose of the Universe*. I was very upset for the woman. And I really thought that I'm so glad that I'm not her. And what a really awful situation she's in and she got married so young. Anyway, all those were the thoughts that led to the play.

You say that you weren't angry when you wrote it. But are you in some emotional state when you write? Or is it all digested and then you just write?

It's not wrong to say "some state." It feels like I'm improvising, because I'm making it up as I'm going. I'm just going to jump ahead for a second: when people used to say *Sister Mary Ignatius* . . . showed great anger, I didn't feel angry writing it. When I'm writing I feel like I'm taking upsetting things and kind of putting them in a context. It's sort of like saying, "Look at what this looks like." And it feels . . . a kind of relief. I must say as I've gotten older, I am more in touch with my anger. And it's not a comfortable feeling, actually. But I think I was not as connected to it when I was younger.

How does it change your work, being in touch with your anger? Or has it?

You know, it may have changed some. If I started to have a dark world-view, I guess it's a way that you use humor to make it less painful. Later on when I met Wendy Wasserstein, we would exchange funny stories about painful things in our families. I guess it's a coping mechanism.

When you read Joe Orton, did you think, "Oh, I can do that. I'm allowed to do that"?

I not only thought that, but there was another permission that I got which is he kept bringing up his Catholic background. And he was slashing and funny about the Catholic Church. And at the same time, I started to see Fellini movies, and he brought up his Catholic background all the time. Up to this point, what I had gleaned from musical comedies—which are mostly written by Jewish people—was that everybody seemed to be Protestant. But I started to bring in priests and nuns because I find the specificity with which Fellini told us things about the Catholic Church very pleasing. It was so interesting because he clearly knew what he was talking about.

In the course of writing a play, do you show it to anybody?

At Yale, we had something called Writers' Workshop, which was three years of playwrights, roughly fifteen people, in this class with Richard Gilman, sometimes Howard Stein, sometimes another guest teacher. And the first year actors. All of them. And the first year directors. You would bring in the scenes you'd written or a full-length play or a half of a play, and the actors would rehearse it slightly—like the night before or earlier in the day with the directors overseeing it. And it was so wonderful to get to know the actors. And Sigourney and Kate McGregor-Stewart were both in my class. And John Rothman was a year before. And I started to write in this style that started with *Better Dead Than Sorry* and *Nature and Purpose* . . . which is slightly Ortonesque, I guess. Stylized, but dark. And I found that certain actors automatically seemed to know how to do it and others didn't. And it was really a wonderful thing to learn, actually. And then there were ten or twelve years when

Wendy and I showed each other our first drafts. And then as time went on, my partner, John Augustine, is who I show my stuff to. He and I have a very similar sense of humor. He's very encouraging. I've never sought out harsh critics. I don't know if other people do. So presently, it's John that I show it to. Or I'll have a private reading with enough invited people that you get a sense of an audience, which is really important to me. I almost always show it when I finish a first draft. And I do more than one draft. Matter of fact when I used to do it by hand, I would do the first draft by hand and then I would type it, and in the typing I would edit and add stuff as I went. I had heard that Noël Coward wrote *Private Lives* in a weekend. I don't know if that's really true, but I decided that I liked it when I wrote a play really fast. So *Nature and Purpose of the Universe,* I think I had one draft. That was it.

And written quickly?

Very quickly. When I wrote those two plays, *Better Dead Than Sorry* and *Nature and Purpose of the Universe,* it actually felt oceanic. I felt this enormous relief. Unlike *Greatest Musical Ever Sung,* which was funny but light-hearted, this was very dark and I felt great release writing it. And also it was funny. It was making me laugh because the setup was this crazy woman would come and just make this woman's life worse and worse. It was very cathartic.

It sounds like playwriting saved you.

Maybe.

Have your writing habits changed since Yale and your early successes?

Well, through most of Yale, I still wrote not in a set way but on impulse. As time went by, I would write down ideas for plays.

Do you do that now?

There was a period when I had a book that I would write things down in. I'm finding that now that I'm older, it seems like longer between plays. I might just write a scene. Actually, on the computer, I would write down ideas to remind myself of it.

How did you make the transition from graduate school into the world of theater?

I don't think people even used the word "networking" at that point, but . . . I had no idea what a fortuitous step it was. After my last year at Harvard, though I felt a lot better, I did not have the courage or gumption to go to New York. I thought New York was scary when I was young. I loved to see the musicals and plays, but I used to get a headache from New York because it's so intense. If I hadn't gone to Yale, I'm not sure what my path might have been. And I remember going to Yale thinking that Robert Brustein ran the school and the rep was rather judgmental. For instance, he was well known for not liking Edward Albee. And I remember thinking, "Gee, I like Edward Albee's work. I wonder if he's going to hate my work." So I went thinking, "I'm going to see if they give me encouragement." And . . . really I just feel so lucky. First of all, Brustein went to see *Better Dead Than Sorry* and loved it. Now the other thing that was funny was that I sort of knew this at the time, but I was in a much stronger emotional state so I only looked at the positive. At first, about half of the school didn't like my work and the other half really loved it. But the next year, more people liked it. And also the one-act version of *Bette and Boo* had more empathy in it and so they started to be less scared because my plays had seemed to them like a mad person wrote them.

On the one hand, the plays—I'm generalizing—seem anarchic. Like the characters will say anything and we have no idea what they are going to do next. And I wonder—especially in a full length—how do you rein that in so that there's an arc? Because they all do have that arc, but the arc is unpredictable. So at what point do you know the arc? Or do you find the arc as you go along?

I find the arc sometimes automatically, but when it's not automatic I will sometimes write the first half of a play and not know where it goes next. Actually, I did this with *Sister Mary*. I'll simply put the play away for four to six months. And then all of a sudden I get an idea. Drying the dishes is one of the times I get ideas. And it's a great time because it's boring. And I remember drying the dishes and thinking, "Sister should kill Gary because he's magically going to confession and she thinks she's going to send him to heaven." And I quickly wrote that down. And then my mother's health got much, much worse. I was living in New York and she was in New Jersey. So basically I was there for, like, four days out of seven. And then when I'd go back, her family was so difficult to deal with and crazy. They were mean, too, but they were more crazy than mean. And when you say you never know what people are going to say, so much comes from my mother's family. And somewhere in the midst of my mother's death I was no longer a believing Catholic or Christian. It was two things. It was a dark view due to all the alcoholics in the family, 'cause it feels like nothing ever gets solved. There are many more alcoholics in my family than I put into *Bette and Boo.* It seemed overwriting if I put them all in. And then the other thing is that we'd all been praying, when I was an antiwar Catholic, for the Vietnam War to end. And after a couple years and it didn't end, I kept thinking, "Well, I'm sorry, what is the point of prayer?" And God says, "I'll allow a few more days of napalm." And it suddenly just didn't make sense. It's so odd that, when I was a child, the Catholic Church had an answer for absolutely everything. Every single problem they would say, "Well, Christ said this." And so I started to think back on all the things that were taught to us as fact. I was taught really from age six that if you didn't go to Mass on Sunday, that's a mortal sin and then you go to hell. This is during my mother's final illness. And I started to write this play where this nun comes out and the important part of the title was . . . *Explains It All For You.* After a certain point, after the sister had done the questions and the little boy had been back and forth, I thought, "I don't quite know what to do with this." And so I put it aside, and then my mother died. Anyway, um . . . at some point drying dishes or being on a train, I suddenly thought, "Oh! What if some of Sister's ex-students show up and they're now thirty years old," which is basically what I was, "and they now come back to say to her . . ." So I thought, "Oh!" I was on the train writing by hand and I startled myself when all of a sudden . . . You know, I have to say I didn't know entirely where the play was going when she starts quizzing them to find out. I knew that one was gay and one was an alcoholic and one was an unwed mother and one had had an abortion, or two abortions.

You're laughing. You still laugh at inappropriate places.

Do I? I do. Especially if I'm in a good mood. Then I wrote all the stuff about my mother's death. And I made up stuff about a rape, but of course I wanted to win the abortion argument! The next thing that startled me was I thought, "This play feels like it's ending, but it's only an hour." And I thought, "I can't make any money with a one-act play." And I almost didn't go forward. I almost put it aside to start another one. And then I thought, "You've just had a year and a half writer's block that's so psychologically unhealthy. Finish it, even if it's a one-act." And then I didn't know that Sister had a gun. Because when Diane brought out a gun, my impulse was, "You can't kill Sister, she's just too strong. You can't." And so I gave her her own gun. Just as a side thing. That's a hard thing for an actor or actress to figure out. And Elizabeth Franz never asked me why. And at some point after she had already done the part, I asked her, "How did you motivate yourself?" And she said, "Well, because of Pope John XXIII, the Mother Superior who wanted us to be more aware of the world made us watch the evening news, which I did not want to see. And there were all these dangerous things happening all around the school, and I was worried for the children. So I had to bring a gun with me to protect them." So many of the best actors that I've worked with come from a place of, "How can I make it work?" rather than, "Defend yourself to me."

I just want to pick up on how you start your plays. What gets you going?

Sometimes, I'd write down a title, like *Nature and Purpose of the Universe,* or I'd write down a topic. And this would just be in a book and sometimes I'd look back and remind myself. Although, truthfully, I think that when a play starts to percolate I don't use the book that much because it would just come up in my head at later times.

For example, let's say Beyond Therapy.

Beyond Therapy to this day remains one of my best-selling plays, which is kind of amazing considering Frank Rich and Walter Kerr didn't like it, which ended it in New York. I mean best-selling in the amateur market because it's kind of cheerful. The guy and the girl don't get together, but it's sort of rueful and lighthearted. And there's part of me that thought, "I want to write another lighthearted play to make some money." That was my impulse. And I was thinking how my parents used to take me to the New Jersey shore every summer for two weeks. And mostly they were fun times. My mother and father liked to fish, and I like the ocean. And then when my parents separated, my mother got work as a secretary and she had enough money to rent a place at the shore, but she would ask her girlfriends to share it with her. And so I thought, "Oh, I want to draw on these happy memories of going to the shore." And I had this idea of merging my memories of the seashore being fun with a sleazy, TV thing of young people in bathing suits getting to know each other and putting a laugh track in it. I'd always wanted to put a laugh track onstage that everybody keeps hearing and is confused by. So that was the impulse. And that was how I started. But by page three, because it was about different people renting together who had only met through their realtors, a serial killer entered, Heath, who had a head in a box, which is an obscure reference to *Night Must Fall,* which is a thirties play and movie. And even though the play is still funny, obviously it darkened from there.

Do you think that other playwrights just write from the beginning and have all the right ideas and go right on to the end?

Well, I thought Noël Coward did.

Maybe it's just an apocryphal story to make all the rest of the playwrights feel bad.

I know. Somewhere out in the real world I would start to hear about other writers' writing habits. And the most intimidating to me were the people who would rent offices outside their apartment and go there at eight or nine in the morning and stay there until four or five. And maybe go have lunch, or maybe eat there. And they would do it every day. And that was so much not what I did. I felt intimidated by it. And I thought, "I must be very lazy." And I started to think, "Well, when do they live?" I mean, if you just keep putting out constantly, do you actually always have the impulse to communicate or something to draw on? So I then become judgmental of those people. But especially from teaching and seeing how different the students are, I've totally shifted to there are just different temperaments. At that time the Phoenix commissioned a play, and I was just having trouble. I would start and I was going through a judgmental phase. And going, "That's awful." Then I would write for ten minutes and go, "That's awful." Wendy and I were at the height of our friendship and we were talking about writing. And then she got this review from Walter Kerr that was stopping her. So we would sort of encourage each other. Left to my own devices, I clearly would procrastinate and procrastinate. So I came up with this rule that I had to write Monday through Friday, not nine to five, but say . . . three hours. And the rule was, if I was hating what I was writing, I couldn't stop. I had to keep going. And I must say, three hours is a long time to write. I probably wrote an hour and a half to two and went and got cups of tea and stuff. But the good thing I discovered is when I would look at what I wrote the next day, I would go, "Oh, that's not as bad as I thought." Or the alternative would be, "Oh, it's good up to here. But then I have the characters do this, but that was a cul-de-sac. Let's throw all that and go back to this place." One of the teachers who made a very big impression on me at Yale was Jules Feiffer, who taught for exactly one year at Yale School of Drama. He wasn't actually a very nice teacher but was sort of right up my alley. I loved his work, his cartoons, his screenplays, I loved *Little Murders* very much. He was a wonderful teacher. And oddly, of all the teachers we had a Yale, he was the most specific. The other teachers would say things like, "Oh, the characters are great and the feeling of it is great but act two sags." But Jules Feiffer would say, "You know, I was really liking it until page seven when they started to say this dialogue. And then it sort of goes off."

Do you ever write with a particular actor in mind?

I mostly don't. I wrote *A History of American Film* with Sigourney and Joe Grifasi in mind. And then nobody would cast them.

You didn't feel you could, as the playwright, press your advantage?

You know, I think I might have, but I thought they were going to cast her. With David Chambers, who I was just getting to know, he thought she was talented. But he thought she just wasn't the right type for it. And so I also feel like if a director is resisting and you force an actor on them, it can make for trouble.

When you say you wrote it for her, does that mean you wanted her to play it or you used things about her that you thought fit the character?

Both, actually. I mean, for instance, there's one joke early on in *A History of American Film* where it's the silent section and she's in an orphanage and the title says, "Loretta is told that she is too tall to remain in the orphanage." And that's probably the only specific Sigourney thing. In *Better Dead Than Sorry* and then in an unreviewed version of *The Nature and Purpose of the Universe* where she played the wife. Both of these roles were unlike her later movie roles. They didn't use how strong she looked. She was very vulnerable and open. And she was very simple with her responses. She said really outlandish things as if it was the most normal thing in the world. So I think that character has a certain deadpan quality or simple quality that I think Sigourney would have done well. Also, I think she's intelligent. And I also think she senses what is good for the play.

What do you do when you're in a rehearsal and, for whatever reason, you just disagree with the director? Or you think they just don't get it?

Oh, it's such a painful thing. It's really nightmarish. Mostly, there isn't much you can do.

Would you talk to the actors directly? Would you in any case or would you only in that case?

Most of the directors I've worked with seem to be pretty open to my comments, especially about actors, depending on their personality. David Chambers was always willing to listen to me, but he didn't want me to interrupt him during rehearsals. So I would do that with him. Peter Schifter was so free and easy, he was fine if I spoke up in the middle of it. I do tell my students that when you're working with a director, it's very bad to go behind a director's back. I have, from time to time, done it. Mostly, I've just been lucky. I remember the actor Jeff Brooks, who was in a lot of my plays early on. He and I were often friends during the productions, and at some point he would come to me and ask me something, and I would say, "You know, I feel like I only have twenty chips to give the director before they've had enough of me." But I'm not going to fight on every single thing. But again, I've been very lucky. I've mostly really liked working with the directors I have.

Do you make changes if an actor says, "Chris, I can't make this work. I don't understand"?

I've not run into that so much. Some of my students do. And I sometimes think it's about personality. Especially now that I'm older and have been around more, I run into that less. I do think it's disorienting. All the actors at Yale really came from a place of, "Let's solve the scene." And one of the things that was fun for me was I ended up getting to do acting at the Yale Cabaret and then sometimes they gave me small parts or supporting parts with the actors in their projects. But it was fun to be with the actors. And we'd be in a scene that felt flat and we'd all discuss how we could make it better and what are the characters looking for and all that stuff. And I really loved learning that. I think I already had a good sense of it, but I liked doing it with them.

Has your success affected the way you write? Did it give you more confidence, or did it make you more frightened or did it just bore you or burden you, or . . .

With *Beyond Therapy*, I got a little scared for some reason. *Sister Mary* . . . had gotten great reviews but hadn't made me money. Also, I had been in a sufficient writer's block during my mother's illness which preceded finishing *Sister Mary . . .* that I think I was afraid that I was going to have another writer's block with *Beyond Therapy*. Well anyway, the Phoenix production had exactly two previews, which was terrifying. And the second preview the newspaper people came to, and the actors were simply off that day. And they were almost all bad, the newspapers were. This is the only time it's been this cut and dry. The magazines came to opening night, and they didn't come out for two or three weeks, but they were great reviews, including the one from Edith Oliver. What she wrote about *Beyond Therapy* was that it was very, very funny. And then she said, "If only he could end the play in the restaurant scene in act two. The audience was on cloud nine. And if he could have just ended it there, they would have gone home happy. But he tried to tie up plot strings. But plot isn't important in Durang. That's not what we go to him for." But my first reaction was the whole review was so nice, I couldn't really get mad at her. I was watching the show a lot because I lived in the city, and one night, Jerry Zaks, who directed, and I were off to the side. And when we got to that scene, I went over to Jerry and whispered, "Edith Oliver wants to go home now." However, as time went by, I thought, "You know, she's right. They're absolutely loving this scene." Claire Nichtern, a Broadway producer, said she wanted to do it but wanted me to rewrite the ending. And I said—and this is a happy thing—I said, "Well, I agree with you. I've come to see that this isn't the right thing and I have this idea. It's very simple; as opposed to Prudence leaving, she sits down and has dinner. It's as simple as that." I might have seen it if Edith hadn't said that, but nonetheless it was a helpful thing that she said.

The first time I've ever heard—from a playwright's point of view—that a critic said something helpful.

Well, it was really helpful. It was almost like that woman at Harvard saying, "You're depressed." She was saying, "The audience is happy now! Don't do this other thing!"

Has your writing changed since you don't live in New York? Not only your writing, but your relation to the world of the theater?

My relation to the world of theater has changed. I don't see as much. I do feel bad about it, but my commute is such that I miss the casualness with which I would go to the theater. You know, just spur of the moment. Or call the day before and just go. And also getting home is a complicated thing. The bus doesn't go that late.

Are you a gentleman farmer?

Well, I live in an old farmhouse and it has a barn. But I don't do too much. And then there are those wonderful flowers that just come up no matter what you do. I love those.

So how has it affected . . . your life or your work or your—

One way that it might have affected it is that I'm not as up on all the other plays as I used to be.

When did you start teaching at Juilliard?

1994. Marsha Norman called me up out of the blue and she asked if I would like to teach with her. And at first I said yes. And then I called her back and said that I was getting scared that I wouldn't do my own work and what if I don't like the students' work. And she said, "Well, why don't you do it and then after six months if you hate it, you can quit?" And the idea that she already gave me permission to leave after six months, I thought, "Oh! All right." It actually changed me. And we actually had a great first year. We just loved our students.

Do you think your teaching has affected your playwriting in any way?

It certainly has affected my knowledge of theater, of playwriting. I credit the students, but also Marsha a lot. She has a more theoretical mind than I do. And so sometimes, she will say what a play is doing, and I won't necessarily have thought of it, but it makes me more conscious of it.

Do you team teach?

Yes, we do. Absolutely. We're always in the same room. And it's almost like running a talk show. I've always wondered what it would be like if we disagreed, and most of the time we don't. And the other thing is I feel like we will nonetheless say things differently. I think we give different things to the students. But one thing she says that I think is fun to keep in mind is, "In the first twenty minutes of a play, the audience wants to know when they can go home." Meaning not out of boredom, but what is the issue that we're looking for and how will it be. And if they're sitting there and have no idea what the play is looking for, they're very unhappy. And then the other way she says it—and I like even better—is, she says, "If you get on a plane to Houston and you end up going to Wichita, you're not happy." The audience wants to be told where they're going. I can't always look at a wonderful play and articulate what the dramatic question is, but much of the time I can. And I actually think when I look back at *Sex and Longing,* I think I wrote from two separate impulses that occasionally went together, but half the time they didn't. And so, I think the audience at a certain point went, "I'm sorry, why are we here? And why are we here so long?" I've looked at that trying to fix it, and I haven't been able to yet.

How do you approach the students? What are your points of interest or entrance into their work?

I have two answers. Marsha and I, like many playwrights, have suffered enough from harsh criticism in the papers. We always end up talking about that once a year to the students to sort of prepare them. A lot of what we do is be encouraging. A lot of the stuff is to be sure to say the things we like. And I think that we do that normally, but it's also sometimes consciously that way. Then I find myself asking, When do you tell the audience certain information? And I'd find that some of the students delayed giving the information. It'd be a long time before you realize somebody is somebody's brother or sister. I mean, just put it in the second page. Don't put it in the fifteenth page. And so, I give a lot of that. I'm not much of a joke teller, but when somebody tells a joke, part of the success is giving the listener the proper setup. And without the proper setup, it's not funny.

How much guidance—or what kind of guidance—do you give the students?

Early on in our teaching, there was one student who seemed a little lost and there was one play that felt so fake, like it was trying to be important, but it felt like she didn't know the people at all and it felt very impersonal and it was really, really painful. And then she brought in a new play that was—I thought—better, although I didn't love it. And Marsha seemed really to hate it, seemed to hate the topic, some combination of sex and violence. We talked about it and we said rather than giving this student negative feedback all the time, why don't we meet with her and try to guide her to some degree. And so Marsha tried by making her more aware of structure. Wendy, for example, wrote so autobiographically and you always know how connected she was and this student's play felt so disconnected from whoever this person was that I told her, "I'm not say-ing to write necessarily as autobiographically as Wendy did. But would you, as an exercise, write about something that you really know well, that's something you've experienced?" And she brought in a scene that was based on something with some of her relatives and it was very good. And, I must say, it made me feel very good. And I could also feel it in the other students. They gave her nice feedback for the first time, and really she kept going that way. And we've had a couple of experiences like that. And now we sort of look back at the few times where we didn't intercede. I must say, mostly we just let our writers go because they're postcollege, and a lot of them already have their voices.

What else do you think you might have been if you weren't a playwright or if there were no such thing?

At Harvard, when I lost confidence, there was also a point where I thought, "Even though I've been doing this since I was young, maybe I'm not meant to do it." And I think I thought that being a social worker sounded ideal-istic. So I thought, "Be a social worker." I don't know why I didn't think psychologist or something, which is actually something I could be.

Would you want to have patients? Would you run a private practice?

I feel that parts of my friendships have been like that. Both ways. And then the other thing I thought, although it's awfully related, I did wonder if I wanted to go into film. Because when I was at Harvard, I saw a movie almost every single day I was there. Isn't that insane? Sometimes, you know, it'd be double features. And I would say sixty percent was because I loved movies and forty percent was avoidance behavior.

Might you have been thinking that you wanted to write movies?

Or being a director. Yeah, writing or directing.

What was your experience of Beyond Therapy *as a film?*

Ugh.

Not good?

Horrible. Horrible. Unwatchable. I've actually not seen all of it.

Did you write the screenplay?

Oh, in a way. The quick version is that Robert Altman—who's charming with actors and was charming with me initially, but I don't think he likes writers very much—I thought he chose such wonderful actors, I didn't want to say no to him. He wanted me to cut it to ninety minutes, which I was open to. Then he didn't have the money. Then he wanted me to suddenly start work on it. And I couldn't for like weeks because I had a job working for a Carol Burnett special. But four weeks in the world of movies doesn't seem that long. So when that was up, all of a sudden he called and said he'd written a budget script, because I wasn't free, but not to worry, none of it was written in stone. And I said, "Budget script? I've never heard that phrase before." Or since. And he said, "Well, I wrote it out so we could know how many interiors and exteriors so we could . . . budget." And I said, "Oh, OK." And there was a part of me that knew not to read it on the plane, I'd be too upset. But I did. All of the psychological connectors were taken out. He doesn't have a great sense of humor. Then when he found out I didn't like it, he stopped talking to me. Then I had to write my own version of it in order to be paid. But I sort of believed that he'd never look at it. I don't know that he did. I think the producers did. I had just met my future partner, John, and he said, "Oh, with those actors, how bad could it be?" And I said, "No, it's really—" and he said, "Can I look at it?" And I said sure, and he couldn't finish. He said, "Oh, I had no idea." It is one of the worst movies ever made.

Did this sour you on writing for the movies?

I've written lots of screenplays and TV shows that have not been made. And so the fact that they haven't been made depresses me. However, I'm also extremely grateful that *Sister Mary . . .* got me in the position that people would hire me to do this. Because I was able to live off of it. So I flip-flop between being grateful and then feeling exhausted, because you take so many notes from so many people. And then, you know, I kept going into these things thinking they would be made and so many of them weren't. And I've been very lucky with plays, knock wood. Well, this isn't wood.

When you write a play now, is there any theater you can automatically present it to?

I've had close relations with a few theaters, so there isn't "one." Thanks to Tim Stanford, I'm still close to Playwrights' Horizon. And I like them very much. And I kept wanting to go back to the Public, and George Wolfe was always nice to me. But I wasn't writing as much. Actually, it was George that gave me the commission. Then he left the next year. I'm working on a play for McCarter, because *Miss Witherspoon* was a commission. Once I moved out to the country, McCarter is like an hour away. New York is ninety minutes away. Longer with the bus. So I started to run into Emily Mann more and we met for lunch and after months went by she asked me if I wanted to do a commission. So this is the second one they offered me.

So it was done at McCarter?

Yes, but also at Playwrights' Horizon. It went really well at McCarter. It went well at Playwrights' but . . . two things. I could feel the audience sitting there, "This is going to be a laugh riot." And then when it was sort of meditative occasionally, I could feel them going, "This isn't a laugh riot." In Princeton, they actually didn't know my work that well. These days I mostly have my agent read the reviews and just characterize them. Then I either choose to read the good ones or not read any of them or something. But with Ben Brantley's review from McCarter my agent said, "He likes Christine and he likes you a lot, but he mostly talks about *Betty's Summer Vacation*." See, *Miss Witherspoon* is about reincarnation. And I think there're some people who just have no response to reincarnation, and I think Ben Brantley may be one of them. Because he doesn't even describe it so it makes sense. It's not like a review that you want to kill yourself over, because he's nice to me and he talks so much about this other play. But it's kind of like you don't even explain what you saw.

But you have a new commission?

I have another political play that I started, and I only have forty minutes of it. But I've been wondering if maybe I should do another political one right away. Five months ago I started something else, which I have two titles for: One is *Chekhov in Pennsylvania*. And then the other one is *Vanya and Sonya and Masha and Spike*. That one gets the larger laugh, so I'll probably choose that one. The McCarter is very patient, as most theaters are with commissions. Anyway, I'm going to have a reading of the first thirty minutes of each of them, back to back, and we're going to discuss which one we feel most drawn to. And that's not to say I might not finish both of them, but we'll choose which one to put up front. I have to write quite a bit more of *Vanya and Sonya* . . . but I am having ideas, which is quite a good sign. And putting them in the computer. I'm finding that when I write things on paper, I can't find the paper. But if I name the files right, I can find them.

Has your writing changed with the advent of the computer?

I've gotten quite addicted to writing on the computer.

You don't write longhand anymore?

I really don't. Now sometimes, I'm on the bus and write. And the thing is my handwriting has gotten so bad that I have to, like, look at it that night and print out the words that I can still vaguely remember but not read. You know, one thing that I love about the computer is that if you're writing something and you go, "I don't think this segment goes here," you can cut it and put it either in a different file or down at the bottom. And when I'm writing, I would have to either circle it or cross it out. I just love that feeling. One of my students started writing on computer. Then he went to typewriting—not even an electric one, he went to a regular one. And now he writes by hand. And it's sort of a reverse of what I did. I must say you write slower by hand, and it's possible that changes how the ideas form. I type very fast, actually. That's another reason it's hard for me to go back to the writing. It's slower.

Does some part of the play come easier to you? I mean in terms of the writing, do you think, "Oh, I've got this character, but I don't have this one, so I'll just sort of mark the place here"?

Oh, you know, I *do* do that. It's something Marsha recommends doing. I haven't done it a lot, but she says sometimes if you don't know the next scene, jump to the next one you know and you can go back. Actually, there was a brief time when Wilford Leach was considering doing *The Marriage of Bette and Boo*. But his favorite scene was the scene of the dead grandparent, the dinner Matt has and the two of them are dead. I was glad to know he liked it, I liked it too. And I couldn't decide where to put it. I think he wasn't sure where it went either. And now where it goes makes sense to me, but I remember when I met with him it was sort of free-floating. I don't think it landed yet. Um . . . I guess the answer is yes, I'm not sure what makes it so. But, yes, there are certain parts that are harder.

Which parts?

I'm not sure what it is. My brain doesn't think in outlines, so I don't always know where the play is going. Once I realized the students would come into *Sister Mary . . .* I didn't realize there was going to be killing. But I knew that there was going to be confrontation.

Do you always know where the confrontations are?

What do you mean? Do you mean in placement?

No, the people who start talking. Do you know if they're in a living room or a on a beach or could they be anywhere?

I would be open to writing a play where the characters are who-knows-where. And actually, I did do a little experiment once. After *Beyond Therapy* I was in this sublet where I told myself I had to write every day. And I literally started with a blank page in the typewriter, and I did not have a thought in my head. I wrote, "He, she, he, she," and they were talking to a baby in a bassinet. And I just kept going and eventually they had names. And suddenly I wrote, "Nanny comes in." And then off I went. I guess as soon as I put "bassinet," it was a room with a bassinet in it. When I was looking for curtain raisers for *Sister Mary . . .* I had a reading where my then-actor friend Walter Bobbie came to see it. And Dianne Wiest read the lead and she was heaven! Walter had this really great remark after seeing it. He said, "I don't think that's a curtain raiser. I think that's a curtain downer." And he was right, it was too dark. I just put the play aside. Brustein got a hold of it and was going to do it on an evening with a Beckett play, and I said—because I'd been having a thought of what if I wrote an act two where Daisy grew up?—and I said to him, "If I were to make this a full-length play, would you be open to that?" and he said yes. And then—this is both a lovely vote of confidence and slightly insane—he said, "I'll schedule it." And I said, "Great. When are the dates?" And he said, "First rehearsal would be in six weeks." And I said, "OK," and I got off the phone and I thought, "What if I don't have inspiration?" And I thought, "I'll just do it." So I just wrote it in maybe two or three weeks. *Baby with the Bathwater.* It was a very good production, Cherry Jones and Tony Shalhoub and Mark Linn-Baker directed, and I actually think act two is better than act one.

How do you go into situations where you have to address an audience, like a regional theater asks you to do a talkback or something?

I find audience talkbacks are somewhat stressful. And also they tend to be during previews, for some reason. Sometimes they're during the run, which is easier. But in previews when you're still forming it, it can be really hard. An early one I remember that I'm sort of proud of myself, but also think, "Where did I get my feistiness from?" was *Beyond Therapy* at the Phoenix. I think we'd opened, but we'd gotten the bad newspaper reviews, and I don't know if we'd gotten the good other reviews yet. But the audience was, nonetheless, kind of liking it. And anyway, some audience member asked me some question that was like, "Well, why don't you do this with your play?" And it really communicated to me that he just didn't like my play and didn't like the style. So rather than answer his question, I said, "Can I ask you what kind of comedies you do like?" And he didn't have an answer right away, and I said, "For instance, do you like *Mary Hartman*?" And he said, "No, I don't." And I said, "Well,

I just don't think you're ever going to like a play I write." And I've actu-ally passed that on to some of my students. Because sometimes people ask a question, when what they really mean to say is, "I don't like your play." And it's kind of like that's the only information. Unlike my positive experience with Edith Oliver as a critic, I don't feel like I've ever learned much from an audience talkback. What I feel sometimes has happened is sometimes the audience has had a good time and they just wanted to hear how you put it together—how did you think of that costume, what did you think it was like to play such-and-such a character, they'll ask one of the actors—that kind of thing. I do think it's kind of odd. I do understand it, though, in the sense that it makes people who go to the theater a lot feel closer to the process.

SARAH RUHL

We're supposed to meet Sarah Ruhl in a room in the Graduate Acting Program at NYU, but next door to the room we're in a class of twenty actors is tap dancing, so we go searching for another, quieter place. Mark Wing-Davey, chair of the program and frequent director of Sarah Ruhl's plays, lets us use his office, so we settle in and wait. Sarah Ruhl is late for our interview, and when she arrives she is apologetic: all three of her children—a four-year-old and year-old twins—are sick and she has left them with a new babysitter. She is visibly worried, taking her cell phone out of her bag and leaving it within easy reach, worrying that she's not sure she can stay long enough for the interview, that she has to get back to them. We assure her we'll be quick and efficient and set a definite time when we'll be done, which seems to relax her a bit. The room we're in is a corner office with lots of windows which look out over lower Broadway and which we can't open because of the traffic noise. It's a bit on the warm side, but the physical world recedes into the background as the interview becomes more and more absorbing. Sarah looks like a romantic idea of a poet: slim, pale, soft-spoken, shy—but as the interview goes on, the shyness and soft-spokenness yield to an absolute firmness of ideas and beliefs. Her answers are often brief and to the point but become more expansive as the interview proceeds. She is, above all things, supremely confident.

When did you have the sense that you wanted to tell stories?

I think I always did, ever since I was little, five or six.

Did you write them down?

I did, or my mom wrote them down for me before I could write.

Was she a storyteller herself?

She was. She's an actress in Chicago. She used to bring me to rehearsals.

So you knew what a play was.

Yes, from a young age.

And did you think, "Well, that's what I want to write"?

No, actually. I always wanted to write poetry or short stories. I never had any interest in being a playwright. I always knew that I wanted to write something. It was when I met Paula Vogel at Brown that I started writing plays.

You didn't go to Brown because of Paula?

No. I just managed to get there.

And you were a writer by that time?

I wrote short stories, I wrote poems.

And you just happened to take a class with Paula?

Yeah, I was interested in playwriting, and I thought it would be a lark. I thought it would be fun. I think through studying with Paula, it became serious. I mean, I think if I had met another teacher of writing at that time in my life who was a poet or in some other genre who said, "Oh, I think you can do this, I think you can make a life doing this," things might have turned out differently. But Paula has such an amazing knack for helping people imagine their own lives and their own livelihood.

As opposed to just being a playwright, imagining a life as a playwright? How does she do that?

She kind of takes you in. I remember when I was a graduate student, she took the three of us when we graduated to her house in Truro on Cape Cod. We sat on the porch and she said, "Look at this view," and we looked at the ocean. She said, "This is what playwriting can buy." I think it was shortly after she won the Pulitzer Prize for *How I Learned to Drive*. So she helps you imagine it, she helps you imagine how it would be.

When you sit down at your desk, do you have a schedule?

I wish. I wish I did. I used to before I had kids. I would write maybe eleven to two every day. And now I just have no bearings at the moment.

You know, we were going to ask you—and we still may—about how your success has changed your writing life. But I think what's much more important is how have children changed that?

You know, I think it makes you a little more miserly about the things you choose to do and how you spend your time, and it makes it just more difficult to shut the door and get out the door.

But before you had children, would you only be a playwright when you were sitting at your desk? When you weren't at the desk, was it in your mind? When you were on the subway, were you still writing?

Sure, yeah.

Can you do that now, or do your children take up that kind of time?

Yes. I do it while I'm changing diarrhea-filled diapers, it's just the vista is different.

Has your children's existence changed what you write about?

I don't find it easy to analyze my own work that way. I'm sure someone outside could look in and say, "Oh, after you had children, your work changed in such-and-such a way." But I don't look back that way.

So you don't see any point or value in having a perspective about your work?

No. I think it's death. I think it's horrible, actually. One should fight that impulse.

Leave that to the critics, right?

I think so.

Just in reflection, you may notice your concerns have changed. Your themes. Where your interests lie. I don't know if that's true. It may influence your life and not your work.

It probably has. I don't know how, honestly.

Do you find the structure as you write or do you have some kind of plan?

I always find the structure as I write. Every structure of every play is different, depending on the story. I know some playwrights have an end always in mind, but I usually hope that if I'm discovering as I'm writing, the audience will discover as they're watching. There's always a panic between the first and second act, where I think, "Oh, God, is this a play at all?" since I don't know the endpoint. But there comes a point where I know the endpoint, and then I rush to the finish.

So you write chronologically?

Mm-hmm.

What if you get stuck? Do you jump ahead?

I usually take time off if I'm stuck. I usually try not to work on it if I'm stuck.

Where do the ideas come from? Are you inspired by your life, something you read, an image, a person?

All of that. Sure.

My main experience was seeing your plays, and when I started to read them, I was struck by—and I don't think I've ever seen it before—the way you write your stage directions and also the way you write your dialogue: in short sentences, each on a new line.

I think, starting as a poet, I'm always interested in how a play looks on a page and how it reads. It's kind of a readerly document. I find most plays very hard to read because of standardized formatting. I hate standardized formatting. For one thing, what it does to stage directions is it turns them into parentheticals. It turns them into blueprints to be disregarded. I mean, the whole notion of what's in parentheses means it's incidental. I don't think stage directions are incidental. It's partly just an instinct. It's how I see what I write. It just makes sense to me. I think maybe starting in poetry, that it's justified to the left and then I hear the rhythm in my head as I'm writing. The rhythm of it is a clue for the designers and actors and director in terms of how long to spend on each image. The same with the dialogue. The line breaks are a clue in terms of how much time to think about each line or how much breath to take.

I found it interesting in the dialogue that there wasn't a pause and yet something happened from line to line. It seemed like a new way for some space to happen before the next line.

Right, exactly.

Does it actually help actors?

I think once actors understand the vernacular of what I'm doing and have done a play of mine before, they really get the punctuation. I'm sure actors could look at it for the first time and think, "What is this?" and be befuddled.

Do you explain? Do you talk about it in the first rehearsal? In a casting session?

It tends to be pretty intuitive. And then if an actor is puzzled, of course we talk about it. Or directors who know my work well will say, "Pay attention to that line break or punctuation."

Some of your stage directions seem challenging to a designer. I wondered, where did you get the—I don't know what the word is—courage, nerve to actually write some of those things?

I think that was really Paula Vogel. She has this great exercise she gives at Brown where she says, "Write a play that's impossible to stage." And it's this great exercise because either way, you win. If you write a play that's impossible to stage, you fulfilled the exercise. And if you write a play that's possible to stage, you think, "Great, I wrote a play that you can stage." You find that it's actually very hard to write anything that's impossible to stage. I mean, if you say, "Then there's a flood, then there's a fire," well, then you do that scenically. If you say, "Then Ahab comes in and kills a whale," then you have a puppet of a whale. I think I did one that had to do with telepathy between actors and audience. I do think it was impossible.

So that influences the style of the play. The one I'm about to quote isn't impossible. It's in Eurydice, *where the stage directions say, "Strawberries and peaches fall from the sky into a lake." So that's not impossible, but what is it? From a designer's point of view, what do you do?*

I don't think anyone's done that particular stage direction. I think that particular one is just a grace note about the tonality of the world and then the designers design around that tonality. Sometimes I cut it if it seems really impossible or not fruitful, but it informs the discussion of the design somehow. I think, "Well, I'll leave it in and see how it catapults the designer."

When you're not present at a play, do you get phone calls, asking, "What do I do with this?"

Sometimes, sure.

Can you explain it, or do you just tell them to leave it out if they can't manage it?

I mean, for me, a premiere is so different than even a second or third production. At a premiere, I would be really intimately involved with the design and then later at a second or third production, I'd say, "Oh, go to it. Have at it. And maybe I'll see it and maybe I won't."

For a premiere, do you stay at rehearsals a lot?

Yes. As much as I can be. I love being at rehearsals. Right now I have a play opening out of town—*Stage Kiss* in Chicago—and I'm kind of desperate. I don't know what to do because when I had one child, I just took her with me, and now with three, it's very hard to figure it out. But I want to be there.

When you go to rehearsals, in what way are you involved?

Well, intimately, I would say. The kind of director I love is the kind of director who doesn't get stern or strange if you talk directly to the actors. Like Mark Wing-Davey. I'll whisper something to Mark, and he'll say, "Just tell the actor." Or Les Waters, whom I've worked with over and over again.

And they're not ever horrified by what you've said?

I mean, if they are, then we'll talk later. Or Les will say, "Let's not do this now in front of the actors." Because, I think, directors can be so much more sensitive to where an actor is in their process and playwrights can know exactly what they want the endpoint to be on the first day of rehearsal. And the director knows, "Save that for week two or save that for week three or four even."

Do the designers want your input?

They tend to. The designers I like to work with. The designers I would not like to work with would not like my input.

What do you do if a director who you haven't worked with before just isn't getting it in a large way?

It's terribly hard. Thank God it hasn't happened to me for a long time. It also makes me wary of working with directors I haven't worked with before. Yeah, you fight with them. You have to. You have to protect the play. You have to learn how to have a constructive fight, a constructive argument.

Do you ever change things because an actor can't do something?

I have. I usually regret it and then I change it in the publication.

I assume that you try to get them to do it, and then if they don't . . .

Yeah, if they truly can't, I'll cut something. And if it turns out there was a reason they can't because they're a really fine actor and they instinctively know it's wrong, then great. But if it's their own weakness, then I'll put it back later.

Do you work with certain actors over and over? I notice Kathleen Chalfant's been in a few of your plays?

Oh, yeah. I just saw her yesterday. I love her. I love Polly Noonan, whom I've worked with a bunch. Keith Reddin I've worked with a bunch, he's also a playwright, a wonderful playwright. Thomas Jay Ryan I've worked with a bunch. Mary-Louise Parker.

Have you written for an actor?

A little bit here and there. I think it's more I start writing something and then I realize, "Oh, this would be a wonderful role for Polly," and that informs the second act.

Do you feel that these actors sort of get your work? Is it the rhythms or is it another level of poetic understanding?

I think it's the rhythm and the emotional honesty that is not about subtext. Being able to be emotionally available to the language and to the thought without any kind of weird subterfuge. It's rare to find those actors. I'm working on this little series of essays that are very short, and one is about subtext where I say that I think of subtext as being to the left or to the right of the work instead of beneath the work. So that the subtext is in the design or in the atmosphere but isn't underneath as a secret. So that if someone in my play says, "I'm happy," ninety-nine percent of the time, it means, "I'm happy." It doesn't mean, "I'm desolate, but I'm telling you that I'm happy." So there's a kind of . . . forthrightness or simplicity about the relationship of the thought to the language.

The Actors Studio is the one that created subtext. In Shakespeare, there's no subtext.

Right.

You did an adaptation of Three Sisters. *Chekhov is always done as if there's subtext.*

And I think that's just the kind of weird inheritance of Stanislavsky's approach to Chekhov as opposed to how Chekhov meant to have it done. I always think, "Oh, if Meyerhold had done all of his work, then we would do Chekhov totally differently." I think Chekhov has an incandescent transparency in his language. I really don't understand how it gets so bloated and weird.

Is it bloated? It seems like it's meant to be really spare with tons going on underneath. So I'm interested to see what your approach to it is going to be with Three Sisters.

It's a very straightforward approach. I worked with this wonderful woman, Elise Thoron, who speaks Russian, and she went line by line with me. I tried to pare it down in the same way that it is in the Russian, where there aren't as many pronouns as in most translations. I think with a lot of translations, it's almost as if they go through the British version out to the American and there's four or five extra words in every sentence.

What was that experience like, adapting Chekhov versus working on your original work?

I loved it. I think it was a time when I needed a little break. It was between two other projects, and so it was almost like knitting or doing a math problem, and I don't knit very well. It was something intellectually completely engaging but comforting because you know what the ending is. It was wonderful to get inside Chekhov's head. I mean, I tend not to work on adaptations unless I think the person who did the original is a complete master and I should be faithful to them and learn from them. I don't want to do a "take" on Chekhov.

Was that a similar experience when you did Orlando?

Yeah, exactly.

How was that different, since Orlando *didn't exist in a script form?*

I mean, with Virginia Woolf, it's almost as if you're directing it on the page, when you move from prose to a play. You just think, "Oh, if I were a director, how would I lay this on the page so it could be done in two hours?" In that sense, it's less writerly. I didn't want to invent much that wasn't there because I think Woolf is so singular and amazing. How could my dialogue possibly compare with her prose? There were occasions where I'd invent dialogue because there's less dialogue than there is narration in the original novel.

Did you see the 1992 movie?

I did.

Did that help you?

Oh, God, no. I think I tried to see it later. I think Sally Potter is a wonderful filmmaker, but to me that was a "take" on *Orlando*. It wasn't *Orlando.* Visually stunning, but to me it wasn't the spirit of the book.

You've had a lot of success, and it came sort of early, it seems. And then the Mac-Arthur Fellowship came early. Did that change the way you sit at the desk?

No, I hope not. I just think the desk is a very private thing. It has nothing to do with anything else. It's a private practice that if I didn't do, I would go quietly insane, whether or not the work is ever done. All the rest of it is nice and helpful. It's helpful to get your plays produced because I think it's sad when plays get left in a drawer. It's helpful to have wonderful actors and designers, because you get to see what you wrote. It's helpful to have money to pay a babysitter so you can write some more. But all the rest of it is kind of silly. I think it's because I started as a poet, where publication wasn't even very interesting or satisfying to me. It was just making the thing. Theater is different because you really don't have the thing until you hear the actors do it. It's not as satisfying, a play in a drawer as opposed to a poem in a drawer.

Did the confidence of having this early success help you or did it not enter into the room at all? One would think the success would have some effect, but maybe it doesn't.

This might sound strange, but I was not unconfident in my private writing process before others said, "Oh, this play is OK, this play is all right." Honestly, it was my teachers who gave me confidence at the desk, not outside accolades like the MacArthur. I mean, the MacArthur is amazing because you have this luxury of having this money to be able to do projects you want to do. It buys you time. But if you get confidence for those reasons, those are the wrong reasons to be confident. When that's taken away, as it will be from me at any moment or at some cycle when people get sick of my work—it happens to everyone—then that would be a sad day for me at my desk if I could no longer write the next play when that happens. I just think you have to keep it really separate.

Do you show your work to anyone? When you finish or at some stage?

Yeah. Fellow writers, a couple of dear friends who are writers. A couple of directors. A couple of actor friends. My husband.

Do you have a place where you can always get your plays read?

The Piven Theatre Workshop was the first theater that ever did my stuff in Chicago, and they're wonderful, and they would always do a reading when I started out. They did my first production. Then in New York, Lincoln Center has really been a home to me.

Do you learn from having your work read to you?

Oh, yeah. I need that desperately at that point. I tend to be very secretive about the play until it's at that point, and then you have to go through this horrible thing of hearing it read and being humiliated and then you can do the rewrite and hear it again and be slightly less humiliated. Then hear it again until it's ready for production.

Have you ever been influenced by what a critic said about your work?

I don't read critics, so it's hard to be influenced by that. I don't read reviews.

But someone always lets you know.

They do. My husband used to read them for me, but then he got too emotionally engaged, and he had to stop. My mother reads them and my agent reads them. They'll tell me, "Oh, this person liked it, this person didn't." Sometimes they won't even tell me. Or if there's a really well-written review by a reviewer whom I respect and there's one special phrase or insight, they'll say, "You gotta hear this paragraph," and I will. But I'll try to hear it while half not listening to it, because I don't want to be terribly affected by it.

It's like you said at the beginning, you don't want to know too much about your own work.

Yeah.

What would you say are your greatest strengths as a writer?

You know, I might almost plead the fifth on that too in terms of this kind of death by self-analysis.

Well, then don't. Maybe that is the strength.

I'm a horse with blinders going through the fire.

Do you learn from audiences? When you're in previews, do you listen? Do you make changes? Do you think about it?

Oh, absolutely. I think you learn where the cuts are, you learn where the staging doesn't work. I don't think I made enormous changes to a character or a plot in previews, but I have said, "Oh, that line is gone, this line is gone." *Passion Play* was so huge that I might have taken a scene out and put one back in. I think in Chicago I did kind of take scenes out, but that was the most radical.

What about when In the Next Room (or the Vibrator Play) *went from Berkeley to New York?*

That was close to done, I have to say. I mean, we fretted during previews. We fretted a lot, but we didn't change that much.

A lot of the questions that we have and we've asked other playwrights are just asking them to analyze themselves, analyze what they do. I think it's a very interesting and unique point of view to refuse to do that.

It's not very helpful, maybe. I think the other part of that is there's a part of my mind that's quite analytical, and if I hadn't become a playwright, I might've become a poet or scholar of nineteenth-century novels and been quite happy to analyze the imagery of wax in *Daniel Deronda*. I like doing that. But if I shone that light on my own work, I think it would be really disconcerting to me.

You do this other thing I think is interesting: at the beginning of scenes, you title them. What's that for exactly?

Sometimes it's to focus the scene for myself. Sometimes it's just for my own pleasure in that literary sense, in the kind of literary tradition of nineteenth-century scenes titles. I love that stuff.

Who are the other playwrights who've influenced you?

All my teachers, Paula Vogel the first among them. Mac Wellman was a teacher and an influence. María Irene Fornés I studied with, and I loved both her plays and her person, and her teaching. Nilo Cruz was a teacher. Then people who have not been my teachers but influenced me: Caryl Churchill, Chuck Mee. I love the old guys, the Greeks, Shakespeare. I love strange plays for the drawer like Edna St. Vincent Millay or E. E. Cummings.

Do you have any interest in writing for TV or film?

Not terribly much. I wouldn't say, "Oh, I'd never do it." If the right project or the right director came up. I think in film it has to be the right director, because it's a director-driven medium, so otherwise what you write would just get turned into cinders and ashes. And TV, I don't know. I just bought an apartment. We just are moving to Brooklyn this summer. We've rented here for the last five years. Anyway, we need more space for the kids now. So I've always been a little "eh" about TV. It would be nice if I could continue in my current way of life.

Are your plays getting done in other countries?

They are. My God. One was translated into Arabic, which I was so pleased about. And Korean. And they've been in Israel. Australia was the latest. I wish I could've gone and seen that one. I used to travel everywhere and see everything. I saw a crazy production of *Eurydice* in Germany once. That actually made me think, "I will never do this again." I would let them put on "crazy" productions but not inflict it on myself by going. It's just a Pandora's box. They'd added a prologue by Heinrich Müller. There are three stones, they'd added a fourth. They'd taken out Orpheus's monologues and written MTV rock songs for him to sing. It was shocking.

Are you interested in musicals at all? Writing a book for a musical?

Yes, that I am interested in. I was working on one that I was very excited about and then suddenly the subject was in the zeitgeist and everyone was writing about it, so we abandoned it. It was an adaptation of an NPR documentary of all things. It was about the first all-female radio station in Memphis called WHER. It was about women, but it was about Memphis and radio in the sixties. So when *Memphis* happened and *Million Dollar Quartet* happened, it seemed strange. I was working on it with Elvis Costello, and I just, you know, love him to death. It was amazing hearing his songs for the first time. He wrote two songs, I had about twenty pages, and then we said, "Eh." I'm saying "eh" all the time right now. My son, who's one, is pointing at everything right now and going, "Eh, eh." I would love to write a musical. I love musicians . . .

I felt that in your work—that you love music.

Yeah, I play the piano badly. I wrote a play called *Melancholy Play* with a cello score. It was always my favorite part of rehearsal to sit with the cellist. The kind of complete subjectivity of music—that it's emotional and not linguistically based, but the objectivity of the musician playing it and whether or not they can do a good job—I love. The musical director will sit with the cellist and say, "You didn't hit the right note. Make that more allegro." And they go, "Oh, great, great," and they have no ego. And the actors are kind of over on the left, full of self-hatred and not sure what they're doing. I just think, "Give me a cellist. Give me a score." I also love about the American musical that it's the American form and it's completely not realistic. To me, it's this great antidote to naturalism: If people are singing about their feelings, obviously you're not in a living room. Obviously, it's not true, it's not real. It's real only in a subjective way.

Just like your plays: they're real, but they're not realism.

Right. Yeah.

They're not exactly the real world. But the actors can still do them.

Exactly. If they act odd and stylized, it doesn't work.

It's a fine line. I think you're fortunate to find directors who can hew to that line.

Simplicity. Directors who love simplicity and who can help actors find that. This actress Maria Dizzia—I forgot to mention her before—whom

I adore and work with her so much. She played Eurydice and Mrs. Daldry in *In the Next Room*. I love her. She once said in *Eurydice*, "Oh, there are no pillars to hide behind." Which I loved. It wasn't Greek in that sense of architecture and pillars and emotionally that you could construct something and hide behind it. She had to be so vulnerable and she was willing to do that.

I know that you don't like to talk about your work process exactly, but how did you do it as a student?

Oh, yeah, it was terrible . . . Well, actually, we didn't get to talk about our own work. Usually other people talked about it, and we had to write notes down.

So you didn't have to explain or justify why you did what you did?

Usually. I have to say Paula is such a brilliant teacher because she too is afraid of excavating too much. So she'll talk about the work formally and break it down formally, but she won't ask you to kind of excavate and make cognitive the more subterranean things going on in the work. She'll just assume that you get that for free, and then she'll deal with the formal elements. I think some teachers can really do harm by forcing students into almost a therapeutic . . . Those who shall not be named, but if we have a beer sometime, I can talk to you about . . .

You just have to fend them off?

You have to either not study with them, or you have to bring in old work that you don't care about anymore and have them talk about it. You can't bring in anything that means anything to you because they will destroy it.

Well, it's not that you necessarily have this grand message you want to give to the masses, but have you ever thought about what you are trying to say as a playwright about the human experience?

No. Absolutely not. What did E. E. Cummings say, something like, "I write about such trite themes as love and death"? Those are all writers' themes. I think we're pressed in this country to think about our themes in terms of how they would sound in a grant proposal. So we're pressed to have smaller issues—I won't name them—but to write issue plays about tinier issues when I think most writers worth their salt should be kind of contending with love and death. But who has a nugget to say about that that's compressible that could be in a grant application or that you could say about your own work? In that way, I think plays should be like poems: irreducible in their meaning. I don't think all playwrights feel that way. I have this theory that the world is divided into Arthur Millers and Tennessee Williamses. One is kind of an architect, that Arthur Miller kind of builds these structures that are amazing, and at the apex of the structure is a line that is the kind of moral message: "Attention must be paid. It's all my sons." And he'd build these amazing structures to contain a moral. So I think morality plays and mystery plays, Miller and Williams. I think Williams is a writer of mystery. It's more subjective, less subjective, and the meaning is more irreducible. It doesn't have a moral. It's more about moment-to-moment experience. When I studied with María Irene Fornés, I always loved, she would get so mad when people would say, "What should I take away from your play?" She would say, "My play is not a restaurant, I do not have a doggie bag! There's nothing you should take away." She was fierce about redirecting the attention to the moment of watching. You talk to people about what they remember from a play. Is it ever even the writing? No. That's the kind of astonishing thing.

Do you think that this same kind of need for the audience to reduce the play to its "meaning" is peculiarly American?

Yes, because I think underneath it we're these pilgrims that are really worried about whether or not theater is useful. If it has a moral, then it's useful and then it's all right to spend your Friday nights doing it. I mean, I think in other countries, there's a less Puritan kind of pleasure in the thing. It's useful because it's pleasurable. So I think the country got kind of divided into the burlesque vaudeville and morality. I think it needs to come back together in the plays because otherwise the only popular form is the cinema. The cinema could care less about morality. Why do people go to movies instead of plays? Partly because they don't make you feel as though you're a sober citizen receiving your kind of communion in the form of a message. This is a little bit of rant. I think New York is especially tough. I actually find it more in regional theater, people kind of sitting forward, thinking, "Oh, I'm here to experience pleasure. I hope it gives me pleasure. I'll sit forward and hope it gives me pleasure. Oh, it's giving me pleasure." I feel like in New York, people go and they're kind of, "This is gonna suck. Watch it suck. Oh, it's sucking. Here it's sucking some more." Watching a play fail is another kind of pleasure in New York. It's kind of blood sport.

I saw The Vibrator Play *in Lincoln Center. What were the audience's responses to that? It was odd. I remember there was laughter, which was wonderful. But I couldn't tell . . .*

The subscription audience was really tough for that play. The things that they found difficult, it was interesting. A man getting vibrated from behind was delicious to them. They loved that. That gave them a lot of pleasure. A woman having sexual pleasure was really uncomfortable for them. A man and a woman having intimacy was really deeply uncomfortable to them. They hated that. Some of them. So it was interesting.

It was different in Berkeley?

Yes, it was. The audience was much more buoyant and less conservative in Berkeley.

Well, isn't there a forty-year age difference in the audience?

Yeah, I mean, I do remember overhearing at one point a woman turning to her sister, "Oh, God, I forgot my oxygen." I thought, "Oh, it's gonna be that kind of night."

LYNN NOTTAGE

We're going to meet Lynn Nottage in the lobby of the Classic Stage Company, which has an espresso bar. It's crowded this morning, and we're sitting at a small table figuring out our new digital recording device while we wait to meet Lynn. She comes in, heads turn, and people recognize her. She spots us, waves, but as she starts to maneuver her way to our table, we rise and steer her to an outside door that leads upstairs to the CSC offices. Artistic Director Brian Kulick has given us a small room in which to conduct the interview. There's a lot of scrambling around to supply everyone with a bottle of water, and, as usual, we're still toying with the microphone. Lynn is dressed in very dark colors. Her hair is done in elaborate dreadlocks. She seems a little wary of the whole procedure, as if we're going to gang up on her, but she is voluble and excited once we stop fussing with the furniture. When she starts talking, she is open and eager to tell us about the personal issues that are at the root of her work.

Your plays are politically and socially engaged. How did that start in your life?

I think for me it started by being a child of parents who were very involved in the civil rights movement and the feminist movement, so I grew up with activist parents, and it was important for them that we be schooled in the vocabulary of social change. And so I think that follows you wherever you go, whether you be a doctor or a lawyer or a playwright or pharmacist—I think that's always a part of who I am. My mother was a feminist, and I was walking the picket lines from the time I was like five years old. She was incredibly outspoken and exposed me to a lot of incredible women like Bella Abzug and Carol Bellamy. My parents' friends were politicians and artists and people who were very socially engaged. I almost feel as though my life is small as compared to the lives that they had forged for themselves. Even though my mom was a school teacher and my father was a social worker, I thought, growing up, that they were at the epicenter of change. Even though that wasn't necessarily true, it looked that way to me.

Did they take you to the theater?

They took me to the theater, and they took me to hear music, because they felt as though music and art were very important components in understanding ourselves. They loved art, and if you've ever been to my house, I live in the house that I grew up in, almost every single inch of the wall is covered with art that they had collected.

Did you immediately gravitate toward writing plays?

You know, I think I did, even though it took many years for me to say that I was a playwright, but I think I started writing at a very early age. Writing things for me and my brother that we would perform for my parents when they had dinner parties. We always forced them to pay attention for five minutes. We'd come down the steps and we'd perform these plays, and they'd indulge us, and I know they were probably terrible. Even in high school I wasn't a theater arts major—I didn't study acting, I wrote plays. I wrote my first play probably my junior year, and it was called *The Darker Side of Verona,* and it was about an African American Shakespearean troupe, and they went down South and performed *Romeo and Juliet.*

Did the play get done?

I actually sent it to the Young People's Playwright's Festival. That was run by Gerald Chapman, an extraordinary person. He didn't pick the play, but he invited me to a developmental workshop for young people interested in musical theater. Four of us were selected from New York City high schools, and we wrote a musical. It wasn't a very good musical, but we did it, and we were mentored by people like Stephen Sondheim and other folks.

Have you written a musical since?

I have fragments of musicals. It's really hard and it's really time-consuming. And it's so thoroughly collaborative that one has to get used to exercising that muscle.

So what do you do when you write? You sit down at your desk . . .

Sometimes. Sometimes I lie in my bed.

Do you keep to a schedule?

My schedule is dictated by having children. I have two children. I have a two-year-old, and I have a thirteen-year-old. I have a daughter who I get out of the house by seven, and I have a babysitter who comes at nine, so my hours are defined by the babysitter. I try to be as productive as I possibly can between nine and three o'clock, focused on writing-related stuff and career-related stuff. Before children became the organizing principle of my life, I was a binge writer. I'd have these deadlines, and I'd wait right until the last minute, and then I'd write five straight days, twenty-four hours a day, but once I had children, I didn't have the luxury. I shouldn't say the luxury, I couldn't do that. I had to carve out time to write, and I'm very selfish about it.

When you're not at your desk from nine to two, are you still writing?

Oh yeah, I feel like I'm always writing, and I feel like my procrastination is an active way of writing. I might go to the library or pick up a book that has something to do with what I'm working on so I always feel like I'm engaged in the process of writing, even though I'm not sitting at my desk, typing with the computer.

How does a play start for you?

It depends on the particular play. In the case of *Ruined,* it began with a conversation that Kate Whoriskey and I had that we wanted to adapt *Mother Courage* for the stage and then going on this journey to Africa and discovering that we wanted to do something very different. Encountering these very powerful African women who shared their stories then inspired me to sit down and write *Ruined.* But in the case of another play, *Las Meninas,* it began with a paragraph in a history book that I read that was kind of funny, sort of curious, and it began this ten-year odyssey really to find whether this story I read about, a romance between Therese, who was the wife of Louis the Fourteenth, the sun king, and an African dwarf who had been given to her by her uncle, was true.

And was it true?

I think so, and at this point I'm probably the foremost expert in the world on this subject. If you go on the Internet you can find me cited. This research is so random. I think I know more about this subject than anyone.

What about Intimate Apparel?

I moved back into the house where I grew up when my mother was dying, to take care of her. She had Lou Gehrig's disease. And so she needed a great deal of support, as you can imagine. *Intimate Apparel* was a play I wrote just after my mother died and after she had gone through this very protracted and quite hideous illness. I wanted to write a play for her. I wanted to write something that I felt she would want to see. I wanted to write a play that was very simple and unabashedly emotional and not sort of shy away from that, because I think that up until that point I'd been writing much more sort of fanciful plays and really avoiding the hard work, which is looking at human emotion in a very raw, honest way and not pandering, and so I wrote *Intimate Apparel,* which I think is very simple but very emotional.

It's very delicate.

It's very delicate. And I say that at the time, it was the bravest play that I could write because it was so fundamentally different from anything that

I had been seeing. I felt there was a style of theater that was in your face, that was misanthropic or cynical, and I didn't want to do that. I wanted to write something for my mother that reflected who she was.

There are fabric descriptions at the beginnings of many scenes throughout the play. How did you come up with that notion? Did you mean that to be a signal to the director or the designer?

For me I think it was because when I sat down to write, I kept thinking, "What material is Esther touching right now and how does that affect the way in which she moves through her life?" And then I thought about the effect: "Is this scene lace or is this scene velvet? Is it more sumptuous or is it more delicate? Or is it cambric, which is a rougher texture?" I was definitely thinking of all those things. It was a clue for the director, but it was also where my head was while I was writing it.

When you start a play like this or any other, do you find it as you go along or do you structure it before you write?

Well, in the case of *Intimate Apparel*, I wrote the first scene and the last scene, and I didn't change a word for those two scenes. The middle was a struggle, and that went through many permutations, but I knew where I wanted to begin and where I wanted to end that play. I wanted the play to begin with a woman sitting at a sewing machine and end with a woman at a sewing machine. In the beginning that sewing machine was a symbol of oppression, and at the end it was a symbol of liberation. So I knew that that was the journey and somehow I had to get that character from there to here. I felt as though that play was much more structured than anything else I wrote. I also knew that each scene was going to be two people and each scene was going to be written around a bed, and I was interested in how that bed shifts the dynamic between two people. This was something I set up for myself. I knew going in that this was my exercise.

Did you do rewriting in rehearsal or before rehearsal . . .?

I did a fair amount of rewriting because there were a couple scenes that weren't working. Interestingly enough, the play was produced at Center

Stage and then we moved to South Coast Rep, and I felt as though it wasn't quite working for me. Even though the play was doing well, I felt as though I hadn't solved the problem, and when I came to New York to do the production with Dan Sullivan, I said, "You know, I'm struggling. I can't figure out how to write this particular scene," and he said, "You know the problem isn't the scene. It's two scenes before that scene. Just take it out." I took the scene out, and miraculously . . . I was like, how can the problem be solved so simply? And I realized that I had this scene in the play that was convoluting everything, and there might have been some writing that I was proud of and I was holding onto it because I was proud of this particular writing, but it had no place in this particular play. And that still remains one of the best pieces of advice that I've ever gotten, because it taught me that sometimes we have to make small sacrifices for the greater good of the play.

At what point do you say, "OK, I've done as much as I can do, and I have to show it to somebody"? Are there people you show it to?

I usually show it to my husband, because I know he'll be an honest critic, and sometimes I show it to my brother, who I call "the man on the street." He has no theater education, so he's going to have a pure, visceral response and he won't mince words. He's like, "It bored me" or "I find that really interesting," and sometimes he'll ask more astute questions than someone who is trained in dramaturgy, because he's not afraid to hide his confusion or his ignorance, and sometimes that confusion will help me figure out what clues I'm not giving him.

And it never gets in the way, personally?

Like what?

Well, that you've asked two people that you're so close with. You never want to wring their necks if they don't like something?

Yeah, it's fine if they don't, and I'm fine with that. I feel as playwrights we have to be OK with that. Not everything is going to be a slam dunk with our friends or our families or with the critics.

OK, they've said what they say, then what do you do?

If it's commissioned, I will do a reading with the commissioning theater, or if it's not a commission, as was the case with *Ruined,* I will take it to a theater or Kate Whoriskey, because she had a relationship with the Goodman, and she said, "I think they might be interested in this play, and we can do a reading." I have to take a few steps back because with *Ruined* we did readings with Labyrinth. I first developed the play with the Labyrinth folks, and that's why there are so many Lab people who ended up in the final production, but the company ultimately couldn't do it because it was such a big show. I did a reading with them. I took it to Lab, and I thought this is a cool, adventurous play, and I thought that the Lab might be interested. So we developed it with them, and when they felt that they couldn't develop it any more, they took it to the Goodman.

A play like Ruined *is obviously researched, and my guess is that* Intimate Apparel *was researched, but a play like* Fabulation *isn't.*

No. It wasn't and it probably shows. *Fabulation* was my vacation from *Intimate Apparel.* I wanted a play where I didn't have to spend hours in the library. I wanted a play where I would literally sit down and every scene tumbled out of the imagination. I didn't know where it was going, and I just let it tumble out, and I would let these characters take me to where they led me, and then it ends.

So you didn't set the character on the course of a downward spiral?

Yes, I knew she was tumbling down, I just didn't know who from moment to moment she was going to encounter until, literally, I began typing on the page. I thought, "Wouldn't it be fun if now she got arrested?" Just seeing where each thing led me, and each step led me somewhere different.

But did you find the tone as you wrote?

I knew the tone I wanted before I set out to write. I knew I wanted to write something that was fun and whimsical and fast and funny. And so I knew that sitting down. The moment I conjured this character, I thought, "Oh, she's funny."

Tell me about the new play that's going to Second Stage.

By the Way, Meet Vera Stark. I'm still in the process of figuring out how to talk about this play, because I'm still in the midst of rehearsal. It's about race. It's about Hollywood. It's about passing. It's about how stereotypes that were conjured during the 1930s continue to haunt us today. But, what is the story? The story is the story of an African American maid working for a white starlet who is auditioning for a film like *Gone with the Wind.* It's a big Southern epic, and this maid decides that she wants to get a part in this film as well, and so this first act of the play is really this sort of fast-and-furious screwball comedy of these two women, one a white starlet and one an African American maid trying to get into this movie, and then we jump to the second act, sort of *Top Girls* or *Sunday in the Park with George* style. It's 2003, I don't know why, just for symmetry. The play begins with the movie *The Belle of New Orleans,* so we actually see the film onscreen in 1933 style, and it's a group of academics critiquing the legacy of that film, and they're also very funny because they're sort of pompous and full of themselves and they all take ownership of Vera Stark to serve their own thesis.

What was the genesis of that?

That play was sort of similar to *Intimate Apparel* and *Fabulation* because I was working on *Ruined,* and I needed an escape that didn't require the same kind of heavy research but would take me to a place like Hollywood 1930s comedy, where I could literally sit down, watch a movie, and that would be my research. But then I ended up doing a lot of research because I thought, "Oh, I'm writing about these African American characters who are only onscreen for two minutes. But who are they once they leave? How are they getting work and how are they feeding themselves?" It just conjured up a lot of questions that couldn't be answered, and I began reading, and it ended up being a research-heavy play even though I didn't want it to be.

So a play is done and you go into rehearsal. Are you there every day?

I try to be there every day unless I have to take time out to answer questions on the page. Sometimes I need to go home because I feel as though I haven't quite figured it out and it would be better for me to spend the time, a full day at home, trying to solve the problem instead of just watching the same problem over and over again with my frustration building. And so sometimes I'll just take time out to look at the script and be with the script to see if it's ultimately what I want it to be.

What do you like in a director?

The last three were developed with Kate Whoriskey. On this I'm working with Jo Bonney. And before Kate I was working with Seret Scott. What I look for in a director is someone who first and foremost is going to be an advocate for the play. I look for who they are and what they want to accomplish as an artist. I look for a director who is as invested in the project as I am and is going to have fun on the adventure. But I also want a warrior director, someone who is going to fight for the words and the ideas. What I like so much about Kate is that I see her so much as a warrior. She will literally go down to the mat for the integrity of the production.

Let's just go back to you working at home. How long will you sit there before you realize it's your problem and not their problem?

In this case it took me a week to realize, "Oh, it's never going to work." I kept thinking, "They haven't gotten there, they haven't gotten there, let me let them sort of struggle through it, and once they get off book they'll be fine." And then they got off book and I thought, "You know what . . . it's not working. It's time for me to look at the script." A lot of times directors will say, "Let me work with it, let's explore, let's see if this is something that is in performance," and a lot of directors will try to figure it out and in this particular case Jo Bonney came to me and said, "I think there is something that is not being activated on the page. We're missing something."

Will the actors actually say to you, "I can't do this"? Or do they just tell you by the fact that they're not getting it?

Yeah, the fact that they're not getting it. Some actors will say, "This isn't working for me."

Will you ever change something right then?

I do. A lot of times someone will say, "This seems really weird coming out of my mouth at this moment in the play." And I'll say, "Oh, you're right." I'm humble like that. I'm not above saying sometimes I make mistakes or there are better solutions.

So you don't have a problem talking to the actor, and the director lets you do that?

I feel I must. I don't like it. I feel like if I'm in the room and I wrote this play, I should have the right to respond to it. And sometimes a director will say things which I diametrically oppose, and I feel it's my responsibility to say, "You know what? I disagree."

So you do that.

I would probably not do that in the rehearsal room. I'd probably do it outside of the rehearsal room or ask, "Can I have a moment to speak to the actors?" or "Can we clarify?" But I'm not going to remain silent if I don't think that the production is moving in the direction that I want to go or if I feel like the director is just misinterpreting something.

It sounds like you have good relations with these directors.

With these I do, and that's why I work with them. I've had directors who will say something like, "Don't pay attention to the stage directions at all," and I thought, "No. There's a reason why this person who is an alcoholic is now taking his fourth drink. Pay attention to that." That drives me crazy.

What will you do with a director like that?

I will tell him that I believe the drama of the play is not just in the dialogue but in the action, and most of the clues for the actions are written in the stage directions, so if you disregard it, you're disregarding half the play.

One of the writers we were talking to said an interesting thing about stage directions: they're in parentheses and parentheses suggest they can be disregarded. They should be written in bold or something.

I don't write in parentheses. I don't use the parentheses format.

Do you work with the designers?

Not generally. A lot of times I'll be asked to look at it after it's been designed, but generally I don't get an opportunity to speak to the designers until after they've met with the director, but that's not true with Kate. She brought me in early, and also I had a relationship with that designer, and we had done several productions together, so we felt very much like a team.

Do you have a visual image of what the play looks like to you?

I will confess to you that I'm not a visually oriented writer. I know that whatever the director and designer are going to come up with is far better than the image I have in my head, which is a black box with actors.

Do you have veto power?

I'd like to think I do. I'd like to think that if I see the design and feel it's not working, I can say, "You know what, I hate it."

Are certain aspects of writing a play easier for you than others? Dialogue or structuring? Is anything easier?

I would say for me that dialogue is easier and mastering structure has been a slow, painful process. When I look back at my earlier plays, I can see myself struggling with storytelling and narrative where I felt like the dialogue had more maturity than the structure of the play. I'm slowly feeling like I'm at the point of mastering both. I still feel like it's going to be a lifetime struggle.

Do you ever feel that the ease with dialogue can be a trap?

I do. Absolutely. I feel I try to solve many of my problems with dialogue, and I ramble on much as I'm doing now, and it just goes on and on and on and nothing will happen. And I think that I can talk my way out of the problem rather than thinking, "OK, what is the structure and how can I rein this in?" In the past I've tended to use dialogue to sort of camouflage the other faults.

Have you ever written a line where one character asks the other character a question and the character says, "I just don't know the answer to that"? And found that it's you as a writer who doesn't know the answer? Do you ever trick yourself into writing your own confusion?

I think I write my own confusion all the time. I get to the point with some characters where I'm like, I don't know where that's going to go, and the character will say something like, "I have nothing more to say. I'm finished." I felt like that with *Fabulation*. She has to have that baby now because I have no more adventures.

Once the play is in rehearsal or maybe in performance, do you listen to the audience?

I may be in the minority, but I believe the audience is the final collaborator, and that's why we do this—because we want to have this conversation with them. And if we're not listening for them, then what's the point? We could write plays and have them exist on the page and not have the interaction. I am very aware of how the play is living and breathing in that audience. I tend to sit in the very back in previews just to watch the movement to see where people are restless and when they're coughing and when they're sitting up and engaged and that tells me something about the way the narrative is unfolding.

Do you believe the audience is never wrong? That if something isn't working, it's not their fault?

It depends on what I'm looking for from the audience. If I'm intending to challenge them and they're sitting back with their arms folded, then that's fine. It really depends on what I'm asking them to do. I'm not looking for approval in the audience. I'm just looking to see how they're responding.

If you built in this laugh and they're not laughing . . .

I've written plays in which I had not intended it to be a laugh line, but every night people consistently laughed, and I thought, that's OK. That is the natural response to this moment.

Do you remember what it was?

I do remember, because it's still a moment that horrifies me. It's a moment in *Intimate Apparel*. In the top of the first act when Esther has never been with a man before, and he takes her hand and puts it on his crotch, and the audience always laughed hysterically. It's such a bold, disturbing act for a woman who is so genteel. I know it's funny, but when I wrote it, I hadn't intended it to be funny, but I accept and acknowledge the laughter.

When you write a particular line, do you ever have a thought about the audience, like, "They'll love this"?

I do. Sometimes I've written things and thought, "Oh, this is so delightful." And it makes me laugh, and it might not make anyone else laugh, but as long as it makes me laugh every time, it's OK.

Some directors believe that there's never anything wrong with a laugh. Even if you didn't intend it, it's fine.

I think that sometimes there can be something wrong with a laugh. There are times when there's inappropriate laughter. For instance, I went to see *Cat on a Hot Tin Roof,* the revival with an African American cast, and there's a moment when Brick and Big Daddy were baring their souls, and the audience laughed for all the wrong reasons, and I found myself really disturbed by it. I thought it was completely inappropriate, but the audience was laughing because they were not comfortable with this unabashed emotion, and they were not used to seeing it, but it made me uncomfortable that they laughed. And I understood why they were laughing. It wasn't like, "Ha ha ha," but it was like, "Oh, God, I'm really uncomfortable. How am I going to respond to my discomfort? I'm going to laugh and diffuse it."

You see that a lot in the theater, that people are uncomfortable and they don't know how to react and they don't stay silent.

The question was, "Is that bad laughter?" I would say that's laughter of an audience that hasn't been to the theater a great deal, and they don't know how to process their emotions, and I bet you if they had seen it again, they probably wouldn't laugh at the same place.

In the case where the laugh is inappropriate, is there a way to cut the laugh?

One would think there is. You mean cut it in the play? I would say in this play there's no way because it's inherent in its nature. I mean, the scene exists. It's a play that's been performed for the last fifty years, and one would not call it a comedy. There are some funny moments, I mean there's when the family that comes on, they're funny, but . . .

Have you encountered a situation that after a play of yours gets great reviews, like Ruined, *which is a play that also has some humor, do you find that people are reluctant to laugh?*

I find that people felt relieved to laugh in the case of *Ruined,* and the play was designed for that, because if I had permitted them to dwell in that very dark place for too long, they would have turned on the play and the characters and would have left the theater extremely angry at me and the world. But what I wanted them to have is tools to understand that in a war zone, humanity continues, and it's OK in the midst of struggle to find humor and humanity and people felt relieved to have it.

So you did that on purpose?

I knew I had to have it.

This is what you're talking about in getting good at structure.

I'm getting better at structure over time. Also, I went to Rwanda for three weeks with a group that was looking at how theater could be a tool for healing. I thought, "When I write this play I want it to be therapeutic so that when people experience it, they feel they can release. Not just an American audience, but if this play was done in Africa, an African audience could release."

Has it been done?

We're in the midst of translating it into Kinyarwandan, and there's going to be a staged reading in Kinshasa, and we were going to do it in Uganda, but in Uganda they don't understand that you can't just do a play and make it happen. There's rehearsal and all sorts of things. They just want it to happen.

Has there been movie interest?

Ruined has been picked up by HBO.

So it's going to happen?

One never knows.

Are you writing it?

I wrote the first draft of the script and am in the process of writing the second draft.

Was this a liberation or was it restrictive?

I felt liberated because it's such an expansive, epic story, and in some ways I felt constricted by the stage because there were so many places I wanted to take the audience, and I feel as though in some ways I can open up the landscape and you can see the mines and the chaos of the mines and you can see the denseness of the forests and you can see the life and vitality that on the stage was confined into one room.

Are you tempted to add things?

I feel I can bring all those characters who were mentioned casually onto the stage. For instance, I imagined the brothel to have many more women in it, but because of the restrictions of doing it onstage, I could only have four women. Here I could expand that world.

Would you show some of the stories the women tell?

I don't think I want to do that because . . . just flashes . . . I still feel as though we don't need to see the brutality. HBO was like, "We need to see it," and I wrote a draft where you see it, and they were like, "This is too brutal," and I said, "I told you. You don't want to see it. It's enough to be inferred and you don't want to see it."

And the power of the words.

And the words. I feel like you don't want to see what's happening to them. You see what's happened to them by the way they carry their bodies and the way they live their lives. You don't need to actually witness that brutal act.

Has this opened up more screenwriting possibilities? Are you interested in that?

I remain open to the possibility, but Hollywood doesn't have a place that's open to stories about African American women. So I may be interested, but it's not going to be easy to venture into that.

Ruined would have to win Emmys.

Yeah, it'd have to do incredibly well and then maybe.

After the play is opened, do you read the critics?

Yeah. I'm a masochist that way. I can't help myself. It's just compulsive.

Do you watch car accidents too?

I do. I'm the one who slows down. I'm that neighbor saying, "What's going on? What's going on?"

Have you ever learned something from a critic?

I feel like there are some critics that are more generous in spirit in the way they write their criticism. Like Michael Feingold, for instance. I felt as though he could be very harsh, but at the same time he could be very generous, and he'd say something like, "I didn't feel like this worked, but I felt like there's a lot of promise, and this is why I felt like it didn't work." I came to sort of trust some of his instincts over other critics who weren't as well versed in how to make a play and couldn't see the difference between a bad script and a bad production and an actor who wasn't necessarily bringing the full potential to the character.

From this vantage point can you look at your work and see an arc? Thematically? In any way?

I do think there are recurring themes in the work. I think unrequited love is something I return to time and time again. Obviously I'm looking at African American women who have been marginalized but not only marginalized, who are heroic women. I like to call them quote, unquote, "ordinary extraordinary women." And I think that those have been the ones at the center of most of my work.

Does it help you or have any effect on you to have this view on your work?

There's part of me that wishes I could just dwell in ignorance and continue to write not knowing what the work is about, if that makes any sense. But I get asked so much about what are the themes in your work and what do you write about that over the years in some ways, it almost feels as though it's confining the work because there's an expectation about what it should be about, and I absorb that expectation and it becomes who I am, and I wish I didn't have that expectation and I could just continue to allow my imagination to take me wherever I want to go.

Do you feel you can't?

It's not that I feel I can't. It's strange. I feel the world around me.

This sort of plays into this other question: since you've been so critically acclaimed and have received awards, does it make you more confident? Less confident?

Strangely you'd think it makes you more confident, but I think it makes you slightly less. And I have had this conversation with one other Pulitzer Prize winner, and it makes you feel incredibly guilty because you're in the trenches with all these other writers, and you think, "Why me?"

Survivor's guilt.

Yes, very much. You very much feel survivor's guilt because, at least as an African American writer, so much of the struggle, so much of who I am, is defined by the struggle, and once that struggle doesn't exist, who do you become? And once you win an award like this, you have to redefine yourself, because you're no longer the person struggling, and you can't say that these are characters not being recognized, because they are.

So what have you done with it?

For me, I continued to work on *Vera Stark*, which thankfully I began before I won awards for *Ruined*. I think it would have been very hard to start a play now, because there's so much expectation.

Another writer said the very same thing. Before the play opens, he starts another one. Joe Papp would say to every writer before a play opened, "Start another one." So you don't have to wake up the next morning, read the reviews, good or bad, and not know where to go.

That's how I feel—I think, "Thank God for Vera Stark," because I was already thoroughly in process before all this began, so I could continue to nurture that process instead of all the concerns, you know, is it going to be like *Ruined*? Is it going to be epic? Is it going to deal with global issues? All those things that stop you from creating.

You mentioned that your worldview comes from growing up with your parents and your sense of commitment in the world. Is there anything else, like your children, that could change how you see the world?

One thing that defines my life is before and after the death of my mother. I happened to lose my mother and have my baby in the same month. It was a seismic shift. I went from being a child to being a mother and mothering my mother and another child, and I'll tell you the thing that was most transformative in my life. Something I never thought I would be able to do was care for my mother with Lou Gehrig's disease. Once I did that, I thought I could do anything, and it empowered me as a woman, but it also empowered me as a writer because I think that so often we're plagued by a lack of confidence and doubt. And after that, I felt like I could do anything, because I survived this horrific journey with my mom. I don't know if you've ever witnessed anyone with that disease.

Did you have a nurse?

We had some nursing, but at that time we had no money. We had someone who came from nine to three, but that's nothing. She required care twenty-four hours, and so it was me.

I can understand that after that you feel you can do anything.

There were times even a year after, I was devastated and I couldn't do anything, but then I found my strength and there was something my mom said. She said, "You must take care of yourself, because if you aren't strong physically and emotionally, then you can't do what you love and you can't nurture others." So I took that time emotionally to get strong, and then I began writing *Intimate Apparel*. And I really do feel it's the play that it is and it has something intangible, because on the page it's very simple. But people who see it have a special experience, because people talk to me, and I think that whatever I was feeling got onto the page, and that's the intangible. And I do think that's what separates good plays from great plays. It's not the technical aspects of the play, because there are plays that are incredibly sloppy, but when people leave they are shattered or devastated or enlightened, because there is some intangible. It's the same thing with stars. You think, why this person? Why isn't Billy Crudup the bigger star and why is Keanu Reeves? Billy Crudup is clearly the better technical actor, but Keanu Reeves brings the intangible: when you look in his eyes, there's something that he's able to communicate.

Or we think there is.

Or we think there is—there may be nothing but . . . After I wrote this play, it seemed to me no different than other plays, and I thought, "Why are they responding? Why aren't they responding to the other play, which, when I wrote it, I thought, 'Now this is a play!'"?

It was very deep, and of course Viola Davis is a vessel for that.

She's an acting machine. She also assimilates changes more quickly than anyone I've ever seen. You come in with pages, and she'll be, like, "Got it!"

But it also makes me think that there's something unconscious about the writing of that play. Is that a place you want to get to again?

Would I ever want to be in the place I was when I wrote *Intimate Apparel*? No. Never again, because it was such a difficult, fraught moment in my life. But would I want to be able to write with as much emotional honesty again? Yes. Absolutely. I feel like that's the goal, but those moments are rare and far and few between.

You hope to. That's the goal.

That's a really interesting question you ask. Would one want to be in that place again? I never want to go through something like that again. I lost my mother during previews for one play, and I lost my grandmother during another play, and I lost my other grandmother during another play, and I became really superstitious, and I thought, "Oh, God, I'm going to have to make a sacrifice . . ."

What do you perceive as your greatest strength?

That's an interesting question because all I see when I sit down are my weaknesses. And the fact that I'm still struggling to find my voice is my greatest strength, because that's what makes every play so different, and I feel like I'm being reborn.

You said something about your curiosity in an essay . . .

I describe myself as a nomad. I search for the water, and I just don't know where I'll find that watering hole. I'm restless and I don't like to sit still, and I think my plays reflect that. It's my strength and it's my weakness.

In what ways is it your weakness?

In that sometimes I feel I should be more focused. I look at August Wilson, for example, who I really admire, a brilliant writer. He had this grand plan and scheme that he was going to follow and he achieved with great success, and I feel like I don't have that discipline in my life. I don't have that kind of focus.

It's not discipline, it's a vision.

He had a vision, and it worries me—where is my vision?—and when it's all said and done, is there any vision?

In a way I think it's for somebody else to say about you what your vision was. If you're inside of your vision, then you can't see what your vision is because you're inside of it.

Which goes back to when you asked me what I'm writing about, and I don't want to say because I'm still searching for what I'm writing about.

PAULA VOGEL

In addition to her career as a playwright, Paula Vogel is the chair of the playwriting program at Yale School of Drama, and so it is in New Haven that we meet her. She greets us at the foot of the stairs of an old building on Crown Street, carrying a takeout bowl of soup. Paula has short, very white hair and is dressed in a white shirt, black slacks, and a smart-looking gray jacket. We follow her up two flights of stairs; she remarks that the building looks like it should house social workers and nuns. "Can't you see *Doubt* happening here?" Her office looks out onto brick walls but is furnished with a good-sized desk and a small round table where we all sit. There are a long and a short wall of floor-to-ceiling bookshelves lined with plays and an occasional photograph: Cherry Jones and J. Smith-Cameron in a production of *Desdemona: A Play About a Handkerchief*; Paula and a very tall Margaret Edson, author of *Wit*. We talk a bit about Yale and the possibility of a new theater building, and once we're warmed up, we turn on the tape recorder and begin in earnest.

Did you go to the theater a lot as a child?

No. Uh-uh. We couldn't afford to go. We didn't have a lot of money, but we did have the radio. We had a program called *Matinees at One* in Washington, D.C. They narrated Broadway musicals every week, and I wouldn't miss it. I don't know what it was. I fell in love with Judy Garland. I fell in love with Mary Martin. I fell in love with the musical stage without ever seeing it. I think the first time I actually saw theater, my parents saved up money and took me to the National Theatre to see *My Fair Lady* when it was on tour. A little later I could go, in high school, and participate in high school theater. It was all from books and the radio.

You acted or . . . ?

Fell in love instantaneously. I was a sophomore and walked into the room. There was a drama coach who seemed impossibly old and experienced at the age of twenty-three. And they were in the midst of rehearsing *The Skin of Our Teeth.* I had never heard of the play. I didn't know what it was about. I was enthralled. And what I did, when it was the summer and I wasn't in school, I would go through the set of Oxford literature, and I would look up every playwright. I just set myself a task. Read all the O'Neill. And then I read all the Albee. This was the 1960s. I read all the Tennessee Williams I could get my hands on. And it never occurred to me to be a playwright, because other than Lillian Hellman, I couldn't find any women.

So you didn't have any role models.

I fell in love with stage management. I loved being in the theater and watching people. For a while I thought I would be a director. But I couldn't act, and a lot of programs said you had to act in order to get into the directing program. I'm very shy. People don't know that about me. I'm fine as long as I'm speaking, but I'm very awkward with my body when I know people are looking at me. And so I just thought, I can't do this. I suffered miseries. I actually acted for two years at Catholic University. My last role onstage I played Sister George in *The Killing of Sister George,* and people said in the post-play discussion, "I didn't believe you were a lesbian." And I thought, "I really can't do this. I'm really terrible at it. I've got to do something else." I kind of tried everything else there was to do.

And that's how you tried playwriting?

I told myself it wasn't writing. I started writing little class plays. For two years at Bryn Mawr there was a class show. I was a scholarship kid, and

I put on *The Beautiful Quasimodo*. I did a musical adaptation of that. I did a musical of the woman who founded Bryn Mawr after finding her love letters to women. I think that may have ended my scholarship. I just started doing it as a lark. I didn't take it very seriously.

Did you have teachers who noticed that you were doing this?

Teachers at Bryn Mawr did. They said, "Take this seriously." They noticed. There were no drama courses. There was no drama program. I transferred to Catholic U, where there really wasn't playwriting either. I just thought, "Well, I'll try a Ph.D. I think I might like teaching." I just had a hunch. And I applied to the Ph.D. program, got in.

At Catholic?

No, at Cornell. Graduated from Catholic. Didn't really, you know, fit in there.

Why'd you leave Bryn Mawr?

A number of reasons. A: My scholarship was cut. I was a little too out. I was a little too rambunctious, and I was trying to actually start a dramatic literature program, which wasn't considered academically viable. The dean at the time said that I was a working class experiment. They decided to give scholarships to twelve girls from the working class. And they let us know who we were. It kind of cracked us in an interesting way. And none of us stayed for four years. We all left, which was a shame, because there were some phenomenal teachers there. And it was a gorgeous campus. It was probably a big mistake for me to go to a women's college. I didn't even choose it. I didn't know it existed. My advisor told me they had financial aid, and I could probably get financial aid, so I tried.

Then you moved on to Catholic U and what else?

Cornell, actually. Ph.D. in dramatic literature and theory—fell in love with the teacher of theory and literature there. And I teach him to this day. Changed my world. He offered one playwriting class, and I had written this one-act about the daughter of Sir Thomas More for him, when I was twenty-three. And he jumped up to his feet, ran to the blackboard, started diagramming it, talking about it like it was a real play. And I kind of turned to him and said, "What are you doing?" "Well, I need to explain what you just did." "Are you for real?" It was very exciting. After class he said, "Look, I can't tell you what to do. It's going to be very difficult for you to be a writer and a scholar at the same time, and I would argue that you should think about the playwriting." And I said, "Yeah, well how would I pay my rent?" And he said, "Well, that's a problem, but I'm just telling you you're a real writer and you shouldn't ignore that." Which was kind of phenomenal. He gave me that gift. So I started writing. I'd been writing but little dribs and drabs, silly little stuff.

Were you influenced by any of these particular writers whom you'd been reading?

Honestly I think I was early on very in love with Tennessee Williams. As writers, I think we have love-hate relations where in a way it's almost Oedipal. At some point you're rejecting someone and then you fall in love with them again. And then another ten years go by and you're having an argument with the writer again. I never ever fell out of love with Tennessee Williams. Arthur Miller I'm still fighting with in my head.

What is it about Tennessee Williams?

I felt that Tennessee Williams was the first writer I knew who was writing extremely layered roles for women. I felt that he knew how I felt when I walked down the street. Every other play up to that point, I felt that women were secondary characters. Not every playwright. I could say the middle plays of Ibsen in graduate school I was absolutely in love with. I was in love with Ibsen. I was in love with Strindberg. Because I felt Strindberg was a really great provocation when I read him. I had to answer him back, and I thought that was really valuable. And I was in love with Nabokov. I read *Lolita* in grad school. So I was kind of wrestling with all of these models. And Tennessee Williams for me . . . much more so than Lillian Hellman. One of the things I did in grad school, I taught very quickly, because they wouldn't give me a fellowship. My chair told me women get married and have children, so we only give fellowships to men. And it was actually a gift because I *had* to teach. So I started teaching intro classes to literature, and I actually got the chance to do early American women playwrights when I was twenty-four years old. I found all of this out-of-print material, from Rachel Crothers on—even before—and started teaching this. I still felt that Tennessee Williams . . . there wasn't any other writer giving me a viable role. Not only Blanche but Hannah, just exquisite in the ways he portrays women. And it's an interesting thing: who's breaking the form? I think we all go through, and I did, a Beckett period. And an Albee period. Where you really are looking how do you distill the theater?

So that was a more formal influence.

Absolutely. Samuel Beckett plays with every element. When I teach here at Yale, it's, "How do you write something that's plot driven? How do you write something that's character driven or language driven?" Beckett is saying, "How do you write a play without plot, without character?" You just see him being very playful. And I think that Edward Albee, for me, is very playful in that way. So then the sixties came, and I started reading Julie Bovasso, Rosalyn Drexler, and then met another love of my life, María Irene Fornés. And once I met Irene Fornés, I felt that somebody was painting on the stage, and she was using the stage in a way that I could intuit but not express. And I found that deeply thrilling. I understood her emotionally. I still find it hard to talk about her cognitively, but I really felt her as a formal painter or sculptor, changing the angles of the stage, changing what a play could be, every time. I have to say, when I talk about my gods, after Williams: Irene Fornés, John Guare, and Caryl Churchill. They gave this huge permission: never write the same play twice. Rip everything you did the last time apart. Start all over again. And so I felt they had their own personal criteria of things they were trying to do in each play that no one had done, in a way that was electrifying me.

OK. So you're in the room, at your desk, how do you start a play?

A lot of research. When I say research, I don't mean about the subject. I mean, What is the soundtrack I can put together so I can feel something as I write? First thing I do is make a soundtrack, like a loop. And I play it over and over and over again.

A soundtrack for each play?

Yes.

So you have a sense of what you want to hear, what you need . . . Are the names of the songs that appear in the script the songs you listen to?

I'll say I wrote this listening to these songs, but I don't expect anyone to use those songs. It's just that I want you to know that I was listening to Janet Jackson's *Nasty* the first time I wrote *Hot 'n' Throbbing,* but I don't expect that to mean anything to anybody. I actually can make myself progress emotionally through the script . . . this is a funny moment . . . this moment makes me feel lighter . . . this song makes me weep. I don't know why. It's the new drugs. I spend a long time trying to figure out how the world sounds. I don't know what the last moment of the play is. I know what the turning point is. Or I actually see a moment. I know that I saw a man holding his childhood self in his arms, drawing his head back, taking a deep breath, and then blowing into the child's mouth, and the child came to life, and I realized it wasn't a child—it was a Bunraku puppet, and I thought, "Oh, great, the last time I read about Bunraku puppets was when I was twenty-three years old. I think I better read a little about Bunraku." It had nothing to do with the play, specifically, or as techniques—

Which play was this?

This was *A Civil War Christmas.* But I started thinking, "Ooh, maybe what would that sound like," so I do research, and it ends up that I actually found a Japanese garage band singing a Japanese song that was to "Good King Wenceslas," which means nothing in Japan but you hear it, you're hearing it in Japanese, and I went "OK, that's it." It's gonna be Japanese garage bands with sounds of Noh drama with the following Christmas carols. And, I don't know, I put it together and that's what I hear, loop after loop after loop.

Do you tell your students that you've done this?

No. Not all the time. Everybody has their own process. I also find images and surround myself with images. So, for example, for *How I Learned to Drive* I went out and got 1950s car manuals. I got a history of *Playboy* magazine. And I got Vargas pinups. I kind of surrounded myself with the Vargas pinups. Something about those poses helped me through the play. And I found my soundtrack. When I say research, I don't mean about the subject.

So it helps you understand the man, Peck.

Oh, absolutely. Something particular about reading this history of *Playboy* magazine and the advertisements in *Playboy* from the sixties . . . how to make a good martini, your sound system. I was kind of cribbing from these ads as I went along.

But your portrait of him is so compassionate. How did you know that you loved him? It sounds like these artifacts that helped define him are not very lovable.

Let me put it this way: I look for artifacts that are cultural. So, for example, I'm playing with doing something about World War II. I feel like we know who we are when we can hear the soundtrack. We get cultural meanings of what it is to be a man and a woman from the radio or from MP3s. I mean, we really do hear generational shifts. And what I'm trying to understand about Peck is how did you make yourself out to be a man in the sixties? What were your guides? The more I read the *Playboy* magazines and the more I thought about it, the more, in a way, the *Playboy* magazines were in contrast to the absent father, in a strange way a very compassionate recipe for masculinity: taking care of a woman's pleasure, taking care of the perfect cocktail, making sure the music is playing. It actually was introducing the notion of sensitivity, the vocabulary of what it is to be a man. That's what I started seeing. And in the interviews . . . I mean, when Jimmy Carter said he had read *Playboy,* I thought, well that explains why he was such a sensitive, loving husband and father. When I'm looking for things, I'm looking for how did these people become who they are in the moment of time that they're living. Not unlike I suppose what actors do. When I say I do research, I'm trying to figure out.

Do you already know Peck, or are you learning about him as you do this research?

A combination of both. Obviously, when I was thinking about this, I thought, "This is my Nabokov challenge." And I thought about Gregory Peck, because I will always have a huge crush on that actor. I think all of us did. And so I actually tried to think of what kind of character does Gregory Peck play. But the other thing that I have to say about this is I do know who Peck is because *I'm* Peck, and it's this that some people withdraw from. He's a teacher. When I wrote it, I was forty-five years old. He cares very much about what he's teaching. That kind of desire. I know that there are playwrights who might not do this, but to me it's the same instinct as acting: you have to find yourself in every character. And so, where are you?

And there are really no villains.

Yeah! I mean, how do you play Iago? I thought a lot about *Othello*. I thought a lot about *Lolita*, trying to do that. I know that when I was younger, I didn't have the same control over my empathy. So, for example, something like *Desdemona*, I had to write three times, because the first draft was very harsh, and the second draft I got a little bit more about Bianca and Emilia, and the third draft I started to feel for Desdemona. And I'm aware that, just like acting, it's a muscle that I think improves with age.

And with understanding yourself better, evolving. So at what point do the characters start talking?

Oh well . . . pretty much when I sit down. What I do, because I teach, is I do my own technique: bakeoffs. I don't do it in forty-eight hours. I find people in this program and every playwright I've ever worked with at Brown and say, "Here are the following things about *Medea*. You can read *Medea*. You can read the following two plays based on the original *Medea* by the following playwrights, but in forty-eight hours you must write a play." I give them a recipe. And they have to write it within forty-eight hours. Read *Don Juan*. Read *Don Juan Comes Home from the Wars*.

You have to write a play with a master–servant swordplay, a statue, a ghost, a moment of coitus interruptus. Go! Forty-eight hours. Whatever comes out. I cheat. I usually give myself two weeks. And I hold myself to it. I mean, I don't come out of the room if I can. I nap and I go through and I play the tape over and over. I don't necessarily get through the whole play, but I get through a substantial part. I think the longest time I've ever spent on a first draft is four weeks.

So you did this with How I Learned to Drive. *Do you remember the five things you gave yourself?*

Yeah. And I gave it to my playwrights, actually.

At the same time?

Yeah. It's a relationship between a younger person and an older person. A moon. Time that goes backward. A radio song of the sixties.

You didn't have the play? You just made that up?

No, I knew the image that my play was going to have. I knew the image had to do with driving because I saw it. It's interesting. When I read Irene Fornés talking about it, I know that moment: you see an image and when you see the image, it's not going to go away. It's going to torment you for years if you don't write it. I knew that I wanted to write something like this, but I had a commission, and I was writing a play about a castrato for Cherry Jones . . . I was going to write her a "breeches" role about the greatest castrato of all time, Farinelli, as a young man. I had this whole thing worked out. And I got a grant for it, and we were going to go to Alaska. And the week before we were supposed to get on the plane, Cherry called and said, "I got the role in *The Heiress*. My first Broadway lead." And I said, "You've got to take that." So I just called up the grant agency and said, "Can I come up with another idea?" And so by the time I stepped off the plane . . . because the car image had been there, and I thought I can do this research very, very quickly . . . and I wrote it in two weeks.

And then what do you have to do? Do you put it down? Do you go away?

I put it down.

Do you show it to somebody?

Yeah. I do. I had a reading immediately. I have about four ideas in my head right now, and I think about them a lot when I'm driving from Providence to New Haven on I-95. I'll carry something in my head for ten years. And then it gets the right moment. Or the image comes. I saw that image of a woman adjusting a mirror, and I knew that was it. I don't know why I knew. With *How I Learned to Drive* . . . I asked the company to assemble everybody together and do a cold read. And actually they asked a young woman who was seventeen to play the role of the teenage Little Bit, and halfway through I stopped the reading and I said, "We can't do this with a seventeen-year-old. Let's stop the reading." I just asked another actor in the room to read the teenage Little Bit. I said to the teenager, "Thank you, you're wonderful, I don't want to hear a seventeen-year-old go to the end of this play." At which point I knew: Oh, you know what, they should not be the actual ages. That was my first thought at that reading. How do we do this without abusing the audience? The first read I thought people hated it. There was this long moment of silence, and I thought, "Oh my God." I always expect to be strung up, like, "Oh, boy, you did it this time."

The first reading was in Alaska?

The first was in Alaska, and the second happened very quickly.

Did you do rewrites after the first reading?

No.

You didn't do any rewrites after the first reading? So this is a four-week period of writing.

I wrote it in two weeks and just went, "OK."

What's so interesting is that it's so structurally complex.

Thank you to Harold Pinter and *Betrayal.*

But this isn't told backward exactly.

There's that wonderful last scene in the car, and you realize that this all started when she was eleven. It is such a powerful, complex moment. Because at the beginning of the play, she's seventeen, and it doesn't seem that bad. He isn't abusing her. She's seventeen, which is . . . well . . . close to eighteen, which is legal, but the eleven-year-old, that scene . . . Yeah. And I couldn't hear a seventeen-year-old saying that. So that was very useful. So I wouldn't say that I changed the play. The second reading happened at the Vineyard Theatre. Doug Aibel put it together, and we were still casting a wide range of ages. And I thought, "I'm not quite sure." It wasn't until auditions when Johanna Day came into the room that I thought, "Oh, they're supposed to be the same age, all three women are supposed to be the same age." I mean, there's a way to look at your grandmother as a sixteen-year-old. There's a way to look at your mother as a sixteen-year-old. There's a way to look at yourself as a sixteen-year-old. They're supposed to be the same age. Again, things like that don't necessarily change a word, but to have the director there . . . I just turned to Mark Brokaw and went, "I think I just found something out about the age, how we can go back, how the time travel will work." Because to hear an eleven-year-old played by a teenager is not going to be permissible, it would be ghastly. You can find out a lot of stuff in auditions. I did cut, maybe, four lines. That was it.

The fact that the grandmother isn't old makes it harder to take. Because you might feel kind of comfortable watching an old woman play the grandmother.

Maybe. And the other way of saying it is that in Adrienne Rich's *A Woman Born* . . . she basically comes up with a premise that in a certain generation no women are mothered, that women only mothered sons and that women remain unmothered in the culture. Now, she was writing back in the sixties. But when I thought about that, it makes a lot of sense to have a teenage grandmother, a teenage or a young mother, and an actual teenager all, sort of, in the same body. So a lot of stuff I found in auditions.

So you went into it thinking you were going to cast an older woman.

Yeah. Until they all walked through the door and we knew we were working with Mary Louise Parker, and you just looked at what happened with the synergy and saw that's absolutely right. Now there are probably productions that aren't doing that. At which point I also knew that I wanted the grandfather to be played . . . I adjusted that after the reading . . . that he has to be played by a young man who can play the teenager as well. It doesn't change lines, but it changes the whole production complex. And I'm imagining that there'll be many productions with eighty-year-olds . . .

Do you know that? Is it still being done?

Oh yeah, still being done.

Do you see any?

No! No, I haven't seen any in a while.

So they don't have to ask permission. They can cast it any way they want to.

I always say, "Whatever I don't know about won't hurt me," so . . . My agent called me a couple of years ago: "There's a place in Germany, we have to close down the play." I'm like, "What? Why?" They were doing the play in chronological order. And that seems very German to me. I don't know why.

Someone told us that a production of their play was done in Germany, and the Germans felt no compunctions about interpolating songs, changing scenes around . . .

They're kind of famous for that. I said, "How's it doing at the box office?" It's doing well, so I said, "Don't close it!"

Wally Shawn told us that Rolf Hochhuth was so outraged about a production of one of his plays that he bought the building and closed down the play.

That's great. It's like that wonderful Chris Durang story about *History of the American Film.* There was a production in which everybody took off their shirt. Why? And he said, "What do you do, put in a stage direction that nobody takes off their shirt?"

One of the questions we were going to ask you've already answered, which was if you'd ever conceived a role for an actor—you've said you were going to do this for Cherry Jones.

She was doing *Pride's Crossing,* and very fortunately—you know—I rely on Doug Aibel all the time. I mean, I think his sensibility as a producer is exquisite, and I think that's because he really understands casting. And he said, "I've got this combination in mind, and let's just hear them, let's just see if they're interested. That was Mary Louise and David Morse. So that really came from him. God bless.

But did you ever think of a role for someone? With Desdemona, *did you think of Cherry Jones?*

Oh yeah, sure. Once we started working together . . . I think about roles for people . . . I don't want to say who they are—I expect they'll never ever do them. At some point, I'll do this one-person show I've carried around for twenty years in my head for someone. I'm not going to say who.

There's a difference between "this would be a great role for someone" and "I know them personally, and I'm going to use certain things about them."

Both. Both. And I actually think that because, as you know, it's a rare luxury that an actor can do a play, that if you tailor it very specifically for the actor, it actually will fit beautifully other actors, so there is a little bit of that, yeah. I think about people all the time.

Has there been an actor in one of your plays who's been so fabulous that you think, "I've got to write something for them again"?

Absolutely. I'm very fortunate. I usually leave off saying, "I hope we get to work again," thinking, "If you don't get the voice-over, if you don't get the pilot . . ."

When you've finished writing, whom do you show your work to?

I show it to friends. Personal friends. "Can you read this when you get a chance?" And of course, wait by the phone. "Oh my God, he hates it, she hates it. They don't know how to tell me!" Now and then I'll back myself into a reading where I say, "Yeah, I'll have a first draft," or I'll have a first act and set the date, and I can always back out of it.

Do you still have Doug Aibel and the Vineyard as a theater?

I love Doug and would show anything to Doug. I mean, not all my plays fit Doug's taste. And you have to be aware of that. And he's a pretty busy man, but, yeah, I feel the Vineyard's a home. I'm trying to adjust here at Yale, that this is my home, so I'm working on something now, thinking it'll be done at the Rep, and trying to set deadlines for that and figure out what that process is going to be. This is a new environment for me . . . I've been here three years. I'm kind of a little terrified in that, you know, you've got your students all around, and I think that's actually the hardest audience to write for.

In what way are they the hardest? Are they judgmental?

No no no. It's that they matter so much. And you're so in love with their writing, or you wouldn't be working with them. And they've been so courageous.

You're most vulnerable to them . . .

Absolutely. I think that matters to me more than anybody. I think it's probably good to write for a place that terrifies you. I'm also trying to think of making a long, long list of places I'd like to work that I haven't. Or artists that I haven't worked with and I'm particularly starting to think about . . . which is interesting, it's new in my life . . . conversations I want to have with younger artists. And I think that's interesting energy.

Do you write for film? Or have you ever?

Yes. And I may again at some point. I have written . . . I did do . . . it was a really great process . . . I did a screenplay of *How I Learned to Drive* for Laura Ziskin. HBO finished two of the Pulitzer Prize plays and then stopped the series. It was *Wit* and *Dinner with Friends.* I was next, and they stopped the series but . . . I've written film. I don't love it. I'm really a theater animal. I love being in the room.

It seemed like How I Learned to Drive *would lend itself to film. Do you feel that a film of it would be reductive?*

No no. It was actually . . . I think I could do things in the film that I couldn't do. It was a very beautiful road trip. I wrote it as a road trip. With Little Bit driving across country from L.A., and the last thing she packs is a black dress, and you don't know why. And the scenes happen as flashbacks as she's driving to her uncle's funeral. I just used the chronology backward, did it with a linear . . . I have to say, I enjoyed taking the trip. I think it would make a very beautiful film. Also, I had these conversations with people: "Oh, what a great idea! Do you think you could change the relationship so he's not her uncle?" I think *somebody* could. Pay me and somebody could.

When you go into the rehearsal room, is it your assumption that the script is done?

No. I assume that there are some plays that I'm never going to get to finish. And I'm OK about that. I mean, it's a very interesting thing. One of the things I talk about to younger writers: you may not be able to finish the script. You may not be in the right place or the right time or the right experience level . . .

But you're in rehearsal and you can't finish it . . .

Well, you know where the flaw is, and you don't have the techniques in your quiver, or you aren't in the right place where you can finish it. So there are plays that I just know I didn't get a chance to finish. I usually work . . . there are only two plays that I didn't really work on a lot and that was *How I Learned to Drive* and *Baltimore Waltz*. And *Baltimore Waltz*, when I went to the room, I'm like, "This is an elegy." I just wrote it . . . did that one in two weeks too . . . It's just the expression of my grief, and I can't change that. I'm not the same person that wrote it, so I don't feel I should work on it. So I just turned to Anne Bogart and said, "I hate to say this, but it's your problem." I mean, I participated in rehearsal but there are times I said, "I have no idea how you're going to do that. I have no idea what that means. It just came out that way." And that's not terribly useful, but I was very lucky.

Wasn't she frustrated?

She was frustrated. I think she was frustrated, probably, by me in that I'm kind of energetic—I can be obsessive in a room. I think I frustrated her, but she knows that I adore her, and I think she adores me. I think we have . . . I think the reason it worked is that we have very different vocabularies and we got plunged into the deep end at the same time. I found out a year later that Cherry Jones was saying, "This play makes no sense." And Joe Mantello was saying behind the scenes, "No, it does, it does. Hang in."

Did Anne Bogart know you before you wrote the play?

We had less than a year together in Providence. She was the first artistic director at Trinity Rep after Adrian Hall. And she was the only person at Trinity that ever called me. I literally spent seven years being told I couldn't meet Adrian Hall because I worked and taught at Brown University, and I was never given an appointment. Adrian Hall probably doesn't even know that. So I just sort of gave it up, and when Bogart got the job, she called me, and I was like in shock. So I went and saw her entire season, and she announced that she was going to do *Baltimore Waltz* at Trinity for her second season. It never happened and I felt, "Well, let's see." And when Circle Rep said, "Do you want to do a workshop?" I said, "This might not be the usual Circle Rep director, but would you give Annie and me the time to do this?" So they gave us three weeks to do a workshop.

I don't mean for you to relate this directly to Anne Bogart, but what are the qualities in a director that you think are most important?

I think Anne retrained one notion in my head, which was really important. And that is that I don't believe the production needs to illustrate the script.

What do you mean by that?

In other words, it's, I think, viable . . . You need to give me enough of a taste of my play world to see if the thing's working, but you can also give me your personal response to the play rather than mine. Why should you be giving me my personal response to my brother dying? You can give me your personal response to grief that you've known. And show me what that looks like. Here's an example: When Annie went with the designer Loy Arcenas to look at ideas for the set, she called me from a hospital, and I said, "What are you doing in a hospital?" She said, "It's in your stage directions. It takes place in a hospital. In a waiting room." I said, "Annie, I didn't mean for it to take place in a waiting room. It happens in a big double bed, and after carrying this big double bed all across Europe . . . it's Mother Courage's wagon is really what I see." She said, "You know, that's an interesting idea. You're going to see that production. I have to show you the Europe I see. You've never been to Europe. Let me take you to Europe." And she said, "If you miss anything from your play, you let me know. I promise you, you won't even remember you're in a waiting room." Which I didn't. I didn't even know you could ask for things like that. The lounge would become Paris, and it literally became the Eiffel Tower. So that notion of using space was something that I hadn't experienced and . . . I wouldn't say that we're aesthetically matched, but on this particular play it was someone else making their own quilt of grief. And that felt exactly right.

To some extent you trusted her to have her response even if it was something you didn't see.

She would say, "Let me show you," and she'd show me. And usually what I was shown was, "God, that's exquisite. I wouldn't have known to ask for that." I think one of the things that Anne and other directors aren't used to is having the playwright in the room. And the real question is, I mean, she sketched something in the workshop and it was so exquisite that when we got to production at Circle Rep, she said, "Now I'm going to throw everything away and we're going to start from scratch." But it was so beautiful. "You've got to forget it now," she said. "That was a sketch. And we're going to make it up with the bodies of our actors." She was absolutely right, but I'd never worked liked that.

Now that you're experienced in playwright–director relationships, what do you look for?

It depends on the play world. What I'm now starting to think is that . . . I'm also fine when things àren't perfect because I learn something. Mark Brokaw was perfect for *How I Learned to Drive*. He didn't see what I saw, and he sat down and said, "Let me tell you what I see." And the more I heard him, I said, "I can see what you see," so we went in that direction. "I don't see slides," he said, "especially at the Vineyard. It's too intimate a space." And he started to tell me what he saw and he said, "We're going to do this very simple, simply with the table." And I said, "Mark, you're absolutely right. Forget the furniture." So I don't think every play I write is perfect for Mark, but there are people, I'm just curious how they work, and if it's not the perfect synergy, if I learn something . . . When you say, "Do I write for actors?" I'm also writing for directors. I'm writing for directors I know I'll never work with. I've written several love poems to Frank Galati. I don't expect on this earth that I'll ever get a chance to work with him. I write directors love letters. It's probably a little embarrassing, and I don't think I'll get the opportunity to work with these artists. There are certain qualities . . . with Anne Bogart . . . I just had this conversation with Sarah Ruhl, I said, "You know you're going to see something about theater you've never seen before. There'll be many other productions." Actually, I did see the production of *Baltimore Waltz* that

I had in my head. I had nothing to do with it. I had no discussions with the director. I only showed up for opening night. And gasped. It was the play that was in my head that I had forgotten. So it does happen.

So you're saying you're not a rigid person and that when someone shows you a different way, you'll risk letting go of what you see, in hopes you'll learn something.

There are two or three things that are sacred to the play, and I cannot tell you why. And I will spill blood over them. I'll say, "This is a problem. I don't know why." And I've had huge fights. I had fights about the fishing scene in *How I Learned to Drive*. It doesn't make sense in the sequence. It didn't fit into my outline, but I literally saw the character doing this. And I took dictation and therefore it's staying in because the character led and I followed. It wasn't in my outline. It makes no sense. And I don't blame David Morse and Mark Brokaw for having trouble with it. It's a big problem. And I'll go into the fight and I'll say, "I've made a big problem, but I'm not going to fix the problem because it came to me and I took the dictation." Anne Bogart said, "It's got to be the Emperor Waltz." And I don't like that song. I hate Strauss. I don't know why. Subsequent productions, fine. But the first time, if you play it, I'll sense the presence of my brother. I don't know why. And I just said, "It's a big problem, but you gotta deal with it." If you're going to be someone who insists on control, write a novel. It's not what the theater is. Your actors and director and designers are writing the production. And you want input, particularly the first time, but I don't have their skills. I don't have their talent. It actually erases what you saw in your head, which is kind of exciting. The character starts to go away and gets replaced by Mary Louise Parker.

So there's the way you hear it when you write and then the way they do it, which widens the play.

And it's absolutely thrilling. You have to believe that life is long and it will get multiple productions. I don't want to be disrespectful to certain estates, but I don't believe it's a smart thing to insist that *Endgame* cannot be set in a postapocalyptic subway station when it is absolutely faithful to the spirit of the play and it makes it relive for another generation. I know there's a huge spectrum, and I'm sure you're talking to writers who say, "No, it's exactly as I wrote it." I may say that I'm not changing the script, it's your problem, but I don't think I should ever say, "No, don't show me."

What do you do, for example, if an actor says, "I can't say this line"?

Occasionally, if it's not important to me, I'll rewrite the line. If it's not important. But if it's very important to me, I'll have a talk with the director and say, "Whooo whoo whoo. I'll buy you a martini after the rehearsal. I think I'm going to sit out this week."

You mean, until they say it.

Yeah. There's a reason for that line . . . I might even say, "Here's the reason for the line." If I know it. But that's not really what the problem is. The real problem is . . . language is something that's very specific, and that is what the writer writes. The writer is writing the language.

Do you talk to the designers too?

Depends on the director. Bogart, Tina Landau, they keep their set design to themselves. Mark Brokaw and Les Waters had me in at the get-go. But they were also . . . which was very smart . . . I actually love when directors say, "Here's what we're seeing. Here's a sketch." I like seeing the graphic design. It helps me if I'm going to be doing any rewriting to see that we're on the same page. So the more you infiltrate with the vision of what that production is going to be, the more I can look at the language. I think it's a very smart thing to do, and I think it's not smart not to share it.

When the play runs, what, if anything, do you learn from an audience? Is the audience right? Is it wrong?

If it's overwritten.

You mean, if the audience is ahead of you?

Yeah. If they're shuffling. If they start turning in their seats. If they pick up their programs . . . I'm overwriting. What it does, when it's working well, is when their bodies are rigid and to attention. And I'm like, "Okay, we're not touching that!" And sometimes people will say afterward: "Oh, it really didn't hold my attention," but they're sitting like this—stiff. There's something else going on. I'm actually fascinated. I've been to see other people's plays . . . Harvey Fierstein's second play after *Torch Song Trilogy*, Anne Meara was in it. *Spookhouse*—that was the name of it. And it got a review in the *Times* that said it was a boring play. OK. I went and saw the last matinee, and I saw people like this, rigid, and at intermission, trying to light their cigarettes with their hands shaking, yet saying, "Oh, I think I agree with the *Times*." Your hands were shaking, your body was shaking. That's not what's happening. Which I always find fascinating.

This leads into our question about critics. Do you ever learn anything from them?

I do read them, which probably is not a good thing. You have to discount both sides. I read them pretty technically. I don't read them if I'm not associated with the production, but I read them if I am. I actually may stop reading them for the following reasons: I'm kind of interested to see how the preshow interviews are landing. This is the advertising executive in me. I like to see what in that interview lands or doesn't land . . .

That the critics are picking up or responding to.

Exactly. You go into every interview with three talking points. There's this and this and this. And you just say it over and over again. The more you can get it in a clear talking point, the better. And sometimes I can do it and sometimes I can't. But that's what I'm interested in.

That's what politicians do, isn't it? I'm going to say this no matter what you ask me.

Exactly right. But you've got to be careful not to praise or criticize too much.

Can you look at your writing and see some kind of arc, in terms of theme or impulses that started you writing, that has changed over time?

I think probably I have changed in my feminism. I still very much feel every day that I'm a feminist, and by that I mean the broadest spectrum possible of both men and women in terms of gender. Which is a different feminism than when I started out, which was very specifically in my twenties when I wrote roles for women, women's stories, women as protagonists. A very different model. From my point of view, writing characters for men is part of that spectrum. I think that's changed.

Has your teaching changed?

I think I'm in a much more direct relationship with my playwrights. Certainly ideas come up. I would not have written *Baltimore Waltz* without exposure to writers like Adam Bock, which people may not be aware of. By teaching several generations younger, you're seeing what they're doing to the form. So I think that Sarah Ruhl had an impact. I think the three women who are in rehearsals now at Yale have had a huge impact. And I'll think of some way to answer them back. In a way I'm looking more now at writing the next play to answer back writers that I love. So that's the arc for me.

What would you say would be your greatest strength and weakness as a writer? What are you good at, and what do you struggle with?

I think I'm really good with structure, the way time travels, and designing that. I think that's my strength. What's my weakness . . .

The things you struggle with—that don't come as easily . . .

I'm right now struggling the most with language because there's been a shift in stage language. I feel the shift in language because of the generational switch. So music, television, screenplays . . . I recognize that the language is English but it's not my generation. And it's that shift that I note, for example, when I'm reading Arthur Miller. I mean, who says, "No one dast speak ill of this man." "Attention. Attention must be paid." It's beautiful, but would we recognize that as verisimilitude? I'm shifting a little on that. I'm finding that a little more difficult. How do these characters speak? I think it's one of the reasons that it's appealing to me more and more to write in different times rather than contemporary plays. 'Cause if I write a contemporary play, I'll be writing as a sixty-year-old, which is different.

Are you working on something now?

I'm writing a new play. I'm playing my tape loop in the car. And I spend a day with what the actual format of the play is, so I spend a day with different fonts trying to see how the space is. I want to make sure that my play looks like no other play on the page. 'Cause when you stop to think about it, you're going to go back to rewrite that script in a year as another play is being written, and you have to be able to distinguish.

I have a font in which the characters seem to speak very clearly.

Oh! Well you're in the Suzan-Lori Parks category. There are writers who find it and stick to it. There are plays I can't write because I haven't found the right font. This is writer's insanity. I have to find the right font. It has to look the right way on the page.

I would think it would help get you back into that head.

Exactly! Three drafts down the line, you see that font and you know what play world you're in. It's Pavlovian.

Our last question: do you think your plays will be performed a hundred years from now?

I think *How I Learned to Drive* possibly. Not for good reasons, in that I don't know how much and how quickly power dynamics are going to change. The other thing that I do believe that I'm in a really happy state about—that there will be students of my students of my students.

DAVID GREENSPAN

Fresh from his success with *Go Back to Where You Are* at Playwrights Horizons, in which he also appeared in the main role, David meets us in one of the offices at NYU Tisch School of the Arts. He is dressed conservatively in a white shirt and dark trousers. His shoes are highly polished. He is, as he has always been, extremely thin and looks cool, even on this very hot June afternoon. His face is sculptural, down to the bone; onstage he can appear young or old, handsome or haggard. He holds his head high. He has extremely nice teeth. His speaking voice is slightly hushed and deliberate. He leans back and is very relaxed as we begin our conversation. His posture—one arm over the back of the chair, one leg crossed over the other—brings to mind Noël Coward at his most languorous.

We'll start with when you first had the inkling that you wanted to tell stories. When was that?

I came to New York just to be an actor and pursue an acting career. And because I wasn't making much traction, I thought . . . I just, I don't know, I just toyed with the idea of performing. And what I was really doing at the beginning was I was just making monologues out of my journal entries, you know, that any twenty-year-old with all the pent-up emotions and drama and the rest of what you write in your journal. So I would kind of fashion monologues—some of them were stream-of-consciousness monologues—and I would do them in the little black holes on the Lower East Side. There's a place called the Limbo Lounge. I did one piece in the basement of a kind of a project right across from Lincoln Center. So this is we're talking 1980. It was in the basement of a project, and they just had a little place for someone to do a monologue so I . . .

You started out in the theater as an actor in L.A.?

I grew up in Los Angeles, did drama in high school, then I went to the University of California at Irvine, and I was a drama major studying . . .

Did you parents encourage your performing or your theatrical imagination?

They supported it. My mother had died by the time I was getting involved in theater. But my father supported it. He enjoyed the theater, enjoyed entertainment and musicals and films. So he was very supportive of it. I never had any resistance about becoming a theater major in college.

Was musical theater your main interest?

I came to New York . . . I wanted to be in musicals because I grew up listening to musicals. I would've done anything. But I was not a very good dancer, and my singing skills are specific and limited in certain ways. You know, as a kid, I told people my father recorded musicals off this radio program called "Broadway Showtime." So they'd be on his reel-to-reel tape recorders. I would just listen to these incessantly. And then when I got old enough, I would go to the library and check the rest of them out that he didn't have recordings of and record them for myself on my tape recorder and would just listen to them constantly. So I was very much—I loved musicals. And I still have a great affection for musicals. So I came to New York hoping to be in musicals.

So the fact that this didn't work out is what led you to concentrate on writing?

Yeah. I wasn't finding that many opportunities, really. I had some, but nothing that—it wasn't consistent in any way. My first job in New York was at this place called the New York Theatre Ensemble, which is that one with the outside circular staircase on Fourth Street a few doors down from La Mama. Some nights you couldn't even get the lights on—it was that kind of place. And I was doing a Lope de Vega play. Or a musical called *The Search for Love,* where I was playing a sheep. The composer's mother made the costumes out of carpet. It was that kind of thing. Also, I got involved with dancers and choreographers, and we were making kind of dance theater pieces where I would write scripts and perform while the dancers were dancing. Just anything I could do . . .

Really, you loved the theater—you loved the whole art of it. But writing. What made you not want to direct?

I did direct my own pieces. And also, you know, I did direct . . . when I worked with the choreographers, one particularly that I worked with most intensely, you know, he would choreograph, I would direct. If the dancers spoke, I would direct them in what they spoke. We made pieces together. I would direct parts of it. We would collaborate on the whole thing. So I was directing from the beginning and acting. I never thought of leaving the theater. It just seemed like everything I wanted to do. I admire people who come out of coursework in playwriting. I didn't do that, and I think it's wonderful to do and to gain that kind of knowledge. But one thing I had the opportunity to do—and they might also after they've studied—I was renting the lights, hanging the lights. You know when I worked with Bill, my partner, he would be making the set in the house. It was that kind of thing. So I ended up doing everything.

Did you think of yourself when you started to write as writing what we think of as a conventional play?

No. If I did, they weren't plays. If I had any notion I was a playwright, they weren't really plays. They were stream-of-consciousness monologues, they were dance theater pieces. It was only when I went back to study acting again. I started taking classes with Terry Schreiber and Lee Wallace. And when I started taking acting again, I . . .

When was that?

This would be like around 1982. Close to around the time when I started doing my own pieces. But I started to take acting again, and that just immersed me more in conventional—I don't like the word "conventional"—more traditional plays. And I directed some of my classmates in a production of *Sexual Perversity in Chicago*. So I just became more immersed in traditional plays, and I think my writing began to take on more recognizably play form where there were characters who were speaking to each other as opposed to just monologues.

The first thing of yours that I ever saw was at HOME for Contemporary Theatre and Art. You had a scroll that was very high up on the wall and you would unfurl it.

Boys Who Like Boys, yeah. That was from that period before I started really making plays. Those evenings that you saw were more monologues or short pieces.

Were there any playwrights in this period whom you admired or read a lot of or saw a lot of?

They were mostly things that I still remembered from college. I wasn't seeing as much theater at that time. You know, of course, there was . . . one doesn't aspire to do it because it's well beyond us or well beyond me . . . but Beckett and Shakespeare, those things, and Chekhov, the things that I read, Miller, Williams. Those were the things that I remembered so vividly. I'm trying to think of what else I read at the time . . .

I was there a lot when you were at HOME, and I saw that audiences really took to your plays. You started to develop what seemed to me like fans. I wonder if that influenced what you were writing? Whether they urged you on in some way?

Well, I don't know if I felt it influenced me as much as it validated, you know, a sense of purpose that there would be some people interested in what I could offer. So, as you know, that was a wonderful place to work, and also it was great because they kept asking me for more work. They had that series *The HOME Shows*, which ultimately my *HOME Show* pieces came out of. So there was opportunity to write for different rooms of the house and create a new piece. And so Randy Rollison and

Denise Lanctot kept urging me to bring in something else. And so I kept writing.

And you would write them and perform them?

Right. Perform them and direct them, at that time, yeah. And they began to take on more of the shape of a recognizable play. *Principata,* the first one, then the *HOME Show* pieces. *2 Samuel 11.*

So at this point you were looking for work as an actor still, or did you do less of that?

By that point, I was really just focusing on performing in my own work or working with a choreographer here and there. By the time I got to HOME, I was really just focusing on writing and performing in my own work.

How do you write? Do you have a desk at home and go to the desk every day and sit there for three hours?

Not necessarily. Because I'm managing an acting career also, there are times where if I'm fully immersed in an acting assignment in someone else's play, my time is limited for one thing, and my concentration is limited because I'm studying and learning lines when I'm not in rehearsal. If I have a deadline for something like an adaptation or something like that, then I make sure I carve out some time. But I don't necessarily sit down to write every day. Right now I'm just rehearsing and learning lines for something I've already written or learning lines for the other solo. So if I do have an adaptation, I'm very good about making deadlines. Or if I'm working with somebody . . . I worked at the Public recently with Nora York, this composer, with Joanne Akalaitis . . .

How is that going?

Well, it's very good. We hope we can find someone who'd be interested in doing it out of the Public or someone else . . . It's called *Jump.* It's based on arias from *Tosca.* This composer has written songs that are inspired from the arias or can be sung with the arias. It also involves the character Sarah Bernhardt, who originated the role of Tosca in the opera the play is based on. So Joan MacIntosh played Bernhardt, and Tosca was wonderful. Bill Camp was Scarpia. We had a great time. Joanne is terrific to work with. It was kind of moving to be back at the Public working with her as a writer.

So you're still developing that?

Yeah, hopefully.

Does the work with Tosca—*did that come from Joanne or did that come from outside?*

In a way, it's sort of like a jukebox musical because there were the songs already written, there were the Puccini arias . . .

How did you get involved with it?

First there was Nora York, the composer. Then Joanne. Joanne liked the idea of Sarah Bernhardt. She could respond to that, and they had a playwright who had been working with them who created a story that they didn't feel was in concert with what they were trying to realize. They just couldn't work together. So they looked around for someone else, and I kind of inherited this project. Of course, I had to discard the other writer's work. What I was left with was the source material of Sarah Bernhardt's correspondence or material about her and the music and lyrics. And then what I tried to do is structure a narrative that I think is in sync with what they're trying to get at and what they've given me and create bits and pieces of Sarah Bernhardt's . . . I've just tried to interweave elements of her biography with the *Tosca* material so that she goes in and out of the play and in and out of the opera because there are opera singers involved . . .

That's handmade for you.

I hope so. You know, it allows her to both play herself and then play Tosca, even though we have an actress who's in her sixties, she's also playing Tosca, who'd be in her twenties. So it's a wonderful pretend opportunity. Then you have opera singers . . .

Joan MacIntosh is still doing it?

We hope she'll do it. The only time she did it was in this Under the Radar Festival at the Public. We had other actresses who did readings. Before, Karen Kandel was doing it and Jenny Bacon did it. Neither were available. Then Joanne had the idea for Joan, and it was such a gold mine. I think it just summoned up in her parts of her emotion and her humanity that I don't think she's had a chance to express. I've never seen it before. The material obviously meant so much to her. It just came across in her performance. It was very illuminating. We hope that we can go on with it, that she can go on with it too. I'm trying to think of adaptations . . . The adaptations I've done for Brian Kulick at Classic Stage . . . I kept myself on a deadline, and when I wasn't fully occupied with an acting job or with acting in my own plays, I just maintained my deadline and wrote.

When it's your own work, do you keep notes? Do you plot first? What is your entrance to the work?

Well, it's often with an idea, and then I'll do reading about it, do some research, take notes, cut out articles, depending on what's interesting me. Sometimes it's based on an idea that I've put down for a while. There's a play actually that I'm working on now that's really only in my head. I've gone to the library to write some things down. It was to do with an actress from the early talkies. Just doing some research on her, on her life, the movies she did, making some notes, thinking about some dialogue. And then hopefully when it's ready, I'll just start writing.

Do you plot it out or know how it's going to end?

Sometimes, yeah. Like when I wrote *She Stoops to Comedy*, ultimately, I knew how it should end and how it should begin. So I wrote it, then I put it down for about seven years. I wrote some of it, a couple of scenes, I didn't like it, I just didn't know where to go, so I put it down for seven years. I kept thinking about it. And then I was acting in a production of *Macbeth* in Cleveland, and I had a lot of time—I was playing the First Witch—so there was a lot of time that I was not called for rehearsal. So I thought, "I think I know how to write it now." And I knew the points I wanted to hit. Because you don't know what everybody's going to say and how exactly it will go and the things that change in the process. But I knew I was ready to write it, and I knew the main things I wanted to hit, and I knew how it should end. And so I just sat down and started writing it. I said, "It'll probably take me about three or four weeks." And that's what it took to write it.

She Stoops to Comedy *is sort of structurally complicated. Was that all worked out beforehand?*

I don't know if I knew it was complicated. I just knew the characters I wanted to include, what their problems would be, some of the issues I wanted to hit, and the points I wanted to hit. And so by the time I got there, I always had something in my head that I was moving toward. And once I hit that point, I knew I was ready to get to the next point.

Where does The Myopia *fit in this? Is that thought through first?*

I started that piece when I was at the Public.

I saw a very early version.

The first time I think you saw it was . . . I read the first act just through the stage directions of the smoke-filled room. And I was planning on doing that with a whole bunch of actors. I thought, "I'll just read it but have lots of actors." But the more I read it alone, it just seemed like the right way to go. So I was working on that for, God, almost ten years, putting it down.

I saw a reading of it at New Dramatists.

Yes, you did.

So you worked for ten years. You were putting it down, coming back to it?

Yeah, well, I wrote the first act. Then I thought, "Well, there should be a second act with all this Warren Harding finagling in Ohio." So I wrote the second act. Then I wrote a fifty-page third act. And I knew where I wanted to go in the fourth act, and I had sketches for the fifth act. Then I did a reading of the whole thing and people were, like . . . hallucinating. It was just . . . I did it in this writers' group, and they just couldn't follow it. So I shelved it, I threw out the second and third act and created this fourth act, which told everything I threw out, plus what I wasn't going to write, and I just jumped into the fifth act, which was the culmination of the story, in which I had some idea what would happen. So I just took a while. But when you saw it, remember I did it in the little white rehearsal room? Then it was pretty much what it was. And I can't remember the date of that. And then the only thing that happened since then was it was trimmed a bit.

But to say you wrote it in three weeks, it would seem to me you needed to know what you were doing.

Three or four weeks, yeah, was about what it was written in.

I'm going to read this question because it's a long question. It's not even a question, it's a statement, and we're trying to think what the question is: A lot of your plays are about the theater, but in a postmodern, self-referential, ironic, meta-theatrical way in which you both love the artificiality and mock it, draw attention to it, and then use real emotions to draw the audience back in. How do you respond to that?

Well, I guess, right off the top of my head . . . What I love about the theater is that it is artificial, but that's the reality of the theater. Theater is really artificial. I think you always know there's a play going on, even as you're caught up in it. And I'm always aware that I'm writing a play. So sometimes that just finds its way into the play. You know, sometimes I think I'm going to write a regular play, and it never happens.

What would a regular play be?

Like a regular play with a regular story. It starts here, it ends there, it's naturalistic, there are characters that are involved in a situation. I thought I was going to write that when I wrote . . . Did you see *The Argument/Poetics* piece that I did? I was going to write a piece about Plato and Aristotle and their argument about whether the theater was good or bad. But it didn't come out that way. I mostly just incorporated a section of *Poetics* and the writing of this guy. Then I made a little internal play about Aristotle imagining a play he'd write about someone like Plato and why he turned off. So it didn't come out as a regular play; it came out as a forty-minute monologue. I think even that with *She Stoops to Comedy*, I wanted to write a regular play, kind of like an *All About Eve* milieu about this actress. Then by the time I got to it, I didn't like the period it was set in, so I just moved it up fast into the present . . .

But what you do when you do that is you actually have the character say, "Oh, I'm going to move this into the present." You say it out loud.

Yeah, yeah.

And of course you could cross all that out and just do that. But that's what I think is so interesting about the way you structure. So the question really is, how does that aesthetic response to the theater influence the way you structure your plays?

I don't know. I told the actors when we did *She Stoops to Comedy*, I didn't want to erase the mistakes. Sometimes there were mistakes, but I didn't want to erase them. I just incorporated them into the play. I thought they were kind of funny. There was this one line I had where I said, "Jayne Summerhouse, she's a treat. I mean a threat. It was a typo." And I just thought that was funny, so I incorporated the typo into the play. And it just seemed to be in concert with the farce and the humor of the play. And even in the recent play *Go Back to Where You Are,* there were just things I thought of as I was writing. There's a line early on that someone says, "Why don't I know this? I should've remembered." And then someone says, "Maybe it's a problem with the writing," because I thought there was a problem with the writing. So I just put it in. And that just informed for me a problem that I thought could be part of the vernacular of the piece.

So when you finish writing something, do you show it to somebody?

Yeah.

Whom do you show it to?

I might have my partner, Bill, read it first.

What might he say?

Sometimes, "I don't get it." Or he'll like it. Sometimes he might say he doesn't understand certain things. So I might think about that. These days, I show it to, you know, if it's a commission, I send it to a theater like Playwrights Horizons. They commissioned the last play. Actually, Adam Greenfield, the literary manager, said, "How's the play coming along?" I said, "Well, I only have a few pages." He said, "Why don't you just bring in what you have and we'll read it?" I said, "Well, just give me a few weeks. Let me see if I can write it." And that's what I did, I did it in about six weeks. And then we read it, and they liked it. Leigh Silverman directed the reading. They liked it and they wanted to do a workshop, then they committed to doing it.

They did a workshop and then . . . ?

We did a two-day reading, then we did a four-day workshop, which just ended in another reading. Then we did the play. Leigh suggested some rewrites, a little expansion of a couple of things, which I did. And then we just did it.

You work with a number of theaters.

Brian Kulick commissioned the two Italian adaptations, so I gave those to him. He'd like to do them both in rep, which would be a big undertaking. They're very loose adaptations. I think of them as original plays because they're very loosely adapted from the source material. And hopefully he'll be able to do them in rep in a couple years. He just did the workshop of one. Leigh would direct one, and he would direct the other, and I'd act in them both.

So in terms of bringing work to theaters . . . in working with Joanne, can she bring you up to Bard to do that?

I've done two things at Bard. I did the Aristotle piece and I did the Gertrude Stein lecture. I'm going to go out to the Getty to do those pieces. I'll do *The Myopia* at Bryn Mawr, I'll do *The Argument* up at Barnard for a day. I go to different places and . . .

And some of the great theaters in the city, you're connected to . . .

I'm very lucky. I have Playwrights Horizons. I have a relationship with the New York Theatre Workshop, the Public, with Classic Stage Company, Transport Group. David Herskovits at Target Margin Theater. So I feel really lucky. Anne Cattaneo . . . it is very nice to be up at Lincoln Center. I mean, I don't think I'll get a play produced there, but . . .

Why do you think that?

I don't think what I write is necessarily geared toward their audience. Maybe something someday, but it's not the kind of work they produce generally.

Do you have a sense of that? I know you like to please audiences. But do you sense different kinds of—do you want to move into other audiences?

Not really. I mean, I'll go where anybody wants me, really. If Anne or André Bishop read a play that I'd written and thought, "This might work," I'd say, "Sure, let's do it." But I'm not trying to write something—unless they commissioned a play, and I'd then have to work very hard to make sure I'd try to write something that I felt would be good for their audience. I mean, when I wrote the play for Playwrights Horizons, I wanted to make sure I thought it was something they could do. But Tim Sanford knows my work enough to know what he's going to get. And Brian I think too. Or David Herskovits when he commissioned something.

So when you've finally got the script and you go into rehearsal, if you don't direct it yourself—

I don't really direct anymore.

Well, is that a recent development?

Pretty recent. My solo plays are somewhat self-directed. You know, Brian Mertes directed *The Myopia*, but a lot of it was conceived by me, the gestures. He just helped refine it and hone it make sure my acting was, you know, properly modulated. But for fuller productions, since *She Stoops to Comedy*, I'm more interested in working with other directors now so I can get more help. Especially if I'm performing in it. With Joanne I did a little directing because she had days where she had to be away and so I stepped in to help direct, then she would reorganize things when she got back. But I don't direct as much. In rehearsal, I'll depend upon the director to offer me not only acting notes but also any ideas of revisions. Because Leigh directed *Coraline: The Musical*, which I acted in, there was a constant sense of, "This needs to be clearer," "I think this is too long," or "How do we make this a song as opposed to a speech?"

Do you have any difficulty if you're acting in one of your own plays, leaving the playwright out when you're rehearsing?

When I'm in a scene, I always work to fully commit as an actor in the scene. So then I'm more dependent on the director these days to say, "I think we need something here or there," if it's the writing. But I'm also sensitive to if I'm not hearing another actor say something I think in the right way or with the right intention, then I would talk to my director. So I can hear things. It's not like I can't hear things.

When you act, you have a very deliberate way of speaking. Is that what you expect from the other actors too? Is that a style in the writing, and other actors either do it or don't do it? Or does only your character do it?

Depends on the play. I felt people thought there was a difference in my acting than other people's acting in the last play. But I thought the actors were doing what I wanted. My narrative tasks were a little different than theirs. I had more meta-theatrical storytelling to do in the play, so they had different obligations. You try to find actors that can be in sync with the play. They don't have to do exactly what I do, but it still has to serve the play. It's hard to know. Mostly it's just whether the intentions or the tone is right. I can be sensitive to that even when I'm acting.

Do you trust the director or do you do both? You trust the director, but you keep your ear open?

I trust the director, especially with Leigh, whom I've now built a very close relationship with. I trust her, and I trust her to hear things. We'll talk in preparation. Or after rehearsal, we'll say, "This could be happening," "Oh, that's a good note." Just talk about things I'm hearing. I don't want to—I want to make sure the actors know who the director is. So I don't—unless it's a reading situation where Leigh solicits or a director solicits my questions. I save those for later.

Do you ever get a sense that the other actors are slightly intimidated or fearful of you as an actor because it's your play?

I don't think so. I try to be very chummy with everybody and supportive. You know, backstage, in the dressing room, we were all a merry band of players. I try to make myself very much a part of the troupe and support their work and support what they contribute to the play. I don't try to do anything that would intimidate them.

Do you have any involvement in the design of the play?

Yeah, I do like to see it and make sure that it's not way out of—it's not something that I think would be out of sync with my intentions. Leigh and

Rachel Hauck, who did the set for *Go Back to Where You Are*, showed me the set, which I fell in love with immediately. I thought it was a beautiful set. So they showed it to me, talked about it. I had a couple of comments, nothing really critical. I thought they were right on from the beginning.

Did you say, "This is the kind of set I want" beforehand?

In the stage directions, it says, "A few chairs." It didn't say anything beyond that. But Leigh thought, "There should be a platform. We need to raise a platform in that theater, or otherwise nobody will see anybody's legs." And we talked about the set, and I said, "You know, something wood would be good." And they just went from there. So I do have input. And if I'm acting in it, of course, all actors respond to their clothes and their costumes and have thoughts about it. They work with the designer in tandem with the director. So, yeah, I try to put my two cents in about the design.

As an actor-slash-playwright in Go Back to Where You Are, *were you excited about where that character was going to go? His big moments?*

"Excited"?

Well, we haven't seen everything that you've done, but it certainly seems to us very different and more emotional and moving than anything else that we've seen.

I don't think I completely anticipated how emotional it would get. But as I worked on it, my instinct just led me there, and Leigh supported that. I think *The Myopia* has big emotional moments, I think there's not the same level of tenderness because it's not a love story, it's more of a nightmare marriage. In the other, because it was a romantic story, it just allowed and called for different emotional territory, as well as the more emotional material at the end, the fear of being alone.

One thing we didn't ask earlier: When you're at the desk or when you're writing, are there aspects of writing plays that come easier than others?

I don't think so . . . Not that I can think of.

It all seems hard?

Yeah, it's all a challenge, especially when you don't know where you're going at first. It's all challenging. Nothing seems particularly easy or particularly . . .

Do you ever get carried away because you have a facility with dialogue? Do you ever get carried away because people are talking in a way that's not interesting and you just have to scrap all that?

Do I get carried away? Depends. I mean, obviously, sometimes you write more than you need. With *The Myopia,* I wrote this long, smoke-filled room scene. You saw it twice. You saw it recently, then you saw the one at New Dramatists. Well, the smoke-filled room scene is now half as long as it was when you first saw it. We were trying to prune it and cut it. We just couldn't do it. Every time we took something out, the rhythm seemed wrong. Finally, I said, "You know, why don't we just start it halfway in the scene?" And so I read it starting at the halfway point, and Melanie Joseph the producer and Brian said, "Oh, that's really good," and I said, "Wait a minute. I lost all those good lines!" And they said, "No, no, that's it." So that's how we did it. We just literally cut it in half.

What did you leave out?

We left out everybody coming into the smoke-filled room, bit by bit. There were toilets flushing, people going into the bathroom, coming out. It went long. There was just more stuff, about the state of the election, the state of the nomination. It was pretty funny, there was a lot of funny stuff, but they felt . . . It was a twenty-minute scene as opposed to a ten-minute scene. So we just literally cut it in half. So there's oftentimes where I write too much. I think that's true for every playwright. You may have experienced this also where you just have to prune back and cut out. Sometimes you need a little more. It just depends. It's nice to get carried away because then that's how you get on fire. When you're on fire, you get something. Maybe sometimes the whole fire has to be put out later, but it does get you stuff, you know, emotional material.

For example, when you're in previews, especially the last play . . . if you're in the play, it must be complicated to make changes, to sense what's working, what's not. Is that an issue?

Probably because of my relationship with Leigh and with Tim being there and Adam was there, a couple of things they thought needed to be clarified . . . I then said, "Sure, I can work on that," and I did. I think we solved the problems. So it's dependent upon the response from the outside eyes. It's true for my acting, certainly. *Coraline: The Musical* was very hard because we previewed a long time, plus there were a lot of musical revisions, and I had to learn some of them. Then you put them in, and you've got to do them that night. Oy. That was hard. Coordinating a musical is so tricky because you're coordinating text and lyrics and song and choreography. So that was a lot of work in tandem with performing every night. This one wasn't as hard. I just had to make a few adjustments. By the time we started previewing, the play was very close. There were just a few things to . . .

Can you tell what's going on in the audience when you're in the play?

I rely to some extent on the outside eyes. That's when you really rely because, as an actor, you may think the audience is not with it. Then you find out at the end that they were or that it was a really good show or that it was a quiet audience but it's fine. To be objective is very hard when you're in something. It's just hard. You always depend on the outside eye, and even the outside eye can use some help from the producer. The director might need some objectivity provided by the producer or the literary manager or friends who say, "I don't think that's working," or "That's really good." Everybody needs, I think, some consultation.

Does the audience tell you something useful?

Yes. Oh, sure. Certainly in moments that you didn't think were going to get a laugh, suddenly people are laughing. Or the worst thing, of course, for any play, whether yours or someone else's, I call it a "cast laugh," where people are always yucking it up in rehearsal, and then it just lies there like a piece of lox when you get into performance, something that's so funny and the audience just flatlines. And you're just mystified, and you're so furious that everybody was laughing during rehearsal, and they just kind of led you on. So now I try to be very careful. I don't believe it until it's there. But, of course, in comedy, you try not to get a laugh, you try to just play the scene. Whatever comic technique, you try to just play the scene. But you do learn things in performance obviously.

Did a critic ever say anything that was useful to you?

Sure. I can think of an acting thing once. I was in a production of Beckett's *Happy Days,* and the critic referred to my performance as "labored." I didn't have a lot to do, but it was "labored." I felt that was right, so I tried to ease off a bit there. Sometimes a critic will see something that you didn't see or they'll read into it something that they see.

What about as a writer?

Yes, sometimes people will refer to something I do as "wacky" or "idiosyncratic" that I wouldn't necessarily think of as "idiosyncratic" or "wacky." So I think about it. Then I have to think about whether I agree with it or not. I don't like to think of myself as wacky. I don't like to think of myself as idiosyncratic. Especially in a clinical sense. But, you know, I'm more likely to know that I'm quirky. And the plays can be quirky in a way. They're odd in a certain way. I think I've come to understand that from the response out of some critics or other people that what I'll write is—I don't mean oddball in a pejorative way or some punitive way, but, you know, a little off kilter. The first one about the "labored" was Charles Isherwood at the *Times,* and I thought he was on to something so I kind of tried to pull back. And Michael Feingold at the *Village Voice,* I remember even in *She Stoops to Comedy* found a couple of scenes a little extended. So I thought about that. Maybe if I did it again, I would shorten them.

Down at HOME, you used to work with the same actors over and over. But you don't do that anymore?

Well, there weren't that many. Mary Schultz, who was originally cast in *Go Back to Where You Are* but had to leave. The other actors who I work with, one in particular, Ron Bagden, he doesn't work as much as an actor anymore. He did a couple plays at the Public, and Mary did also. But they were the two I was closest with. You know, Kathleen Tolan doesn't act as often, she acted for me once. I've acted for her. I kind of fall in love with actors, whether it's actors I'm working with in someone else's play or mine. I always think, "Oh, I want to do the next play with them." And sometimes it works out or doesn't. That's fun.

Do you write for actors other than yourself?

Yeah, I think of actors who I think would be good in the play. They're in my mind. Mary Schultz is someone I've done that for. Sometimes it works out that they're there, sometimes it doesn't. I certainly had Mary in mind for the last play, and it was emotional that she couldn't stay and it was for her too. But I think of actors sometimes. I also think of myself and where I'm going to be in the play. I'm in my mind when I'm writing.

But you haven't written minor roles for yourself or supporting roles?

No, I'm often the principal character or the protagonist. But even when I wrote *2 Samuel 11,* which I didn't perform—I'm sorry I didn't perform that one—the protagonist, certainly in the first part, was Bathsheba that Mary played. Only in the second act did the actor take on the multiple roles. So in the first act he's certainly the supporting character, he has no lines. It's all her.

Do you ever look at your career—so far—as a writer and see if there is some kind of arc, some direction that is now clear that you're going in?

Not really. For the most part, the plays have gotten shorter, and that's all I can think of. I try to be a little more refined and hone down.

Well, you started out with monologues.

Yes, and they were more autobiographically oriented. That isn't as true anymore. I mean, they're certainly personal experiences and feelings that are incorporated. But now I try to be more of a storyteller of other stories that mean something to me or that come from me somewhere but aren't detailing specific parts of my personal life.

Are your plays done by other theaters around the country?

Occasionally. *She Stoops to Comedy* has gotten done. It was just done recently in Texas. I saw it at Woolly Mammoth. I saw it at a theater called the Evidence Room in Los Angeles. I've seen *Jack* done a few times.

And you've seen them. What is your response to the performances of the characters based on you? Ones that you've played.

It's fun in a way. Sometimes I think, "Oh, that's not exactly what I had in mind." But that's OK. Also, you know, I'm happy to talk to people about the play and be of any help I can. Sometimes they invite me to go to rehearsals and see things. Woolly Mammoth, I went a few times and gave Howard Shalwitz, the director, thoughts and notes. But he did a beautiful production. I thought some of it was better than what I did. I saw the production in Los Angeles. I thought it was very successful, and I thought it was quite good. I saw *Dead Mother* in San Francisco, I hadn't seen that play in a long time, and they had quite a success with it. It was old, I thought, "Aye aye aye, I wrote that, huh?" But they did quite a good job. I just appreciate people doing the plays, and I'm happy to be of help any way. Nothing outrages me, really.

Most traditional playwrights obviously want to see their work translated, done in many theaters. Is that an impulse of yours? Would you like that?

I guess so. Some of the early plays, there's nothing anybody could do. People do the HOME Show pieces. *Dead Mother* has been done a few times, *She Stoops to Comedy*. I don't know if anybody would do *The Myopia*. That'd be hard to let go of, frankly. The recent play I hope people do it. Yeah, I want people to do it. But I'm not going to . . . That's my agent, that's people that word gets around. I'm not going out and shopping it around. Even *Dead Mother*, which, you know, incorporated a lot of feelings, it was a story that never happened. Some people have an interest in it. I'm not going to try to write so it gets done in every regional theater. I'm not writing for that. I'm just trying to write a play that . . . would come out of me and people would enjoy. But I'm not writing with commercial interests at heart. Maybe no playwright does that unless they're really . . . Maybe a few do, but the playwrights I've acted for, I think they did write because they have an idea and they want to try to express something and perhaps, given the accessibility of their writing, may get done more frequently than my plays, which is fine. I guess if there's been a trajectory, it's been more in my thinking, which is less about trying to get established and more just trying to make a contribution, trying to give people an enhancing experience and give them a good experience. I just read this wonderful autobiography of Stefan Zweig. He talked at length about wanting to make a contribution, and that was very resonant with me. That's a very noble ambition. Less about having a lot of people do your plays and more just trying to contribute something and to put something out there for people to enjoy. That's my trajectory—try to develop that thinking and hopefully write the best piece I can write.

One thing that I've noticed with some meta pieces is that there is a distance between the emotions and the medium. And I didn't find that with your work. What techniques do you use to try to bring that warmth to the audience instead of being a little more distant?

Part of it is I like to bring the audience in on the joke. You know, like the line I quote, "She's a treat. I mean a threat. It was a typo." I think I just meant to bring people in on the joke, bring people in on the artifice that's being revealed. It's more to reveal the artifice, to reveal the fact that a play is going on there. Again, one of the last lines of *Go Back to Where You Are,* the character Bernard says, "I wanna try, to see you that is." And then the character I play says, "This is a play." So in a way, it was meant to say, "This could only happen in a play, and it is a play." I wanted the audience to remember it's a play. But also it's meant to incorporate how fearful he was that it may not be true, maybe it wouldn't work out. So I tried to always think about not only letting people in on the joke or letting people in on the artifice, but also that there is an emotional stake behind it, you know? I don't want to push the audience away. I want them in on whatever is going on. And that's as close as I can get to it.

So that is kind of basic to your writing?

I like the unembellished stage. There's a line in *The Myopia* that says "the impoverished stage." I don't think it's really impoverished. Just . . . I love the directness for the actor and the script to the audience. Not a lot of things in the way. I enjoy it when I see other people do it. I've acted in so many different kinds of plays that have more technical requirements . . . But I love the simple, direct relationship of the story, the actor, and the audience.

It's interesting that it doesn't alienate the audience when you do something like that. In fact, I think it brings the audience closer to the play. I think the audience feels like the play has just thrown its arm around the audience and said, "Come on, we're all in this together." Rather than there being a separation. It could be alienating, but it isn't.

I love audiences. I want them to have a good time, either from a poignant moment or a comic moment. And I do love the theater. You know, we all say we love the theater. But I love the process of it. I love the hope of entertaining people. I really consider myself an entertainer. I don't mean in terms of just, you know, something empty, although I love kind of thoughtful frivolity. But something, you know, where to engage people and let them have a good time, either to be moved or to laugh. I love that about the theater. In fact, there's the last lines in *She Stoops to Comedy* you make me think of at the end of the play where she says, "I'm going to leave the door open. I could leave it closed, but I think it's more interesting to leave it open. And besides, I trust you all completely."

DOUG WRIGHT

We meet Doug Wright in the second-floor classroom at New Dramatists, a building on West Forty-Fourth Street that is a converted church, just down the street from the Actors Studio. Doug is an alumnus of New Dramatists, and this room is comfortable and familiar to him. The narrow room has a long conference table and fireplace that probably hasn't seen a blaze in a hundred years. Doug comes in and greets us affectionately. He is an extremely affable fellow. His manner betrays nothing of the dark rage of his play *Quills* or the eccentric gothic humor of his libretto for *Grey Gardens*. He is tall and sturdy, heavier than he'd like to be, according to him, and even more articulate than we expected about himself, his work, writing, the theater, and just about anything we asked him to talk about. His love of language, apparent in many of his plays, is also obvious in the ease with which he speaks.

Did your parents encourage your creative side?

My mother always loved children's literature, so she used to staple together pieces of construction paper, and she'd ask us to dictate text to her—to tell a story—and she'd write it down along the space of the paper like, "Johnny went to school early in the morning," turn the page, "He took an apple in a paper sack." And then she'd give us crayons and ask us to illustrate our pictures on the blank space of the page.

Was she a teacher?

No, she grew up with teachers. Her father was a school principal, and her mother taught piano. For a long time when the nest was empty, she managed a children's bookstore. It was a passion of hers. So I think it was ingrained in us at a very early age that telling stories had some kind of innate worth.

How did you connect it to playwriting? Did you see plays?

Yeah, and I think it was when I realized plays were actually written. We went to see children's theater on occasion, but the first grown-up play we saw was Howard Lindsay and Russell Crouse's *Life With Father* at the Dallas Theater Center, and there were children in that play because there are children in the cast, and I saw them acting onstage, and I thought to myself, I could do that. And then I realized that plays had to be constructed and written. And in her never-ending quest to encourage her children to read, my mother would take us to the Dallas Public Library and check out anything we liked. She wasn't terribly prohibitive and didn't oversee our selection that assiduously. I remember when I was about nine or ten plucking down a Tennessee Williams play from the shelf, and it just blew my little mind, and I think Mother's attitude was, "Better that he picked an American classic than common dreck." I don't think her knowledge of Williams was that exhaustive, so I don't think she really knew what I was reading.

What was the play?

I think the play was *The Glass Menagerie,* and that's when I started to voraciously read plays. This is so pretentious, but I had worked through most of Williams and a good deal of O'Neill by the time I was in middle school.

This is twelve?

Probably fourteen or so. This is not to suggest that I understood them in any way—that I was truly up to the task. It was grossly premature and gave me enduring nightmares, but it was still pretty formative.

But the thought that you could do this . . .

Yeah. This is perhaps a silly anecdote, but I remember that my mother and father—they have a lovely relationship, but they had a fight on this particular day, and so my mother grabbed me by the hand and said, "We're going to the library." She loved to go to the library to do genealogical research, which was her passion, and she let me wander the stacks, and I was in the sixth grade, and I went to the theater section, and I plucked down *Oh Dad, Poor Dad, Mama's Hung You in the Closet and I'm Feelin' So Sad,* by Arthur Kopit, because it was such an evocative title. And I sat there and read the whole day. And full of the fight my parents just had and my mother's retreat to the stacks of the library, the Byzantine perspective of the play felt very true to life at that moment. And now I sometimes volunteer to lead workshops at the Lark Play Development Company, where Arthur Kopit is extraordinarily involved, and it's a great thrill that I get to sit next to him. It's a pinch-me occasion.

Would you say that he was a serious literary influence?

I would say one of them, yeah, absolutely.

What were some others?

Certainly the key ones. I don't think you can grow up in this culture and pretend that those gentlemen didn't wield huge input . . . Lillian Hellman . . . sort of the playwrights of the Golden Age.

What about television, did that work in any way?

We had an interesting television stricture. We were each allowed one hour a week. I remember that we weren't allowed to watch *The Nutcracker* at Christmastime, because my grandmother thought that the men's tights were too revealing, and you could see their behinds. Which was probably formative in an altogether different way, but I always chose *The Waltons,* and my sister always chose *Little House on the Prairie,* and my brother always chose *Star Trek.* So I think I sort of fetishized John Boy Walton for a long time.

When you work and actually sit down, do you have a schedule? Are you a good boy every day?

I get up in the morning and fill my coffee cup up and head upstairs, and the first question I have for myself is, "What is the most overdue?" And that informs the day's agenda. So, I'm not a good boy. I think panic is a very reliable muse. A deadline rather than my own discriminating tastes usually determines when something's finished.

But when you began, you didn't have deadlines.

I didn't and it's a curious thing—I wonder if other writers agree, but when time to write was time stolen from earning a living or going to school, whereby the precious hours you carve out of the day to sit by yourself and draw the windows closed and be mischievous on the page in hopes that maybe someday it would see the light of day, it was delicious. When you're fortunate enough to be doing it full-time as a profession, it loses a bit of that. I feel guilty saying this because I'm so privileged to be spending my days writing—it's such an honor—and yet when I had to make the time and wasn't afforded the time, I was always more punctual.

Did you get more done?

I got more done. It flew more readily, and it wasn't encumbered by expectation. I was doing it for myself on a whim. Now I think I redraft more. I'm more inhibited when I sit down because I know there's this figure at the end of the day that I have to please, whether it's a resident theater that's commissioned a work or a commercial producer that wants a musical or a film director I'm asked to write a screenplay for. There's someone sitting in judgment, waiting. That was never the case before, and the writing was more free, it was liberating.

There's a trade-off.

Yeah.

Does the fact that someone's waiting, in any way, fill in for that kind of expectation?

I think so. I know the pressure of writing for someone specific can some-times energize me and lead to maybe better writing faster. I think that's possible.

So what do you do when you start something? Do you structure it? Do you start at the beginning or do you start at the end? Do you have a theme in mind or a character? Or an image or an object or a piece of news?

I think it's almost different for every single piece. I think they all have had their own peculiar genesis. One general rule for myself . . . I think it's the artist Marcel Duchamp who said, "To conceive of the work is glorious but to execute it is drudgery." And so I try and know just enough to start, but I don't want to know every twist and turn and even necessarily my endpoint because I want the adrenaline that comes with discovery.

So it surprises you as well.

Yeah. I think when you are fully engaged in the act of writing, all your synapses are firing. The only state that comes close to this is when as a viewer you're completely swept away by a completely consuming play or a movie that reaches out from the screen to envelop you, and you can't wait to see what the character's going to say next, you can't wait to guess the next narrative turn. That's where you are when you're really in that zone, writing, and you're a vessel for a story that's spinning faster than you can shape it.

Are you still finding that happens?

It's what we always pray for. Not daily, maybe once or twice a year, but it's like that hit of a potent drug that makes you a lifetime addict—that feeling is so fantastic.

Then what do you do about rewriting? What's that process like? Is it different in terms of a play or screenplay because that's a whole different process?

Definitely. This is a little pedagogical, but I think writing a first draft is like excavating clay, and you want really high-quality, dense, pliant clay, and redrafting is actually semantic, and so you want what comes from plundering your own subconscious and whatever research you've employed to do the piece, and then when you rewrite is when you really take full authorial responsibility for its shape.

Do different muscles come into play when you write Quills, *for example, than when you write* Little Mermaid? *Meaning, something original as opposed to an adaptation.*

Absolutely. I would say that when I'm writing a wholly original play, I feel like an artist. When I'm adapting something, I hope I'm a really responsible craftsman. And there are those times when I've done an adaptation and tumble into that alternate fantastic reality and suddenly felt like it was mine. And you hope for that, because that's what yields the best writing, ultimately, but I can't say it always happens. I think that when you're adapting something, you're really applying all the rules of your craft to translate something that may or may not be innately theatrical and make it so. Which is different than sort of plundering your life experience or interior psychology to forge a work that's born of your DNA.

So Grey Gardens *would be both or would be adaptation? You so refashioned it.*

It's my hope. And I would posit that *Grey Gardens,* the source material was a complement, but I still had the requisite freedom to fall headlong into my own writerly imagination. I hope it was.

Was it your idea to have that first act?

Truthfully Scott Frankel had come to me and said he loved the movie and wanted to musicalize it, and I said, "You can't." It's completely nonnarrative—the movie is brilliant, but it's constructed with psychological portraiture, which film can do, but a musical needs a story. And I said, "The very thing that makes it such an enduring documentary is verisimilitude, and to place these very artificial, over-the-top, outrageous women in the over-the-top world of the theater is a redundancy. So the very thing that makes the film special is going to undermine you onstage." And he listened very closely and he said, "That's terribly interesting. Can you come back in two weeks and tell me again why we shouldn't do this?" So I went back two weeks later and I said, "Here are the other problems." And then I went back six weeks later and I said, "The other thing you're going to run up against is . . ." and suddenly by the end of about fifteen weeks, we had a first draft. Part of it was Scott and Michael Korie, our lyricist. They went out to dinner, and they said, "How can we nail this down?" And suddenly Scott had an idea and on one cocktail napkin he wrote 1943, and on another cocktail napkin he wrote 1976, and they brought the two cocktail napkins to our next get-together.

On the other things that you do for hire, do you choose them because in some way they do speak to you?

I think filling a blank page is extraordinarily difficult. So if it doesn't speak to you in some primal way, you're not going to be able to dig up the requisite clay. So when I'm taking assignments, they do have to speak to some unresolved issue in my own life or some historical fascination I have or some philosophical question that I'm engaged by, or it's simply too hard, you can't do it, you can't do the work. It's like saying, "Yeah, I'll drive to Chicago tonight, but I don't have any gas." So you can't promise anybody that you'll take the trip.

Are there some aspects of writing, whether it's original or adaptation, that come easier for you? That you can look to in your art and say, "Well, at least I can go there when I'm stuck."

I so urgently wish I could say yes. I don't think I can. I think it's all hard.

Dialogue?

I guess. I don't know if it really answers the question, but I do know that when I'm stuck working on a play, if I allow myself to skip ahead to a scene of maximum conflict, or if I'm sort of dutifully writing scene three, and I'm really excited about writing scene four, I'll allow myself to skip to scene four, and then in the act of doing that, I usually find that I don't need scene three. I'll try and find a place in the text of maximum conflict and go there.

Where you're drawn into the script.

Yeah.

Were there any strictures or orders from Philip Kaufman, the director of Quills, *in terms of what he wanted in the adaptation?*

Absolutely, that was my very first screenwriting experience, and I made a deal with myself early on and that was: I am going to participate fully. I'm not going to be precious or censorious. The movie may be brilliant. It may disappoint me, but by the time it's shot, I will know how movies are made. I will know how to write a screenplay. Happily, Phil and I often saw eye to eye, and I had a remarkable time on that movie. Writers are usually thrown off sets; I actually had my own deck chair with my name on it, and I was there for the shooting of every single scene, and I got to cultivate relationships with the actors. There were times when Phil let me run rehearsals, because he was dealing with technical concerns, and he really allowed me to collaborate, and in thanks to that, I gave ground on some things. So when I look back on the movie, there are things about it that I adore, and there are things about it that in retrospect frustrate me a little, but what I know is that I was on the front lines making the choices too, so I can own it. So anything that works brilliantly in it, I'll claim some small measure of success, and anything that's a mistake, I was there making the mistake too. I felt thoroughly implicated in the making of that movie and thoroughly included by Phil, and at the end of the day, I think it's a great relief and a privilege to be able to say that.

I just watched it again, and I thought it was fabulous.

There were certain things that were pragmatic, which we agreed about. The play is much more violent, but it's sort of hyperbolic stage violence, which has a sort of almost-camp humor about it. In film, violence becomes literal, in the theater it's somewhat hammed or removed—it's a metaphor. In a film, it's, "Oh my God, somebody got their hand chopped off." So we had to temper the violence in the movie so this didn't become a bloodbath. Also, in the theater, dialectic often holds the stage because it has dramatic power lines running through it, narrative power lines, but dialectic or debate on the screen usually curdles, and any kind of philosophical plant you want to log on a camera has to be embedded in the storytelling. So that meant that the film isn't nearly as discursive as the play, and as a result I feel like some of the complexity of the arguments about censorship in the interest of distilling them for a narrative and visual attack, they get a little simpler. And that's one thing that frustrates me when I watch the film, and yet I feel that it's so true to the tone and the style of the piece. I'll never forget—you asked about other authors that influenced me, and one person I'm always quick to cite is the late, great Charles Ludlum. And that play in particular owes a huge debt to him.

In what way?

It's based on historical materials. We took extravagant liberties with it. It's sort of shot through with a kind of arch humor. It has certain camp affectations that it uses pretty shamelessly to lob its point, and it asks performers to go to really bold, audacious places without apology. And even Geoffrey Rush came up to me at the craft services table, and we were about to shoot one of his major scenes, and he said, "It's Ludlum. It's all Ludlum. This part is that intersection of King Lear and Norma Desmond. And both of those characters used to do that all the time." So his spirit is really present.

Is there some point when, if you feel uncertain about something, you'll show it to somebody?

Yes, I'm chronically insecure, and I'm always calling my partner, David, upstairs to read something off the screen. You be Big Edie, and I'll be Little Edie, and we read it together. David's probably the only one I involve in that minute detail. Usually I won't show it to anyone until it's the first draft. And sometimes I have a lovely assistant, an actor who comes in and works for me one day a week to do filing and dry cleaning and things like that at my indulgence, and I actually will give Jason a couple pages to read and say, "So what do you think?" Those are probably the only two people who see unfinished drafts.

What do you want to hear from them? Do you want them to say, "OK, this works," or, "This is why I'm confused"?

I want them to say, "It's fine, keep going." I want incentive to keep working more than I want to fix the problem, and if they can just say, "Yeah, that's a moment. You've captured a moment. What's next?" I usually want some type of reassurance, which isn't to say later when the draft is done I don't want everybody's rigorous eyes, and I don't welcome challenge, because I think I do. Oftentimes, when it's in process, what I'm really asking for is a kiss and a nudge.

It helps you go on, and that's the point. When you finish a first draft, are there any theaters you show it to or any producers who you have a relationship with that would want to see your work immediately?

I guess so. Usually they've been sort of committed in a way when they were begun, so there have already been directors sort of involved. People who have been my informal dramaturgs: Christopher Ashley, he's at La Jolla, he's a dear old college friend. Moises Kaufman, because we grew up together at New York Theatre Workshop. I'm very good friends with screenwriter and playwright Bobby Harley, and I usually take my Hollywood pieces to him, because he has a lot more experience there.

He did Steel Magnolias.

He's had a very successful career in film, and I'll go to him as kind of a big brother figure and say, "Did you ever work with so-and-so?" and, "What's the latest you've ever turned in a first draft?" He'll console me. In the theater it's probably Chris and Moises, and I've had the pleasure of working with Michael Greif a bit, and he's usually involved early, while I'm still writing, so he, I would say, is pretty formative.

Do you ever write for a particular performer? Do they give inspiration, say, he would do it or she would do it?

There have been certain journeys I've taken where actors have implicated themselves early in a workshop process, where I realize their indispens-ability to the project. With Jefferson Mays, I didn't really have a text, I just had the research, and he started to read the research off the page, and I knew I found my actor, so it's almost fair to say that I wrote that piece for him. And similarly we were at Sundance with the first act of *Grey Gardens*, and Christine Ebersole and Mary Louise Wilson were just revelatory. So we knew early on that they would play these roles. So I've written for spe-cific actors in that context. I don't often sit down with a blank page and say Debra Monk and John Slattery. Let's start. That's just not part of my process. I usually start to cast it when the roles start to find themselves.

In rehearsal do you ever adjust things because of what an actor's bringing to it or, conversely, not bringing to it?

Yeah, absolutely. You hope for that fabulous fourth week in rehearsal where their knowledge of the character outstrips your own and they be-come a true resource for finishing the draft. Because you can see five or six or eight people in your imagination and in the last four weeks only one. So the goal is for them to surpass you, and you need that. There are also points when the actor hasn't landed a point in a scene where I will go back to the text and make the point more explicit. And that's not necessarily because the actor's failing me in any way, but you want a play to achieve a certain sameness from production to production and performance to per-formance, but if this actor can't make this land, maybe you need to chal-lenge yourself to make it more explicit, so when it's done in Oshkosh two years from now, and you're not even there, the line hasn't lost its point.

What about when you're in rehearsal? Do you have to deal with the director who's pushing you to do something because you're not getting something? How do you deal with that—people who aren't coming up to your vision?

It's learning to fight productively. Moises, who is one of my dearest friends on the planet, and I were having problems, and I thought he was making a huge mistake conceptually, and I really resisted a lot of what he wanted to do, and I was keeping it inside, and I was sitting in the back of rehearsal getting more and more tense. And he said to me, "I'm Latino, you're WASP. Be Latino. Just be Latino with me." He had life-size pieces of furniture that flew in and flew out, and he really wanted to make a spectacle, and so I just exploded and I said, "It's doll furniture! It has to be doll! There's nothing amazing about showing twentieth-century history with all the stagecraft in the world. If we can show twentieth-century European history with doll furniture, we're doing something." And his face lit up and he went, "You're being Latino!" So it was mostly Moises's generosity of spirit and patience, and he taught me how to fight in productive ways so that rather than hold on to your ground, the two of you, if it's a good collaboration, will leave your own ideas in the dirt and push through to a third idea that's even better. And I think he was patient with me and taught me that lesson.

What qualities would you like in a director, then? Or do they vary with the project? In terms of working with someone, what's most helpful?

It's interesting. There's a part of me that always feels like they're false designations, because certainly on a journey of a play like *I Am My Own Wife* there were times when I directed Jefferson and times when Moises made such an astute dramaturgical contribution to the piece that I feel like he was almost authorial. It's extraordinarily complicated. As a playwright and a good member of my guild, I think those designations are more important to forge an etiquette and to build the business of theater, but in the rehearsal halls they're always semifluid. I guess I want a director who won't tell me what's wrong with the text but will show me, and if there's a rusty scene and he reads it on the page and he's suspect, I hope he doesn't stop rehearsal and say, "Go home and do a rewrite." I hope he says, "Let's put it on its feet and let's see," and in the act of trying to make it work, it will expose what is rotten to the core, and I'll be forced to go home and rework it, and I won't have a moment to log a complaint that, "Well, she read that line wrong." I have to take responsibility for it. I learn more watching a director mount my work than I necessarily learn talking to him or her about it.

What about an actor? What kind of actor do you like working with?

I would say if there's a moment that's confusing you, try it fifteen different ways. And if you can't make it work, it's my problem. I much prefer that to an actor who resists.

Fifteen different ways is a lot.

I do think—you may hear this from other writers—I do think that the development craze in the country has created a false perception that everyone involved in the work is there to fix it or make things better, and as the playwright, you're the patient and you're surrounded by expert medical staff and they're all going to breathe life into this sick puppy. And so increasingly actors who have been there for twenty seasons or have been out to Sundance feel their role is diagnostic and not participatory, and I think that's really dangerous. I think actors teach you about your play by acting it or attempting to act it and failing. Those are the actors I most like in the room. My experience with those kinds of actors has been extraordinarily rare because I think we have an epidemic in the other arena.

Are there actors you won't work with because they don't deliver in that way?

Yeah.

Do they know it?

I hope not. Anyone who in good faith labors their way through your text using whatever resources they have at their disposal, you owe a little piece of your heart to, but certainly there are actors whose processes dovetail with mine and actors whose processes interfere with mine. You only learn that by working with people.

You mentioned a couple directors you love to work with . . . what if they're not available? How do you decide on a new one? What do you have to do to get to know them before you get in bed with them, so to speak?

This is a provocative thing to say, but I directed an evening of my own one-acts at the Vineyard Theatre in 2001, and I got the best reviews of my writing life for those pieces. They were modest in scope—they weren't ambitious and I'm not suggesting they were necessarily the most interesting things I wrote—but I do feel they were the purest expression of me onstage, and similarly I just adapted a Strindberg play and directed it out at La Jolla—*The Creditors*. Again, the critical response to it and audience response to it was very affirming. And I know there's a huge bias against playwrights directing their own work, and my sort of flip response is if Betty Crocker can write the recipe, chances are that she can bake the chocolate cake. There's a certain truth in that. I didn't come to playwriting through literature. I didn't have a particular fascination with putting words on the page per se. I knew at an early age from that production of *Life With Father* that I wanted to be in the process of making theater. I wanted to act in things, and I wanted to direct things, and then graduate school required me to check a box, and I said, "OK, to direct somebody needs to give you a play and a space. To act, somebody needs to cast you. To write: paper and pen and you're doing it. This is where I'll put my chips." And so I got halfway through my career as a writer. This is all I'm doing. It's disappointing. I want to do more. I think if your impulse isn't to write plays but to make theater, and you happen to write a play, I don't think you should be shy about attempting to direct it. So I'm getting increasingly emboldened.

You said that when you directed these one-acts that it was the purest expression of you. And just to play devil's advocate, is it possible that there is more there that could be revealed by a director, not you?

Possibly. I guess I would say by the time you have a guaranteed slot at a resident nonprofit in New York, you have been through six workshops, three directors, two casts, multiple readings by your colleagues, and the play has been examined from so many angles, it's hard to enter that slot without a pretty impressive store of information, so it's certainly, I guess, the dream for every playwright that the director not only achieves dramatically what is written but pushes it even further beyond that, to touch the sublime. I have been gorgeously served by directors. There have never been situations when directors said, "Complete my next sentence." I guess this is an argument against directing your own work: there has been a compelling tension between us and that's something that in directing your own work you don't get. But I don't know that I always believe that. I can be in a room with a designer, and the designer can say to me, "I know how you see it, but look at it my way," and they can completely re-invent the space for me, and at the end of two hours I can be sold on it.

But that's the important point—that there's another force in the room that can challenge your vision and see where else it can live and how else it can live. It's very hard when you have all the marbles.

You're right. If there's enough opposition . . .

If there's a designer, and not a young designer who is going to say, "Yes, whatever you want, Doug Wright," but instead, someone who can say, "No, look at it this way." . . . Otherwise I think that in my experience it's very rare that a writer can really direct his own work as well as, not anyone, but someone special.

Well, *Creditors,* for example. There I am, second-time director, with Su-san Hilferty doing my clothes and Robert Brill doing my set. So it's more likely that I'm the junior member of the staff, and Kathryn Meisle and Omar Metwally and T. Ryder Smith and, you know, like people kicking my ass with Chris Ashley looking over my shoulder. There have been a lot of times, so many times, where I have been, earlier in my career, where you're in a room and you're speaking English and the staff is speaking English, and there's this person in control who's speaking in rapid-fire Polish. And you find that's when the 3:00 A.M. phone calls from the ac-tors start coming and they don't stop. I went through that so many times early in my career, and it's so liberating to be able to have a direct, simple conversation with an actor.

What is your relationship with actors when you're not directing?

When I'm not directing, even though I think that roles are sometimes in the rehearsal hall in context, I think they need to be specific and explicit and in the rehearsal hierarchy, they need to be acknowledged. If I have a problem with an actor and I'm not the director, I go to my director, I go to Michael Greif, and conversely, if the actor has a problem, I want them to go to Moises or Michael Greif or the director. So I do think that it is a dysfunctional family that's constituted for eight or twelve or thirty weeks. Somebody has to be the mommy and somebody has to be the daddy and that's how it functions.

So it doesn't seem indirect to you if you're having a problem with the actor and the actor is having a problem with the line that you need to talk to a third person?

I think the director has to be engaged. I think sidebar conversations get everybody in trouble, and I just think that's the protocol in a way. What you don't want as a playwright is for your cast to distrust the director. So if you distrust the director in an overt way or don't engage the director in every issue that you have, that sends a signal of distrust, and I think the family starts to break down.

I think that in a relationship with Moises I would assume, or with Chris, if an actor had a problem, they would go to the director and then maybe the three of you could talk.

Oh, absolutely. I've had countless conversations with actors one-on-one because oftentimes you go to the director and the director says, "Talk to him. Take five minutes at the next break," and you do. I think it's important to involve everybody.

Do you attend every rehearsal?

No. I think it's something playwrights have to learn and same thing for directors. A choice you prescribe for an actor is a target they have to hit. And sometimes they'll hit it and sometimes they won't, because they're trying to please you. A discovery they make for themselves in a rehearsal or to trust their impulse in the moment is a choice they will own performance after performance after performance, because they arrived at it in their own true way. So as a playwright, you have to be generous enough to step out of the room and allow for that to occur. And as a director, you have to allow them to flounder through a scene until they get their own foothold, because if you tell them what to do too early or push them too fast, they're trying to hit a target, and so as a playwright sometimes the most generous thing you can do is just leave it alone.

Do you find it frustrating if you are in the room and sometimes they're just not getting it? For your own sake do you leave the room?

That happens too. You want to time it in such a way that your departure doesn't send a message of its own. Like, you want to give people time and space to fully engage in their own process, because that's how you'll get the best results, and you have to have a lot of diplomacy and tact and a great deal of patience. It's like when I bring in a draft of a challenging scene, and everybody starts tearing it apart. It's like, let me live with it for two days and figure out for myself why it's wrong and bring it back. And you don't want to chastise actors, you want the rehearsal to be a place of rhythm and responsibility, and the more you put strictures on it, the less you stand to gain. And again, it's like the other thing I was saying is that storytelling when an actor's knowledge of a character surpasses yours. If you inhibit them too much, that's not going to happen.

So when it opens, what is your attitude toward critics? Do they change your mind in any way?

My strict maxim is that critics are paid to keep abreast of my work, I'm not paid to keep abreast of theirs. I think that a critic's function is to educate and alert the buying public. I think very few critics would profess to be in the business of forging better playwrights, and if they do, I think that's egocentric and misguided. I think that writing a play is an enormously personal and hugely invested affair, and you go to those people for critical feedback who you know in your soul have your best interest at heart. If you were going to buy a house, you would go to a parent or a sibling or a spouse and say, "Should I buy this house?" And with your best interest at heart, they may say, "Sweetie, you can't afford it." They may say, "It looks gorgeous, but the foundation is broken." Or they may come down very hard on you indeed, and it may be challenging to hear, but underneath that is a fundamental interest in your betterment and your welfare and your enrichment, and those are the people who should criticize your play. And I don't mean that you give it to people who will glad-hand you. Give it to people who will challenge it down to the play's very core and who are interested in your success. And I don't think there are any critics right now who can claim that relationship with a particular playwright. As a playwright, I don't read them. As a potential audience goer, sure, I think they're writing for that particular instance. When my playwriting hat is hanging on the hook, sure I can be an audience member and read a critic and decide if I'll see it or I won't. But if I'm a playwright, it's masochistic.

They always say that the review will be on the street in the snow, and people will be stepping on it in two days.

I'm talking not necessarily of the terror and impact of bad reviews. Good reviews can turn your head in a foolish way.

And what do you learn from the audience?

So much.

And do you make adjustments accordingly?

Oh, yeah. Absolutely.

Are there examples?

I do think that sometimes you learn more from a candy wrapper than you do from a post-play discussion. But audiences are unforgiving and almost always right, and yeah, I make cuts if I think I'm losing the audience. If the audience was really engaged in a moment, I'll examine it and I'll make sure I'm maximizing the moment. If an audience is confused, I'll clarify, but I think they're crucial to the evolution of any work.

But you get this from the way they're responding, not because they say, "Oh, Mr. Wright, I was confused in that scene."

I don't want to discredit well-intentioned comments from audience members, but I would say sitting among them and taking the temperature of the room beat by beat is useful. I find that post-play discussions are usually about providing a service to the subscribers or for the profile of the theater or to educate the audience about the making of the play, but usually by the time the post-play discussion begins, the audience has told you everything you need to know.

And there are other things at stake—there's performance and some in the audience want to make a point or be the smartest one in the room. I think sitting in the room and really feeling what's going on is . . .

So crucial.

Do you sense that your success has made it harder for you to write the next piece or easier?

It gives you greater faith that people will care if you write the next piece, and that's a beautiful thing, a wonderful thing to know that the potential readership for the next piece will increase so it may have an array of opportunities it didn't have before. I don't think it makes things necessarily difficult. I don't want to lie and say no, I have high expectations for the next piece that I may or may not meet. I don't really believe that, because no one ever reviews your present efforts by giving you credit for your past ones. So I think the glory of the Pulitzer Prize and the Tony was one thrilling moment in my life, when for a brief time the consensus among most literary and cultural people was that I might be able to write. And that's what it was. That's how long it lasted, and it buoys me and it buoys my ego, and it makes me think that people care, but it doesn't mean that I'm, as they say in reality shows, getting immunity anytime soon.

It can also do the opposite. There's a sense sometimes in the theater world, "OK, what's he going to do next?" and not in a friendly way.

I guess I feel like I'm delighted that *Grey Gardens* happened. I'm delighted that *Mermaid* happened. I'm pleased by a Strindberg, and I'm glad that I'm over the hump of follow-up work, and I think one of the great gifts of that, we were certainly talking about *Grey Gardens* at the time *I Am My Own Wife* was having its great success, and I didn't have the luxury of writer's block or fear because I had a composer and lyricist waiting for a book and so I just had to keep moving—so it blissfully presented that safety net. I also have to say that since *I Am My Own Wife,* I haven't written a straight play born wholly in my imagination that I did all myself. That may be my hedge. It may be that subconsciously I have had some reaction, though, I don't want to pretend I haven't. But I'm glad I pushed through that moment.

It makes me think that maybe it's an American thing that each thing somebody does needs to be an advance over the thing they did before. That the public doesn't look at this is a body of work, and it just goes on and he's going to write other things for the rest of his career, but it has to be better than the thing before.

I don't know that if in my career I have been labeled with a certain subject or certain writing style—that I've created expectations like a wonderful writer like Neil LaBute or a writer like David Mamet. I've worked on a pretty diverse plate of projects. I think a lot of people don't realize there are things I've done, certain things they've seen bear my name, and I think also I've had a very, I don't want to talk about them too much, but in terms of the critics, things that have gone well in New York; curiously, *Quills* was reviewed during that brief respite when Vincent Canby was the theater critic between Frank Rich and Ben Brantley. And *I Am My Own Wife* was a second-string review from Bruce Weber, which put us on the map. And the only times I was reviewed by Brantley in a large-scale way were *Grey Gardens* and *Little Mermaid.* So there isn't any one critical voice that has punctured me or chartered me. Some writers must face that pressure—I haven't felt it.

Was it instinctive in any way, this diversity of projects?

As a writer you do see possibilities. Early on with *Little Mermaid,* my dear friend Tom Schumacher said you're an unusual choice for this, and I said the sea urchin and the Marquis de Sade have more in common than Disney wants to admit. And if you look at *I Am My Own Wife* and *The Little Mermaid,* well, the transgender community rallies around *The Little Mermaid* because it's a tale about an individual who has to change everything that she has below the waist to get the object of her affection. So, you know, the worlds may seem like disparate stories, but to me . . .

Did you just make that up what you said about The Little Mermaid, *or does the transgender community actually rally around that story?*

They love that story.

Can you look at your writing and tell what kind of evolution there has been in terms of form? Has there been? Is it en route?

I would say this might be a slightly different answer, but I hope it still addresses it, and that's that I see an evolution in myself. I think for a long time, like a lot of young writers, I wrote from a place of rage. I was a young gay man growing up in conservative Texas and ticked off, and a play like *Quills*, for all its humor, it's an angry, angry play. And I think there are other angry plays. There was a piece that was in New York called *Watbanaland,* but it was a deeply angry play.

I loved it.

Thank you. It's one of the ones that doesn't get mentioned. And then *I Am My Own Wife*—writing it was a real act of love. So I think I look back at the play, and rather than having the perspective as a literary critic who might divide things, I think I see a growth into genuine adulthood, which is to accept people's ambiguities and failings with greater equanimity and less fury. And I hope that means my characters are becoming more well-rounded and engaging and the play transcends diatribe. I used to think that in order to write about something I had to have a maniacal energy that anger provides. And now I write from a place of love, which sounds so corny, but I really think it's true.

What are you working on now? Are you working on anything?

I am working on a couple things. Another musical, hiding behind my collaborators. It's a really fun piece about a little cult documentary film called *Hands on a Hard Body.* There was a contest at a Nissan dealership in Longview, Texas, where they put a new hard body truck in the parking lot, and people were invited to place their hand on it, and whoever could stay standing and keep their hands in place on the truck for the greatest duration of time won it and got to drive it off the lot. It was an economically depressed town, there were several people who came out to enter the contest, and the dealership never dreamed it would last over five days. People have collapsed from hunger, exhaustion; they had psychotic breaks. The journey of these people around this truck is like the dance marathons of old. It's harrowing and funny and surprising. I love this movie, and I was finally able to get the rights. And Chris Ashley at La Jolla was kind enough to commission it. And, so that's, we're about to do a three-week workshop here in New York.

Do you ever want to write the lyrics?

No, because I've worked with lyricists who are too good. It's kind of funny, it speaks to the peculiar nature of our profession, because I'm much quicker without any compunction at all to say, "Yeah, I'll direct one of my plays," despite the odds you cite so truly, and even though I'm a writer and I traffic in words, you ask me if I'd ever write lyrics, and I say, "That's a lyricist's job." I'm not sure I have that aptitude.

What do you see as your strong points as a writer and your weak ones?

I think I write actable roles with characters with big appetites that actors get a charge out of performing. That's what I'm proudest of. Where I get frustrated is I'm very slow. I'm not a fast writer. And, sometimes when I say "hide behind my collaborators" for this musical, I think I have been shy to get back to a straight play. And I think, those are the things that vex me the most. In terms of the qualitative nature of the work—

No, we don't mean that.

I think like it's just, again, the critics who we find so irritating, literary folks are better able to do that.

Do you think your plays will be done in one hundred years? Or fifty?

I really hope so. And I only say that because in a sentimental way—it's a terribly sentimental answer—but my partner, David, and I don't have kids. This is our legacy. And if all of us as writers didn't have healthy enough egos to believe that, we probably shouldn't be doing what we're doing because it's so difficult, so I can't say they will be. I can only say I hope so, but I think we're in it for that gain.

WALLACE SHAWN

We are to meet Wally Shawn in the second-floor classroom at New Dramatists. Wally arrives promptly, looking slim and cheerful, glad to see us, glad to be doing this interview. He's warned us ahead of time that he's about to go into an intense work process with his longtime collaborator Andre Gregory for a possible production of Ibsen's *Master Builder*—Wally will be playing Solness—so this is the last time he's going to have this kind of free time. We hope the tape recorder is working; we're always nervous about it. This is our one shot with him. As the tape starts, he also warns us that he won't use any proper names in the stories he tells, which is fine with us. His answers to our questions are long and thoughtful, and in fact we're mostly quiet and have to restrain ourselves from prompting his answers, because until Wally decides to say something, there is silence and the temptation to fill it is great. Listening to Wally talk, one is struck by how the rhythms of his speech so clearly find their ways into the mouths of his characters—that Wally's unconscious, which he talks about as the deepest source of his work, is communicated very directly when he speaks.

What's the first play you ever saw?

I believe it was *Jack and the Beanstalk*. It was in New York. I was five, six? Some kind of children's theater. I think I went with my mother. I don't picture my father going to *Jack and the Beanstalk*.

Did they generally take you to the theater as you were growing up?

I know that I went with my parents to *Peter Pan* with Jean Arthur. Never got over it. Boris Karloff was in that. An overwhelming experience, and certainly my father was there too. Probably I was seven, but by that time I'd probably been in a play at the Dalton School. You know, I don't really care anymore what people think of me . . . Fuck them. I came from a privileged background. I've written about that. It's not a secret. At that time, Dalton was a very radical, progressive school. It had bohemian teachers, including left-wing people, people of varying sexuality. I think people of varying sexuality almost dominated Dalton. And the theater program was delicious, it was fantastic. And I was in a Christmas pageant. I was a shepherd and exposed at that time to the lights, the costumes, the bohemian teachers of theater who made no effort to hide their bohemianism. Now subsequently, Dalton had a revolution and it became a much more conservative school, which was devoted to getting people into Harvard. But in my day, Harvard was not mentioned. And this Christmas pageant was very beautiful. Particularly for the lighting, the vastness of it all, the ropes that hold things up, the curtain. So I was into that even probably well before I saw *Peter Pan* with Jean Arthur. And yes, my parents took me to the theater, but my father was not a devotee of plays. He liked musicals, but prewar musicals. He despised the Rodgers and Hammerstein, he loved Rodgers and Hart.

What was it about Peter Pan *that so amazed and stayed with you?*

I think it was her performance. Maybe I've always associated theater with sexual experimentation or something. After all, Jean Arthur was a girl! She was playing a boy, and she was flying. It was . . . she was . . . I mean, to be honest, it was her sex appeal that was absolutely overwhelming, that still is affecting me as I'm remembering it right now. And that was sixty years ago. Sex appeal combined with a certain panache that she had.

Did this affect you as a writer? Was this the kind of dramatic spectacle that made you think, "I want to write"?

I don't think I was thinking of writing at that time. I mean, I was in a play at school where I was quite funny, and it was probably the best time

I'd had at school until, I would say, nine. And then, when I was ten, a teacher said, "Well, it's OK to be the class clown." And actually I competed for the role of the class clown with another boy who was more into physical comedy, and I was more into—I don't know—less dangerous comedy, for which I would not be punished. Really, he was much more courageous. But she said to me, "Well, why don't you do something more seriously? Here's a book. Write a play about this." It was a biography of Socrates. So I wrote a play about probably the most dramatic episode in the life of Socrates: his death. My friends played his disciples. Naturally, I selected the leading role for myself. And, well, I think that sort of set the course for my life, in a way. There were some twists and turns away from it, but it was a philosophical play and that's what I write, in a way.

Were there other writers whom you read or whose plays you went to that had an effect on you?

Oh, yes. I had been going to plays with my parents and with my mother sometimes. I saw, for example, Paul Newman in *The Desperate Hours*, where he took Karl Malden and the rest of the family hostage. *Inherit the Wind* with Paul Muni. And there was a marvelous play sort of for children, *Mrs. McThing* with Helen Hayes. She was not my absolute favorite in that play, but I loved the play. But then when I was twelve, I went to plays with Edith Oliver, before she was a drama critic. She was my very, very close friend, I would say. Edith and I went to see the Lunts. We saw *The Great Sebastians*, in which they played magicians. That was mindboggling. I still haven't gotten over it. They came out into the audience before the first act began and did a magic act in front of the curtain. It was a great experience—one of the great, great moments of my life. And while you could say, "It isn't true," or "He's lying," but in a certain way I had a personal relationship with S. N. Behrman, who was a great playwright of the twenties, really, but by that time, he was not writing plays anymore. He and I frequently had lunch, and he would talk about the theater, and it had an incredible effect on me. But then when I was twelve, other friends of my parents took me to *The Iceman Cometh*, which was at Circle in the Square, with Jason Robards. This was, like, five hours long. My life was turned so upside down by then, I went home and I memorized the speech of Hickey, where he describes murdering his wife. And then the next year, my God, the next year, there was *Long Day's Journey into Night*, the American premiere, with Florence Eldridge, Fredric March, and Jason Robards again. And that one I saw with a friend, and then I dragged my parents to it. I said, "You have to see this." And I think my father thought it would be a nightmarish experience, and I'm sure it was for him. And I said, "You know, this is exactly like our family," which neither of my parents particularly appreciated. And I read all of Eugene O'Neill's plays when I was thirteen. And then next year when I was fourteen, they did *Endgame*. I believe Alvin Epstein was in that. And *The Chairs* and *The Lesson* were done at the Theatre de Lys the same year. So all these things actually happened in the history of New York theater when I was thirteen or fourteen.

Were you writing at this point?

I was writing some plays . . . they weren't very . . . Well, one of them that I wrote at school with a friend was sort of ambitious and serious, and some of them were more just my impressions of my family, should we say farcical, comedic, but the thought of doing these plays had never come up or I hadn't thought of it. But then my brother and I, when I was twelve, we started doing puppet shows every Christmas. And sometimes more than once a year. And those were unbelievably ambitious, huge events.

Did you think of being a writer? Did you think of it that way?

Up to the age of about sixteen, I took it for granted that I would be an artistic person of some kind. It was taken for granted because that was sort of the world I came from, or that's how I interpreted the world that I came from. I'm sure there were periods when I was absolutely certain that I would be a writer. When I was, say, fifteen, I was 100 percent sure that I thought I *already* was a writer. And even when I was a kid, I didn't acknowledge being a kid. I didn't have any interest in it. I mean, if some mother said to me in a group of kids, "Well, just play," I didn't even know what they were talking about. It was frightening or horrifying to me. I didn't get the whole thing about being a kid. A few times I explicitly said to my parents, "Well, I don't understand, who are you and why do I have to listen to you? I don't get it! Why? What is the explanation? I simply don't . . . I see that you're *here*, we're all living in the same place, but why? What's going on? Why am I supposed to do what you tell me to do?" But then when I was sixteen, I turned violently against art, and anything having to do with the spirit or human feelings, and I not only stopped being involved in those things myself, I discouraged other people. I proselytized. But nonetheless, there was a compartmentalization going on. Because the puppet shows didn't stop. The puppet shows could not be interrupted by mere psychological changes, they were just . . . they just couldn't stop. Then when I was about twenty-one, I had another psychological upside-down.

This is after Harvard?

Yes, well, after college, I went to India for a year. And in India, I flipped upside down again, and I gave myself permission to be a writer. I made a very conscious decision that it was OK. A year earlier, or two years earlier, I would have said it would be immoral to do that. And in India, I decided, no, it would actually be permissible and even appropriate. So I sort of gave myself permission.

Well, what led to that? Or how did that flip happen?

Well, we could fill the rest of this whole interview . . . but I can summarize it in a sentence without going into the psychology of it. I had felt all during my college years and my last couple years in high school, I had felt that a person should serve humanity and that art was enjoyable for those who did it or those who experienced it but that it was not really appropriate to devote your life to it and certainly not for me. I had gone to India expecting that I would see only things that horrified me and that I would be encouraged to devote my life to alleviating the poverty of poor people. But in fact I was more struck by how happy I was there, how much it seemed to me we had to learn from people in India. Clearly I realized we had a terrible spiritual problem or psychological problem, and a writer might be allowed to get involved in helping people in that way.

What's your day like? I mean, your writer's day. Do you have to write every day?

Quite honestly, I haven't had six days in a row that are the same, really, for about forty years. Except when I've been in a play and had a rehearsal schedule.

But when you're working on a play. I know you take a while and you take your time, but is there a schedule . . . some days you do, some days you don't?

Well, there have certainly been periods when I've worked every day on the play. Certainly. That would tend to be in the latter half of the writing of the play. People who would hear this would be repelled, but I have some very pretentious attitudes about my writing, and there's no reason why anyone else should think, "Well, how funny." In my mind, there's a very clear distinction between making things up and somehow receiving mysterious inspiration from, you know, outer powers or something. I don't really believe in outer powers, but I do believe that the unconscious is real. Some people don't, but I feel like I could prove that the unconscious does exist, and I do think that the world that you live in and the other people climb into your unconscious. So they're speaking also through that mysterious force that seems to come from outside. I've had very little experience with commercial writing, but it's possible that if you said to me, "Well, I'm going to give you a situation and you're going to write a scene, and you have an hour to do that. The two characters are going to be a brother and a sister, and they're going to be in a kitchen, and the mother has just left all of her money to the sister, and they're talking about it. And I want you to write a scene," I might be able to do it. I've just never done it. But that would be an extreme case of what I would think of as making things up. I would come up with something, but it would be from a very shallow layer of my mind. I don't consider that that counts. I mean, I almost feel the way somebody would feel if they plagiarized something and feel it's quite a good passage, but I don't think I should use it in my book because this other guy wrote it. My writing is mostly composed of things that come from a deeper level in me, even though the person reading this might think, "Fuck you, we don't care about this and where your stupid plays come from." But I am pretentious. I always have been, and I don't care. That's how I think. So in the early stages of writing a play, it's not, for me, about logging the hours, really.

OK, it's not logging the hours, but if you give yourself a schedule, do you tell yourself, something will happen, so something will?

Well, I do believe it's a good thing. I exercise the kind of self-imposed discipline in which I would say, "All right, for the next three hours, for the next two hours, you, meaning me, are not allowed to do anything but write. I mean, you can't read a book or do anything else. Either you do nothing or you'll write something." I do believe in that. I think it's a good practice or exercise. Have I imposed those types of rules on myself in recent years? I don't think so. I think I sort of go on the assumption that whatever I'm capable of, I'm just going to do. And I can't really do it any faster. I mean, my last play, I spent ten years writing it. And the previous plays, I spent five years writing. And I just don't think I'm capable of speeding up the process. Because there is no process. It's so mystical and mysterious that I wouldn't know how to rush it and I don't have any feeling, "Oh, I could have written twice as many plays." I couldn't have, of the kind that I wrote. Sometimes I imagine, what if I lived in an era when there was only Broadway—there was no such thing as the avant-garde—and if you wanted to write a play, the only thing that would come into your head would be that a lot of people would see it . . . all plays were commercial plays and they all had to face the discipline of an audience. After all, when I was a kid, I so adored Mr. Behrman. I adored him. So if such a thing had been what was possible or the only thing, maybe I would have tried that, maybe I would have written many more plays than the strange methods that I use. But the methods that I have used . . . the first part of it can't be rushed, and then the next part, yes, you can work all day once you . . . I mean, speaking of when I say you, I mean me, because it's just my own game, I don't know anyone else who plays it, but yes, in the later part of writing, I can work all day because I have some kind of idea, I have the material, what it's going to be, so the question is, what is it, and how can it be made to be what I think it is.

So what might start you off? I mean, an image, a word, a person, an idea . . .

Well, I don't really start off. It's just like my attitude to give away the secrets of my life, but basically I don't know what I'm doing for . . . well, let's say this last play, well, for all of them, you could say, say it took five years to write *Aunt Dan and Lemon,* which it did. Now in that case that's the only one in which I was reading books with the very strong feeling that they had to do with the play . . . but even so, I didn't know what, really. And I was writing, and I didn't know what I was doing for, let's say, three years. I wasn't working on something. I just had a notebook and put things in it. I didn't know what I was doing.

But do you find that unbearable? Or bearable? Or exciting? Do you just have faith that if you keep jotting things down, someday they'll become something?

Well up until *Aunt Dan and Lemon,* I had a belief in my own ability. Not even ability, to be honest, I had a very high opinion of my ability. I thought that I was definitely . . . I mean, when I wrote my first play, which was when I completed my first play, I thought, "Well, you know, this play, I'm going to devote the rest of my life to writing plays because this play is so extraordinary." That play was a play no one had ever seen. It was called *Four Meals in May.* And I thought everyone would recognize this play for what it was. But actually nobody did. Nonetheless, with *Aunt Dan and Lemon,* I really believed that I was doing something, and if other people didn't get it, they were wrong. Eventually I would be accepted. I mean, when I was fourteen, even thirteen, I knew that Samuel Beckett was a great playwright. I argued the case for Samuel Beckett with some distinguished people who said that his work was absolutely ridiculous and absurd. A few decades passed. Those very same people became devotees of Samuel Beckett, said he was the greatest writer of his age. I thought similar recognition would take place in my case. That in my early days, people would say, "Well this is ridiculous nonsense," and in my later days, people would say, "Well, isn't that funny? In the old days, people would say, 'We don't like your plays,' and now they're great." So yes, at that time, I had total confidence that whatever was written in the notebook would turn into something fantastic. Now since then, I have an agnostic attitude about my writing. Society did not turn around. I had the opportunity to go to the memorial service for Harold Pinter in London. It was a ceremony, a beautiful, astoundingly well-done ceremony in which about twenty-five wonderful actors did pieces of his work. Ian Rickson directed it. I have to say it was absolutely amazing. And I pictured when I was twenty-two, or let's say twenty-five, I pictured that I would die and people would do that for me. Now it's turned out, I'm pretty close to the age that Pinter was when he died, and people feel basically what they did when I was twenty-five . . . with some improvement, in a way. It's gone in a positive direction, but anyway, I realized when I was in my forties, certainly, that it wasn't going that way, and I became agnostic. Because it's hard to believe that everybody is wrong. I mean, I'm a conventional person. I can think, "How could everybody be wrong?" So if you say to me, "Wally, you know, you wanted to be a writer. You tried, but your work . . . it didn't . . . you thought it was terrific, but it wasn't, really," I would say, "Well, that could be true." Whereas when I was forty, I would say, "I'm afraid you are wrong. You will see, after my death people will come around and you will come around, if you wait long enough. You will be attending my memorial—by the way, I don't want to have a memorial. Just so the two of you know this, it's on record—I would be very, very upset. I mean, I don't care if it's hate-filled, or love-filled, I don't like them. So I've never actually had the fantasy of having a wonderful memorial, but I'm just using it as a humorous example. I thought that when I was forty that you too will turn around and see that it is terrific. But now, maybe they will, maybe they won't.

That's so startling because one of the things we were going to ask you was if the success that you had early on made you more confident or more fearful as you went on to the next piece of work.

I think because I came from a world in which a lot of the people I knew were really accepted by society and honored, respected. I mean, I won a couple of Obies because the eccentric Ross Wetzsteon liked me, and John Lahr liked me—he used to be at the *Village Voice,* and Joe took me on. I suppose we need to identify Joe Papp. Joe took me on and my plays were done at the Public Theater. But my fantasies about myself were so elevated . . .

When we told the editor of this book that we were going to include you, he said, "Oh, you're going to get Wally Shawn! How great!" So you have to know that in terms of people who write and people who value playwriting, you are considered top drawer.

I'm actually, I'm disgracefully, nauseatingly ungrateful. I mean, this is a characteristic of mine, and I regret it. I mean, it's true that the people that I grew up with were respected in many cases by the general public. They were known. Now I'm going to try to disguise what I'm about to say without naming it. You're not going to give the specific date of this interview so . . . I was working with a group of people on a television program, in a city that is not our city, and they were all in the field of entertainment, broadly speaking, but none of them knew that I was a writer. And of course I meet, being an actor, an enormous amount of people in airports, and they have absolutely no idea that I'm a writer. Then, one guy, in a customs line, a desperate-looking man, said to me, "I just want to tell you, I really like your writing. Your plays." I said, "What? That's unbelievable." And then we were—it's too boring to explain and could never be written down on paper—but we were in a zigzagging line, which meant that he was ahead of me, so we would cross every time the line zigged or zagged, and the rest of the time, we were pulled apart. So I had a long time to think about what was said, because we had a conversation that was broken up into about eight parts. So, I thought, "How the fuck would this guy have heard of my writing?!" So I said to him, "Are you also in theater?" And he said, "Yes, I'm a playwright." So I do feel honored. I am very grateful that for some reason, I am taught in theater schools. Maybe the people who teach there, I don't know, but a lot of smart people who go to drama school to study playwriting or acting have heard of me. Which is very, very gratifying and extremely wonderful, and I have had, compared to ninety-nine percent of the people who write plays, I've had great fortune and success. My plays have been put on, they've been done by wonderful actors and directors, so the complaining that you hear, it can't be justified. I'm just telling you how I feel . . . but don't worry, I've been cut down to size. I mean, I don't fight it anymore, and I do recognize that my plays are quite odd, so I don't expect people to like them. I mean, out of ten people who ask me, "Are you doing anything these days?" I meet people all the time, of course. Why, it happened to me only half an hour ago. People who say, "I haven't seen you much recently. Are you still working?" But if I have a play on, and I meet ten people who say, "Are you up to anything these days? Anything I could see?" Six times out of ten, I'll say, "I don't think so, nah, nothing really." I won't say, "Oh, I have a play on! Down the street! You should see it!" Because I know they wouldn't like it. And what's the point? That's now. I've actually matured and sensed that I know I can't really predict. Because some of the people who I think wouldn't like it, they might like it. And God knows, a lot of people who I think would like the play, they don't. And that is a painful experience I go through every time.

When reading a play like The Fever *or* Aunt Dan and Lemon, *which really just takes you on a very interesting journey, but at the end, I'm gasping. And as an audience member, when I saw them, I didn't feel like applauding. So what do you think should happen at the end of those kinds of plays?*

Well, that was actually my goal. Certainly with *The Fever.* And in a different way with *Aunt Dan and Lemon.* With *Aunt Dan and Lemon,* I really and truly wanted to provoke thought rather than provide a pleasant entertainment. And with *The Fever,* I was trying to write something that would not even be interpreted as an attempt to amuse but would be taken as one person speaking honestly to another person. And that was why I didn't want to do *The Fever* at first in a theatrical building. So your response of gasping rather than applauding was the dream response that I hoped for. I mean, I'm not knocking it, because I think if somebody can do something that is delightful and pleasing, well, I mean, I'm totally obsessed with Noël Coward, and if you can do something that's entertaining and pleasing, I realize that is an astounding and amazing gift. I wasn't trying to do that with *Aunt Dan and Lemon.* Or *The Fever.* I was trying to make people think of the real world, not just think about my play and whether it amused them.

Maybe this is one of the reasons you're more appreciated in London, where the habit of theatergoing is ingrained in the populace . . . whereas here, theatergoing for most people is more going out for an evening of entertainment.

Yeah, that's been a source of anguish for my whole life in the theater. And of course, it's not just that they want to be entertained. It's a somewhat narrow view of what entertainment might be. I mean, because you know, there are things that I would find entertaining that apparently the typical . . . I mean I think of my most recent play—we won't get into that, but it has an entertainment side to it that for me, if I were watching it, I think I would enjoy, but that's not the typical audience I've encountered.

What was the response when it was done in London?

Well, it was different every night. There were some nights that seemed like it was the greatest hit in town. It was full, anyway, a hundred seats. But it depended on who was there. There were nights when it was joyful and uproarious and people were affected by it, and there were nights when it seemed like it was the biggest disaster since *Moose Murders* or whatever.

Is there any chance of it being done here?

Well, somebody has to pay for it. It seems like it's ahead of our time. We're offering something, but so far society has a whole has not flipped to gobble it up. I happen to believe in it. From my point of view, that's like a . . . one of those things, people say, "Oh my God! His painting couldn't even be shown in the exhibit! It had to be in an attic." But I think there are a lot of people who would say, "Well, an attic is too good for that play."

This play is called Grasses of a Thousand Colors.

I don't want to talk about it on the record, because for one thing, it's a story that isn't over and it's constantly changing. And perhaps before my death, that play will be done.

Or maybe before the publication of this book! It seemed to me that with this play, and Aunt Dan and Lemon, *that you draw an audience in and the audience thinks it's going to have a nice time. And I think it's very interesting that then the audience is taken on a different ride.*

I feel that *Aunt Dan and Lemon* was uncompromising in its roughness. Of course to me, both *The Fever* and *Aunt Dan and Lemon* are objects that have a certain aesthetic. I mean, you know, to me, that's what writing is. I'm in the artistic field, in my opinion. But *Grasses*, to me, is brutal, but also, to me, is attractive. It's less uncompromisingly brutal. It's brutal—it's no less brutal—but it also is attractive, and, well, I would have enjoyed seeing it. I mean, whatever it was that I got out of seeing Jean Arthur. And here with Miranda Richardson, Emily McDonald, and Jennifer Tilly—they were providing that to those lucky people.

Do you ever conceive a role around a particular actor? I mean, did you conceive that role around Miranda Richardson, or did you just hope to cast her?

I think there have been times when certain actors have helped me to write the play in my head. I mean, in my mind, Barry Humphries should have played my part in *Grasses*. We're all young, maybe he will one day. He considered, but he said no. But having Barry Humphries in my head playing that part helped me to write the part. But the only time that I have actually totally consciously known it was a character that I was writing for a specific person was *Aunt Dan and Lemon*. Linda Hunt. And the other time was when I wrote a play for Andre Gregory's company, *Our Late Night*. In both cases, the actors didn't have a delighted reaction that I had hoped for. I would almost say—if I had the self-discipline and I ever did it again—I wouldn't tell them I had them in mind. I think it does a funny thing to an actor. I mean, a guy came up to me yesterday and he said, "I just want you to know. Everybody confuses me with you. They all think I'm you." Now this guy, I sort of . . . at first, I sort of just gasped and couldn't speak. I managed to get it together after about twenty seconds and say, "Oh well, that's very flattering to me." But in a way, I didn't think so. I wasn't totally sincere when I said that, and I hope he never reads this interview, I hope that if he does, he doesn't remember that. But it wasn't totally sincere. There was an element of, "Oh! Is that how people see me? As being that? Like him?" And I think the actors, for whom I said, "Oh, I wrote this part for you," I think the actors felt, "You did? Why? What in the world do I seem like to you?" Of course that isn't the way it really is, you really aren't that way. The point is, I had this dream of you being this way, you're an actor, you're supposed to change. Anyway, nobody took it that way.

You've used Larry Pine in a lot of your work. Do you write for him?

Well, I did write the part in *Our Late Night* for him. But no, usually, the characters that I write are . . . you know, it probably shows some of my weaknesses, but I don't, I mean, there's no question, I don't write good characters in the way that some people do. I believe it as an article of faith, I believe that you use your disabilities, and it helps you do what you can do. What *you* can do.

Do you show your work to anyone during the writing process?

No. It's all based on secrecy. Quite honestly, I could work for nine years on something, and I think if someone went in and read it, I might say, "Well, I'll throw it out, then." I think I'd almost completely lose interest in it. I think I'd think, "Oh, well, it's nine years, just wasted."

So when it's ready to go, it's ready to go.

Well, no, I don't think it can't be revised. Every director I've had has had some thoughts, and in rehearsal, things can change. I mean, I'm not a brilliant, on-the-spot rewriter because, you know, obviously stuff that's written in a rehearsal is by definition the stuff that you make up out of your head, it can't be deeply inspired. So I know those passages. I mean thirty years later, I look and I know which ones they were, and I remember how that came about.

I just want to go back for a moment. You're saying that if someone saw your work before you thought it was ready to bring to a director—

Well, I suppose there are a couple of people who are in my life who might get a first look. But for me privacy and secrecy are terribly important. You know, you can say, well, you know, what a jerk, but it's true. I can't deny it, it's very, very important to me. You know, some people are helped by describing their work to others while they're writing it. Some people really need to do that. And certain things benefit from that. But I don't know, writing isn't that for me.

At the time I saw The Hotel Play *at La Mama, I thought, "How did he ever have the audacity to write a play with eighty characters that cannot be double cast?"*

Well, none of my plays had ever been done when I wrote *The Hotel Play*, so why not? I mean, it wasn't as if, "Oh, well, this play might not be as successful as the others." None of my plays had ever been performed, and I submitted them to every theater in England and the United States. They'd all been submitted. But at that time, I was somewhat naive—I didn't even know that people had agents, much less that *I* have one. You know, I just brought things around. In 1970, for nine months, I took classes at the HB studio in acting, because I thought a playwright should know about acting. I also sent them my plays. And I went in the office and I said, "Well, I don't want to be an actor. I'm a playwright, and I'd like to study," and a woman who worked there—because I was a student there—instead of actually just sending the plays back to me, she actually spoke to me and said, "We found these rather bizarre." And she gave me at least the respect of saying, you know, that they didn't like them much.

Your plays are very different, each from the other. And some of them are conceived to be done in a physical space that is very different than any other. Like The Fever *is done in living rooms, or I saw* The Designated Mourner *in a deserted men's club in the financial district. Now, how does that come to you? Was there some reason that was related to the play?*

Well, yes, it's ghostly. I mean, the play is about people who have died, and it's taking place after all this violence. I mean, it was perfect. Thanks to Mrs. Bartos and Scott Rudin, we were able to do a production that was exactly what we wanted it to be. That's a privilege that painters have, novelists have, to actually do it not as a compromise, but there were no compromises. We did it exactly in the way that we wanted to do it.

Who is Mrs. Bartos, may I ask?

Celeste Bartos is a philanthropist, mostly gave money to art, although there's a very beautiful Celeste Bartos room in the New York Public

Library. She mostly gave money to visual arts. She is a very sophisticated, hip woman, was a friend of Andy Warhol, and she was a fan of Andre's and mine, and we went to her and we asked her for money. We said, "The play was done in England, it got terribly good reviews, we can send it to you tomorrow." She said, "Oh, I don't care about that." I mean, those days are apparently gone. But yes, for a great deal of money, we were able to do a production that was exactly the way we wanted it. But to be honest, productions that are rushed or done in what we call "regular theater," the compromises are so internalized it's not even a *conscious* compromise. You've got your opening night set months in advance, there's absolutely no alternative to making the costumes before you've rehearsed the play. I mean, you can't design the costumes after you've been rehearsing for a while. You have to have a certain number of people in the audience, so that means you have to shout or you have to mic yourself. It's just inevitable that there will be some compromises. If you don't want any compromises, then Mrs. Bartos has to be enlisted.

Was it done in a similar kind of space in the London production?

No. In London it was done at the Cottesloe, at the National Theatre. David Hare directed it. So that was not in a weird building, because I've had a bad time in the theater buildings. I don't like the idea of anybody going to something of mine and being totally out of sympathy with the entire enterprise. I mean, I would just as soon not have even one person in the audience like that. Whereas, sadly, we have to be honest . . . a lot of my early experiences . . . My God, you know, the play that Ron Van Lieu was in, and Kathy Tolan, I mean, that had an audience capacity of a hundred, and if there were three people who appreciated it out of a hundred, I'd be surprised. It was basically—there might have been three—who were looking at it and saying, "Hmm, that's kind of interesting. It's kind of smart, there's something I like about it." And 97 percent of people saying, "Why is Joe Papp doing this trash? And making me go to see it? I can't believe it. I'm going to write him a letter." And with *Marie and Bruce*, I would stand outside the door, and people would be walking out. "That was the worst play I've ever seen!" For me, that is like a completely pointless encounter, and it's one that just has no value. It has no point. So if there's any point to get the people who just want to have that amusing experience, who are not looking to see something that's slightly different . . . I mean doing it in a strange place can weed out those people.

We've talked about London and New York. What was the reaction to Aunt Dan and Lemon, Designated Mourner . . . *was* Marie and Bruce *done in London?*

Yes, Les Waters directed it. Well, yes, it was really different in London because, you know, it's not that we have to worship everything about England, but it is true that the expectations that theatergoers have are much more . . . what can I say. I'll start that sentence again. People who go to see a new play at the Royal Court or at the National, their expectations are wide open compared to what you would find here. If they're going to a new play at the Royal Court, they don't know what it's going to be. They're interested in seeing a new play and seeing what's going to happen. I mean, of course if they think it's trash, they're disappointed. But it's not supposed to be necessarily familiar. They're people who like to see a new play. And at the National, certainly the people who came to *The Designated Mourner,* they were into it.

Would you make any changes or rethink something based on an audience response—especially in London—or would your director encourage you to?

Well, I have mixed feelings about it. There are passages in some of my plays that I think are important and part of the story that I'm telling that are boring to 200 percent of the people in the audience. Now I have a mixed response. Sometimes I think, "I'm sorry. I know you're bored by this passage, but it's terribly important to the story that I'm telling and you have to listen to it." And sometimes I think, "Well, you're not listening. You win." And I have to take that passage out.

And have you done that?

Yes, because not even one person is listening, and having tried out that passage, they have voted so resoundingly against that passage . . . I mean, obviously if an entire play were that boring, I myself would have to say it's not a good play. It might be a good, I don't know, piece of writing in some form. But a play should not be boring. I mean, for one thing, out of simple politeness, people are trapped in a theater in a way you could not say by any other art form.

Dance.

Well, dance, yes. You could say, well, dance, certainly. Although dance is usually much shorter, leaving in between dances is not insulting, whereas leaving during the intermission of a play is insulting to the actors. So a person who has a conscience about how the actors would feel wouldn't walk out even in the intermission of a play because we do see you and hate you and are hurt by it and never forget it. I mean, I remember the people who've left my plays and—

People you knew?

Yes. It hurts me, and I have walked out of a couple of plays in my life. I mean, it takes a great deal to make me leave, but on a couple of occasions, it has happened. And in both cases that come to mind, I was genuinely unsympathetic to the way the play was being presented. It wasn't just that I was bored. There have also been some plays that I didn't walk out of, but I instantly fell asleep completely involuntarily. They were like being hit on the head by a mallet.

The work that you do as an actor is aesthetically very distant to the work that you do as a writer, and I wondered if that helped you, to keep that separate.

Well, I mean, I've acted in a lot of my own plays, so I don't know how distant—

Oh, I meant in movies.

To me, I'm somewhat similar to what I am in my own plays, but maybe not. I mean, I don't feel any different as an actor, although there is this very strange thing that if I'd never become an actor, I'd have never discovered that there was anything in me that could be enjoyable to a lot of people. Amazingly, I became an actor, and it turned out that the average American finds me funny. I mean, they don't have an opportunity to anymore as much, because tragically, the sitcom is not what it was. It's not the major form it was, and that was where I would say my, I don't know, *strength* as an actor was. I felt most comfortable, and I think I did quite a good job on those sitcoms. It was very natural to me, I mean *The Cosby Show,* and then *Murphy Brown.* Two episodes of *Taxi* that I did, and I was very comfortable doing that. I did two pilots with Gene Wilder, and we were pretty funny together.

What I meant was that the aesthetic world that you live in when you're doing sitcoms is so different from the aesthetic world when you're doing plays.

Oh! Yes, yes.

So is it just a relief to be away or does it help feed them or what does it do?

If I would live long enough—and I wish I could—I might bring it all together. But I don't know if I'll live long enough. I mean, for me, yes, it's unbelievably pleasurable and refreshing to do these acting things, and if I was only just involved in my own world, my own imagination in my own life, that might be unbearable. I think it is a wonderful thing for me to be able to get out of that and, you know, do these things that are so incredibly different. I mean, some of it I have enjoyed more than others. One in which I was, in a way, employing writerly talents. I did one episode of Kirstie Alley's TV show called *Fat Actress.* Did you ever see that? I played a diet doctor. It was improvised. I mean, you know, they wrote a paragraph that described the scene, and you sort of worked your way through the paragraph, but you made up your own dialogue. It was bliss. And it's pretty funny. If you see the episode . . . I'm the diet doctor, Doctor Koi.

Like the pond.

Like the pond. And that was a little bit of one's writerly abilities.

You've worked with five or six major directors. Let's talk about what you like first in a director, what you look for.

Well, the director really creates the performance that people see as much as a movie director, but somehow that's not acknowledged. Somehow in a film everybody knows it's the director's vision, but because actors have an instinctive desire to please the director, I would say probably even those actors who denounce directors and say they hate them, the directors' taste and aesthetic are put on the stage, and that is what people see. You supposedly wrote the play, but what you are looking at is really the spectacle created by the director. There've only been a very small number of directors with whom I've had a feeling of aesthetic kinship and understanding, really, and I'll tell you who they are but . . . no, I won't. I won't make a list, but I've had only a limited number of directors who've done my plays, because I just have not felt on the same wavelength . . . well, excuse me, I should hasten to say most directors wouldn't want to do one of my plays.

I knew you'd say that.

People who like my plays obviously are people who have something, say, an education that we have something in common, but there have only been a handful that I've really wanted to entrust. And there are different qualities that directors have. Some have a clarity of mind, which can make the whole thing marvelously lucid and comprehensible, which is a beautiful thing. Some have a beautiful imagination, they create a beautiful work of art. Because the theater could be seen as a work of art. And some have a deep psychological insight into life and can get actors to bring insight to a play. Of course, if I thought I could do it, I would. But directing is a special talent. Do I have it? I don't know, I'd have to find out, and by the time I'd found out no, I would have ruined the play I spent five years writing.

Have you worked with directors who don't get it?

You know, there have been people who've even done my plays who I didn't know, though not often. My plays aren't on the regional circuit. *Aunt Dan and Lemon* was done, you know, several times. The others haven't been, really. In Germany, *The Fever* was done probably by fifty different actors. I mean, there are fifty German actors with that text in German in their heads. I must have seen three or four. And, you know, directors over there are a big deal. And they are revered much more than writers. They're revered as gods, almost. And they can take legally unimaginable liberties with the play.

With the text?

Yes, they can do anything. They can say, "We are presenting *The Fever*, by Wally Shawn," and they can take out 90 percent of it and put in texts by other writers, songs, they can do anything.

There's no legal recourse to a playwright there?

Well, Rolf Hochhuth picketed one of his own productions and then bought the Berliner Ensemble, the building. He found out who owned it, he bought it. And he said, "Well, now you cannot do my play in there anymore." So I've seen, you know, I've had the experience of seeing at least one truly outrageous production of *The Fever*.

I saw Aunt Dan and Lemon *at NYU twenty years ago. Paul Weidner directed it.*

Did I see it?

I don't know, did you?

I don't think I was told about it. But I've seen it done by students. Marvelously, I must say. Because there are a lot of very interesting people who show up to do a play in a university. Maybe they're not even going to be professionals. They bring something very interesting, not to mention energetic.

In rehearsals, do you get involved with lights and costumes? Do you put your voice in, do you talk to designers?

I have my own strong preferences about the aesthetic side, but usually, I don't know, I'm guided by the director. I mean, you know, with both

The Designated Mourner and *Grasses,* the process of working on the play was over a long period of time. Donna Grenada, our costume designer, was someone that I introduced into the room . . . and of course Eugene Lee and Andre go back probably forty-five years. Whereas Andre and I only go back forty years. Eugene and Andre are very, very bonded, and of course Jennifer Tipton worked with us. She is credited in the program as "co-creator" of *The Designated Mourner.* In other words, she was involved with the entire process over a period of years.

Just to go back to the question about the writing and the acting. Have you spent more time acting than writing in the last ten years?

No, because with the acting I only had small parts, and it just takes the time that it takes. I mean, if I'm hired for two weeks, I work for two weeks. That's a pretty good gig. You know, the days are long gone when someone would say, "Let's hire him for nine weeks." You know, I've gotten away with a lot. But there are limits.

Well, there's Toy Story 1, 2, *and 3. That must take lots of time, doesn't it?*

No, for each of the films maybe the first session was four hours. Certainly I can't do more than four hours, nobody can. It's just you alone, and my part is all screaming because I fancy myself the most emotional of the toys. I mean, I am used to express emotion. Some of the other toys make sardonic remarks, I'm screaming. So four hours, you go through the whole movie and then maybe you do it again eight times. You revise. But those sessions are less long than four hours, they might be two hours. So altogether, you might spend, I don't know, twenty-four hours doing one of those. I mean, it's quite intense. You're in a little booth with like ten people directing you—one director and nine people directing the director.

You talked about your writing—that it comes from a deep place in your unconscious. Where does your acting come from?

Well, certainly doing a cartoon, it's completely from that. There's nothing in the room, except you're in a dark room in a little booth, and you have your line, "Don't throw that rock!" It's your imagination, it's completely out of the unconscious. You don't have time to think, you don't have time to do anything that Uta Hagen described in her book like what did the character have for breakfast.

Now what about your Vanya on 42nd Street, *which I must say was very good. Really good, really serious acting.*

Well, we worked on it for four years. By the way, that's not a secret. We rehearsed that play for four years because it was never an equity production. So, you know, fuck you, that's it. It was four years, not every day, we'd rehearse for a few weeks, then we'd go away for a few months. But it was over a long, long period of time, and Andre is a great director. And then it was filmed by one of the great filmmakers of all time—Louis Malle—so I'm very, very proud of it, and I sort of don't remember that I didn't write that one. The acting was . . . you could say the same part of me that writes. We're going to start rehearsing tomorrow on *The Master Builder.* We've been working on . . . well, now, that becomes questionable, because maybe we will do it publicly in New York as a play, so maybe I should say, "We've only rehearsed *Master Builder* for three weeks!"

But you've worked on it, it's been on your mind, people have gotten together on and off for years . . . but is it going to move to a production?

We had a fantasy for a long time that it would be a movie, and now we've abandoned that, and I have, let's be honest, tweaked the play so that we can do it. In other words, you know, sue me. I'll be dead soon, fuck you, sue me, I have made some changes. I have tweaked it so that we can do it. And so that we can do it anywhere. It will be very simple. Very, very simple.

Is Eugene Lee designing it for you?

Yes, and Julie Haggerty is Mrs. Solness. And what can I say, it's going to be . . . well I think it's going to be pretty great, but some people probably won't like it, I don't know, but it will be our most accessible work, I would think, because that play is electrifying.

What I love most about the Vanya . . . it was the first time I understood Vanya's relationship with Yelena. It was just wonderful because you always think, he just bothers her, she doesn't really like him, but now you realize she enjoyed him, they had fun. It never made sense until I saw your version of the play. Of course, most of these plays are rehearsed for three weeks.

The truth is, if you get down to what I really believe in theater, I think you can't really rehearse a play within three weeks and expect to really get everything that you should.

Do the plays you write get rehearsed for more than three?

No. Many of my plays get done in a short rehearsal period, and that's why in particular I need to start out with a director who knows where I'm coming from and has a deep connection. That at least has to be there so that the three, four weeks are not spent saying, "No, actually, that's not me at all." And there are some directors whose rhythm is fast, who wouldn't want to rehearse a play for years. And of course I've had some of the greatest experiences of my life doing plays quickly.

With Andre as director?

I don't want to mention specific plays, necessarily, because it's a losing game to get into comparing them.

What kind of critical response do you get in London?

Well, there are a lot of critics in London, so it doesn't matter what any one of them thinks.

Does it matter to you?

I would complain quite a bit about the reviews I got last year. I mean, one of the things I think is fascinating is that there are a lot of people who reviewed *Grasses* who had reviewed *A Thought in Three Parts* in 1977. In each case, they had the same opinion as they'd had back then. There's a guy who writes for *The Telegraph*, I think his name is Charles Spencer, who said, "This is the vilest thing I've seen on the British stage," thirty-three years ago, and he basically said this is a worthless piece of trash thirty-three years later. Michael Coveny, who at that time was the editor of *Plays and Players,* not only loved *A Thought in Three Parts,* but called me up and said, "I loved it, and I want to print some of it in my magazine." And thirty-three years later, he loved *Grasses.* That was sort of amusing and interesting.

So much for change.

I mean, there were some people who were different. But I didn't feel, "Well, these guys are geniuses and our guys are dopes." I didn't feel, "Oh, the British theater critics are so elevated compared to American critics." That's just not true. American critics in some cases work harder on a review. They pour more of themselves into it. Occasionally with an English critic, there's a laziness in their writing. There was a guy who used to write for the Sunday *Times,* John Peters, who wrote some very sort of atmospheric reviews of me. They were good. There was a guy in the *Financial Times* who wrote about *The Designated Mourner* who said something like, "I don't think I completely can tell you about this play that after one viewing I totally understood it," which a critic has never said, which I thought was incredible. There was an American who was living there, who wrote very deeply, I thought, about *Aunt Dan and Lemon.* But I wouldn't say that reading my reviews in London, this time, I thought, "Ah, how magnificent the English critics are compared to those Americans."

Do they ever help? I mean, do they show you something in the play that you didn't know, or did they respond to something you didn't think people would respond to? Were they ever useful?

I am so vain. I used to give people my plays in the old days, and I would say, "I'd like you to read this, but I never would want to know what you thought about it." I was just that arrogant. It's really wrong of me, but I sort of feel I've spent many years with this, and so I did this for a reason. Now that's flatly a mistake and wrong, because actually someone that just walks in and sees it very definitely has the right to an opinion, particularly about a play. I feel about a poem somewhat differently. If someone reads a poem once, and the poet has been working for years on it, that's stupid. I mean, the guy's view is not worth much.

If there's a unanimity of opinion in the critics about a passage or a section or a scene or a character . . .

No, that doesn't ever affect me.

With the Tony Awards, the award for best play goes to both the writer and the producer. But there are instances when it's a terrible play with a great production or a great play with a lousy production. Do you think critics should read the plays as well as see them before they write a review?

Both in England and America it's become quite customary for critics to have the script beforehand. But for anybody it's hard to judge. Was it a wonderful play? Or a wonderful performance? Or a wonderful performance of a terrible play? It's not easy to tell, even for people who've spent their lives in the theater.

SUZAN-LORI PARKS

Suzan-Lori Parks is an artist in residence at the Public Theater, and it's to her upstairs-down-a-long-corridor office that her assistant guides us. Suzan-Lori is standing in the doorway, waiting for us, hostess-like. Her hair is in a mass of dreadlocks. She's dressed for work in a dark, soft-looking shirt and trousers. Her office is dark too, lit by table lamps. She asks if we'd like something to drink. We say no, but she can tell by our hesitation that we're being polite, and she insists and goes and gets us each a bottle of water. She apologizes for the mess her office is, but it's not really a mess, just a large collection of books and manuscripts and papers and magazines. Suzan-Lori pulls chairs over to her desk for us, then settles in. She points out with pride a framed letter from James Baldwin that hangs above her desk. She leans in toward us, eager to begin.

This interview is about how you work and how the play goes from the page to the rehearsal room and afterward.

You know that show I'm doing, *Watch Me Work.*

Yes, talk about that.

Well, I started doing it in September. It's a show about how Suzan-Lori is working. It's called *Watch Me Work,* and I tell people that the "me" in the title is "you." So basically it's not about *my* process. It's about the audience, *your* process. The audience is invited to come and bring their own work and we also stream live. We have people in the lobby of the Public Theater two days a week, and they're online in our online community. And they write or do their work—whatever their work might be—and they're with us as we work. Then they email and tweet me questions about their process. Or people in the live audience. So it's all about working.

They're writing and they're talking to you?

What I do is I sit for an hour. I sit with my typewriter and I set the timer and I work for an hour and they work for an hour. It's a play, and we create audience participation. They are writing, for example, while I'm writing. OK. The timer goes off. Bling! And then we create dialogue. They ask me questions about their work. You can imagine the questions they ask: "I'm a playwright and I'm having trouble with characters." Or, "I'm writing a novel," or "I'm writing a song," or "What do I do in rehearsal?" Whatever they want. They email us from all over the country. We've had some emails from Turkey. All over the world they've emailed us. So it's all about working.

It's on television?

It's on the Internet. We live stream every day and it's also archived. A lot of folks can't watch it live. There's a woman who just emailed us that she's going to somewhere in western Africa and wants to keep her work schedule so she's going to watch our archives as she goes to Africa, and she's going to email us questions as she goes along. So we've formed a community. I'm sitting around going, "I want to do a play and it's going to be called *Watch Me Work,* and it's going to be about me working onstage. It's all about work and how we work."

So who were your influences? We know James Baldwin spurred you on. How did he do that? What did he notice in you, and what did he say to you?

He said, "Have you ever tried playwriting?"

What was the context? You were in class?

Yes, I was in a class. It was a conventional creative writing class. Sit at the table sort of thing. And it was a short story writing class, and it wasn't a playwriting class. A short story class at Hampshire College, where he taught. His very first, he said, his very first creative writing class ever, so there I was with fourteen other people, and when I read my short stories, I was very dramatic, kind of thing. I didn't know, you know, I just felt that I wanted to act out the whole thing, the characters and whatnot. And after a couple weeks of me doing this, he said, "Ms. Parks, have you ever thought of writing for the theater?" And that was, that was his question to me, and I felt horrible at the time, at that moment, because I, other than, you know, Sophocles and those dudes and Shakespeare, I didn't know anything about theater. I was not a theater person. I was in love with literature, meaning, literature to me at that moment in my life, as a second-year college student, narrowly defined literature as poetry, novels, things like that. So I wasn't thinking theater. Theater to me was hanging out with people who did theater. To me, they were people who wore funny hats and spoke, "Dahling, dahling." They were all from, like, Long Island or something. And they had very affected ways of dress and very affected ways of speaking, and I didn't want any part of that. I was a writer. I wasn't a phony.

Had you ever been to the theater?

Oh, sure. My dad was a big opera fan and stuff like that, but sure I'd gone to theater, but I just remember very clearly looking across the green—you know, I went to Mt. Holyoke College and so there are these lovely greens and lawns at Mt. Holyoke College—and there are these people, these theater people, and they were so phony.

So did you take this comment as an insult?

Totally. Totally. He was saying, "Get thee to a theater. You don't belong with the writers, you're one of *those* people." Because I like to act things out. I got very excited about writing and when I read a lot and got very excited? So, at Hampshire College, where he taught his class, you weren't to give grades. It was an alternative, hippie school so you wrote evaluations, but my school, Mt. Holyoke College, needed a grade, so he wrote, "An utterly outstanding and beautiful creature who may become one of the most valuable artists of our time." That was my evaluation. That was what he thought of me, which I learned at the end of the semester, and I was like horrified and humbled, and you sort of go, "OK, if Mr. Baldwin says so, maybe I'll try."

Were there others along the way who encouraged you?

Sure there were. Everyone you meet is wonderful and helpful. But I was in the presence of the sun, you know the SUN. While there are lots of stars out, it's . . . it's daylight and I didn't really notice them as much as I noticed him. I mean, other people along the way have been encouraging—people like Mac Wellman. I'm going to forget everybody now. August Wilson was encouraging.

Were you influenced by these people's work? Baldwin wasn't primarily a playwright.

You know, I was influenced more when I came to New York. I hung out a lot at the Poetry Project and was influenced a lot by Poets Theatre. I was into that kind of scene at St. Marks. Mac knew that scene but wasn't really a part of that. I didn't know anything about him until later on. After I started doing my kind of thing, including bells and all the weird stuff I was doing before. But he was very encouraging. Jeff Jones was also very encouraging. Laurie Carlos was very encouraging. And then the greats along the way. August Wilson. Ntozake Shange, Adrienne Kennedy gave me a lot of love and encouragement along the way. But no one like James Baldwin. I didn't go to grad school partly, mostly, because I took that class with Mr. Baldwin. When I was a sophomore or junior, 1983, whatever year it was, I had that sort of experience and I thought I need other teachers, but I cannot imagine sitting . . . I've been given my note. I got the note. It's right there. Fold it up. Put it in an envelope. I got the note. I know what I have to do. So I just have to go do it. It kind of burned my mind, burned into my mind, and gave me a direction and I just went.

A young writer doesn't often get that and maybe doesn't get on that path.

I got on the writing path, but I think the path I'm on . . . I feel that my writing is a vehicle to create understanding. It's not to create more writing. I'm not saying this as well as I could. I got on the path of being called because James Baldwin is such an enormous presence. In my childhood too for Valentine's Day, when I was a fourth grader or fifth grader, they gave me *The Fire Next Time.* "Here are some books." They always said you all are the ambassadors of your race, my brother and sister too, so we always felt like we were called to represent, and when he called me to represent capital *R,* as a writer, well ha ha it doesn't start with an *r* but it could. It's a big thing, so I didn't need another teacher.

Can we go from the sublime to the mundane? Are you on a schedule every day?

Sure. It's five o'clock in the morning, I get up. I write until 6:30.

You get up and go right to the desk.

I actually write in bed. I love it. I get up and I write sitting in bed.

You write with your hands.

Yeah, I write with my hands. I'm doing many projects at once, like so many writers, and so it's, "So what am I thinking today?" Then I go to yoga from 6:30 to 8:00 and I practice yoga and it's really helpful.

You do it at a studio?

Yeah, I do it at a studio. It's vigorous and athletic—all those good things. So then I come home and I write again. I usually work at home. And then I go to readings. I don't work here because I'm very aware that I love to sit down and I love to yak yak yak, so I have to stay home. I don't try to get work done here at the Public. I tend to be Chatty Cathy in the hallways.

Do you have a structure in mind when you sit down to write a play, or do you just follow your pen?

It depends on what I'm writing. Like *365 Days/365 Plays*, it was just: put it down and go and see what came out. It was just an active thing every day, not any planning, pick up whatever's in the air. Sometimes in the security line before a plane I would write . . . I wrote wherever whenever.

Did you ever face a day in 365 *where you didn't have something?*

Oh, sure, sure. Or I was writing something that was awful. That happened a lot. Or going through the motions. In longhand or on a computer. Or a typewriter. When I do *Watch Me Work,* I write on a typewriter.

So you sometimes go from the end or the middle?

It depends. For *365* it was very, "I didn't know what I was doing till after I figured that's what it is," but for other plays I know the whole thing before I write it. Like *Topdog/Underdog*.

For Topdog/Underdog *you knew the whole play?*

I knew the end. I knew the brothers are not going to move.

So would you call that an idea?

No no. Ideas feel like . . . it's a feeling, the word. It's very personal. Ideas may feel like they're located up here somewhere, like, cerebral, you know. When I first felt it, it was like WHAP! Feels like you've been hooked by the great fisherman. I have this thing. The sky is blue. God's in a boat with lures that are dangling down into the world and when he laughs, like that, you've actually been hooked. One of the lures is hooked in your gut, God in your mouth. You've actually been hooked by God and the great fisherman or fisherwoman, fisherperson. I'll say fisherman, shit, and that's the feeling. It's the feeling of being hooked. So it's not an idea, but it's something real—you have that hooked feeling and you go from there. But that was that play. Not every play is like that play, you know? Some plays start in a canoe. Like *Fucking A.* You'll hear all my dumb stories! I was on a canoe with a friend, and I shout out to her, this is another hooked feeling, "I'M GOING TO WRITE A RIFF ON *THE SCAR-LET LETTER,* AND I'M GOING TO CALL IT *FUCKING A.*" It's that same feeling of being hooked. Get back to land. Oh. This might be a good idea. It's still a good idea when I'm walking on land. Hmm. What do I have to do? What do I have to do to write that riff on *The Scarlet Letter.* I had to read *The Scarlet Letter,* and I never read it before.

So what did you think it was?

Oh, I heard about it. Like, I heard about, try to think of some novel you haven't read but you heard about. You know, I've heard the story. It's like I haven't read it, but I've heard about it. So out of that joke, basically . . . so, that's the answer. I don't get an idea, I get a joke. I get a laugh.

What about The Book of Grace?

Another laugh. That's like a laugh. You know I'm directing it. I'm going to Austin in a month to direct it. Some people from the Zachary Scott Theatre in Austin came to see it, and they loved it and said we want you to direct it, and I said OK. That was also a laugh, very disturbing. But that play's so openhearted to me. The heart of that play is so open and longs for . . . it's such an invitation for all of us to participate or be included in *Grace.* A very sort of wild play, and it's very musical and it's getting better, and what we're doing, I decided, I did a little bit of a rewrite and we're going to cast it differently, which I think will help.

You know what I think is interesting in your plays, especially the more recent ones, is how there seems to be a really unique voice, but it's not at all the same from play to play. With certain playwrights you can always tell that this is so-and-so's play. I don't know that we can ever say that about your plays.

I've sometimes maybe often wished that I was the writer who could be more—not regular or consistent—but more recognizable from piece to piece. I seem to become reincarnated from piece to piece, which is very strange, and, yeah, I can't write like I used to, because I'm no longer in 1999, when I wrote *Topdog/Underdog.*

But also the content seems to suggest, or the way you've written it, the content and the form are completely wedded. The only thing that is the same is the power and passion in all.

That's what I'm realizing, that's what I said when I said, "I'm realizing that writing is the vehicle for me to bring love and compassion to this world." So I do it by, "Let's look at two black men who are alive in a room together who are brothers." Let's look at this, let's look at another, and that's why *The Book of Grace* is the closest one to me because it's that beating heart, that attempt to include everybody in this concept of a better world.

It also seems to be two other things. No, not about race, but something really larger. But aren't all of your plays as you write them, "the play."

Oh sure, sure, sure. I'm working on *Porgy and Bess* now, so that could be the play, and I'm working on a new novel, so that could be the thing. But no, in *Book of Grace,* we cast the best actors, stellar actors, A-list actors, actors I loved who loved the play, but we cast it wrong. Looking back on it, it was miscast.

Why do you think so?

So many people thought the play was about race. Everybody thought I was trying to talk about race. A lot of people in the talkback were like, "Why aren't you talking about race? Why are you trying to skirt the issue of race?" It's not about race. "But the father's white, the son is black, and the mother's white. Why are you trying to skirt the issue?" And I thought, the way they're seeing it, they're not seeing father and son, they're seeing white man, black man.

And they're seeing it written by you.

And that too, I suppose. If it had been written by somebody else, it'd just be white man–black man. I don't know. Would it just be father and son? I don't know. But it occurred to me that the play doesn't support that discussion, so we'll just make an all-black cast or in the future racially homogeneous, because it doesn't support that. It's not about race. They did it in another city, and I said, "Please cast it homogeneously," and they didn't, and I've got interviews on the phone talking about what, about race, and I'm like, "What do you mean?" To me it always looked like a family, but I think to the majority of the people it was a commentary on a racial dynamic, and I was like, "Huh?" But it's OK. We live and learn.

The only other writer whom I can say that you're like in how different the voice is from play to play is Caryl Churchill.

I love Caryl Churchill. We shed our skin, and I don't know what makes a writer do that. I'm not sure. You know, we have an extra fold in the brain. You know you're conscious because the brain is folded, and the writer must be folded on top of the fold on top of the fold. It must be fourfold, because you hear the voice of God.

Do you wonder sometimes when you're writing, "Who am I?"

And that is the question, the one question in my work. Who are we? And what are we doing here? That's the question. Who are we? That's it.

Do you have to live in that world, and if you do, how do you get out of it? Like when you go to dinner with somebody.

I know! I suppose . . . I have a system . . . I mean, I've gone to dinner with writers, and then I've gone to see their play, and I'm like, "Oh my God, they were doing a rewrite at dinner." They weren't talking to me—they were working out their play. So I have a cool kind of . . . I have a way to compartmentalize and contain. I believe I do or maybe I don't, maybe I'm just bullshitting myself. Or, yeah, I have to live in the world. *365* is weird. I had to live in a variety of different worlds, and then it was hard . . . I had to go out and be with hundreds of thousands of people while doing the play. And that was difficult. So many artists doing fantastic things, they would take off their clothes and part of the play is about licking whoever's in the audience and whoa! After a year of that I was just like, "Whoa!"

So the play is there and you're halfway through, you leave it, and the next morning you can just enter it?

Yeah. It's just waiting. You build a really good door—sometimes it has to be a fire door and really good windows—and so much of playwriting to me is like architecture. Sometimes a path back. There are all these things we do as writers to create. I mean, yeah, right now I'm working on a novel, *Porgy and Bess,* and *The Book of Grace* . . . so there's different rooms in my brain.

At what point when you're at the desk do you think, "OK, I've gone as far as I can go"?

Topdog was three days. You expect this is how to do it, not to think. That usually takes a while. It depends. My process is not every time, and writers say this all the time, they say every time they sit down, they start anew to write. It's like, "Oh shit, I just learned Chinese, what do you mean, I'm in Japan now? What do you mean? I just learned Japanese, I have to learn Arabic now? It's a totally different world. Oh, I'm on the moon? I thought I was on the Nile. The Mississippi."

Where do you keep the work on all these things?

I have inboxes. Like with my novel. I have inboxes. I have the draft of the novel. It's on a chair. On that inbox is another inbox, and that's *Porgy,* and on another chair is *The Book of Grace* with all the notes and the plot, and on top of that are some bills I have to pay or something.

Let's hear about Porgy and Bess.

I'm so pleased. Seventy-six years ago it premiered in Boston—I want to get this right—it premiered in Boston, but that's where it started, and now Diane Paulus is helming a reimagination, a revisitation, a re-anything. Number one, *Porgy and Bess* is beautiful and wonderful. It's a great opera and means a lot to American culture, and it's one of those great incredible institutions, great incredible shows. The Gershwin estate wants it to be viable for the musical theater, so it's going to need some tweaking. So where I'm tweaking, I'm adding some scenes.

Are you working from the original play?

I'm working with the libretto. The original libretto. Of course, we've reread the novel and we've reread the play. DuBose Heyward is a wonderful writer. The novel is beautiful. I just think he didn't have time to continue work on the libretto, because Gershwin died two years later. If Gershwin had lived, he would have kept tweaking on it, and I think he just ran out of time, and I think it's up to us to pick it up.

OK, let's talk about a new work. Once you've got a script, it's ready to go, do you bring it here to the Public?

Oh, sure. This is the home, so I bring it here, I would bring it to the Public, Oscar or Mandy Hackett. Just like with *Topdog,* it was my home when George was here, and the first person I called was Bonnie Metzgar. It was the same thing then. I would bring it here first, and we'd take it from there.

So now let's get into the process of being in rehearsal. What do you think are the qualities that are essential for the director?

They have to love the play, and they have to get along with me, which isn't hard. And they have to be able to work really, really well with actors. I suppose they have to have a vision for how the play will sit in the world and why it's important to do now. The same kind of thing you would ask if someone was directing an old classic, you know: why do this play now? They have to come to a new play with that feeling. Also they should have some kind of understanding of the world of the play and the world in general, but the world of the play is helpful, but not an understanding that would obscure the world of the play.

Can you cite an example?

The Book of Grace was set in the Southwest or Arizona. I wouldn't say, "The director has to be from Arizona." You know what I'm saying? They don't have to be from anywhere in particular, but having an understanding of Southwest culture is helpful, so they don't see it as a novelty, "Whoa, those weirdos down in the Southwest," kind of thing. But also an understanding that doesn't obscure the world of the play: "I know exactly how they are, and I know exactly how they're supposed to be." Well, we're not doing anthropology. It's a play. That kind of balance is healthy.

Do you like for someone to really get into a dialogue with you about it?

Sure.

In rehearsal do you like to talk to actors?

Oh, yes. Definitely. That's what my NYU class Loving the Living Playwright is about . . . getting the writers comfortable talking with actors and being comfortable—being sort of one in charge in the room. In rehearsal I do very much love talking with actors, and the director I tend to defer to only because it's confusing sometimes when a writer is always taking an actor aside. I don't think that's appropriate to the process, and it mucks up the work. I prefer talking with the director and having the director communicate the vision that is ours joined. Like Jo Bonney and I worked on *Father Comes Home from the Wars*. It was a very wonderful collaboration. I would talk to her, she would talk to me. Or with George when we worked on *Topdog*. That was hand in glove—that was a seamless, amazing collaboration working with George C. Wolfe on *Topdog/Underdog*. We very rarely talked about what the play means and the sociological implications, not at all. Just, what are the guys doing from beat to beat to beat. It was absolutely beautiful. I love working like that.

Is that your assumption when you write a play? That there's no meaning to discuss or to work on? That the meaning is with the action?

Yeah! I'm gonna hang out with you guys all the time! You guys totally get it. The meaning is for the scholars to glean. That's their job. You're an audience, so you're paying but you're invited into the process to glean meaning and to create the conversation around it. The world that it reflects is you. You're supposed to tell us what you see in the mirror.

There's this thing you do where you put in the name of the character and then right below it the name of another character and then sometimes repeat it. How do you explain this to the director and actors? Is it a way you control time? Or is it that you want the actors to be still and just be?

Both are right and both feed into the emotion . . . it's an emotional marker, like spells. They're spells, it's like a laugh . . . Number one: I was told in high school that I shouldn't be a writer because I was a poor speller. So I put spells in my plays, which is a huge ha-ha-ha for me, a joke. And number two, magic spells. And number three, spell as marker of time. Like rests in a spell. So the way I explain it to the actors is we just do it. I say what we're going to do is, not that it has to be done this way onstage, let's do it here, look at each other. We just sit and look into each other's eyes. And that's a spell. It's a moment of deep, intense connection with another character onstage that precedes an emotional time. And it's silence. Now, a director could fill it with action. A character could have one with him or herself like *The Book of Grace,* when Buddy changes his name from Buddy to Snake, he has a spell. He's connecting very deep within himself, within his core. So it's a spell when an actor has to reach into his core, and connect within himself, most often before a deep, emotional turn. He will connect with himself and change his name. So that's an example. Or Lincoln and Booth will look at each other.

So what do you do if you get an actor who's not doing it?

That's OK.

It's OK?

Yes. They're there for all time, and if they're sometimes missed, I don't mind. Actors are like, "I'm not feeling it here." It's OK. Just know if you do feel it great, if not, that's OK. No worries. It's something for all time. It's a monument, it's a marker, it's a milestone. There it stands, but you can walk by it.

There's nothing in the way dramatic literature is written before you, to let you know you could do this.

Line breaks in Shakespeare. That space, whoa, we're back again. Whoa! We're back. But to me, I want to see it more verbal. It becomes a visual thing. Like the line break would be a visual thing. You mark space which is absent, and here I'm marking the space with a column.

It's a great idea.

It's pretty, too, right?

Yes, it looks good.

That's important.

Yes, it's truly a graphic representation of what you're talking about.

I think the first time I started doing it was Lincoln and Booth in *The America Play.*

It's like concrete poetry.

That's what I'm talking about. I came up in poet's theater. That's what my thing was. And the way the coffee poets really use words and space and also Charles Olson projected verse, the way the typewriter could be used to create the page and the silence and the sounds really is important to me, so why not do it in regular theater.

We were going to ask you if you learn from an audience, and you mentioned this. But during the preview, do you make changes?

In the best . . . I'm not learning from the audience, I'm learning from the play. I'm not listening for where the audience laughed—ooh, more of that—I'm not one of those writers. There are a lot of great writers who do that very effectively. I'm more like I'm watching the play and watching the actors, and I'll learn a lot from the actors and the director and producer who's coming night after night, but not from a one-off audience person. I mean, maybe if the audience didn't understand a line, that's a note, but I generally don't write in response to what an audience member has to say, unless they're invested on the team kind of thing.

So you just listen to your piece with people you trust. Everyone else . . . they haven't been through it with you.

Only because I've seen *King Lear* done really poorly. So we see King Lear and the actress playing Cordelia may be a little sleepy or whatever. Someone says, "I'd change that line, man." I learn from the play. And I learn from my collaborators. The directors, the actors, the producers, the designers. I don't really take notes from the audience, no. The thing about *Grace* and race, that was very particular to the casting, I wouldn't say it was a response to the audience.

What would you say is your greatest weakness and your greatest strength?

Let's see, my greatest weakness. See, that's a trick question. Because then I'm going to go home and work on it. If you shine a light on it, then I'm gonna have to work on it, I have to fix it. My greatest weakness, I would say, it's that I don't work fast enough. Um, um, um, oh, I don't know, I mean, maybe, maybe, maybe, I want to write more. That's my weakness. Maybe I'm not as "think-y" as I could be. I'm not as "idea-y." I'm more like laugh-y, ha, ha, ha. I probably could do better if I were more, you know, up on the sort of . . . I talk to writers sometimes and they read the *New York Times* and they can digest. It can mean, what things mean and I'm fascinated. I'm like, "Wow." I'm a little slow. I think that's my greatest strength. I'm a little mushy and slow.

Mushy?

I'm a little . . . I feel deeply, which makes me a little slow. I feel very, you know . . . I'm not as quick. I'd like to be quicker of mind, I'd like my mind to be a little quicker, but I'm a little, what? Country, I suppose. Or more country.

Is your career, if it can be said that it has an arc, do you see yourself starting one place and going to another?

Just so you know, because they won't know this when they read it, you used one hand and you made an arc like the one in St. Louis, right? The

Arch, the Arch. It's beautiful. What I'm going to do is I'm going to put two hands in the middle of my chest and bring them both out in different directions. It's an arc. It's the same thing, but I'm making it because, just because, I'm doing at the same time. I'm doing *Watch Me Work*, which is a solo performance piece, made up on the spot every day for free. Anyone who wants to come down to the lobby in the Public and play with me can do so. It's kind of what I call lowbrow downtown stuff, and we're doing *Porgy and Bess,* which is high on the hog working with the Gershwins and Mr. Heyward. And what you said about changing voices, I'm doing voices out of both sides of my mouth. I'm doing downtown and uptown at the same time, and so I'd just like to continue that. And that's an arc.

So rather than going from A to B, it's going inside.

Yeah. It's going out. It's going A to Z, and it's, you know what I mean? Where, I don't know. It's going from . . . anyway, I'm playing with A and Z. I'm wriggling the endpoints to get to the middle. I don't know. It's fucked up, this idea of timelines. Maybe I'm just doing more. I'm able to do more. When I started I was doing downtown exclusively, and now I'm doing more uptown stuff, but I haven't stopped doing my downtown stuff, which I love.

OK.

This is kind of confusing. This will make sense soon. It's the world. This is the world.

I like that it's coming from the midpoint of your chest.

Or just the beginning of time, you know what I mean? And it's encompassing all. It's kind of embracing everything or trying to.

What part of you does your novel speak to?

It's the part of me that wants everybody to be the director and the costume designer, they have to do it all. They gotta do the art design.

You do as a novelist.

No, you say it like, for example, *Oliver Twist.* You say, Oliver Twist, he's a little kid with short brown hair. A little kid with short brown hair to you isn't how it is in my mind, so we're all thinking something different. We all cast it. We cast the whole thing, and that's really fun. Also I get more specificity in the novel. I don't know. I love working on my novel. I loved writing the first one, and I put songs in it, and I'm doing the same thing with the second one. I love it. There's a sense that it's portable. It's finished and it's portable. They can take it and they can experience it. They don't need a whole group.

What about screenplays? Any interest?

Yeah, screenplays. Writing original screenplays and adapting. Like I adapted *Their Eyes Were Watching God* for Oprah four years ago or something like that.

They're hard to get done.

It depends. Everything is hard to get done or hard to write. I'm really in love with doing this downtown/uptown thing. I love it. It's something else. It's sort of, I can represent in a very deep way when I do *Watch Me Work* in the lobby, what am I doing. I'm sitting in the lobby giving a free class for people. It's very very important for me to do that. For the Public Theater, for New York City, for the world. Yes. Someone like me can be present for someone like "I don't know what's your name over there" and invite you in and support your process. I don't even know you, but I'm going to support you. I'm going to show you. I'm going to represent the human race, not just the black race—but the human race.

DAVID HARE

We'd just about given up on the possibility that David Hare would be part of this book. He lives in London, we live in New York. The chances of him coming to us were unpredictable; of us going to him: nil. Luckily for our book, he was scheduled to come to New York for a long weekend in early fall to give a talk and present a playwriting award at Yale, and he emailed us the news. On not too short notice—long enough to reread most of his plays—we were able to snag a few hours on a Sunday afternoon in late September. We met at The Public Theater, where several of his plays have been done over the years, in a large conference room on the second floor. The offices were empty. Quiet prevailed. David was right on time, marveling at the changes that had happened in the neighborhood since the last time he'd been there. He is tall and was dressed in dark colors, his hair shaggy. He has an immensely friendly presence. His face opens up when he smiles, which he does easily, and he is eager to elaborate on even our simplest questions. At one point during the interview, he talked about the fact that he finds all people interesting, and he certainly made us feel that. Our conversation was rambling and discursive and roamed freely over the course of his impressively long and distinguished career. On several occasions we had to turn off the tape recorder so he could relate a particularly juicy and hilarious not-for-publication story, which he did with relish.

Do you remember the first play you ever saw?

I was brought up on the Sussex coast—a town of twenty-five thousand, so there was a repertory company. In the 1950s there was a completely different culture . . . every small English town had a repertory company. We were by the sea, which was why we had one year-round. Sometimes in the summer there were two theaters presenting plays, mostly murder mysteries. Mostly by Agatha Christie. An awful lot of those things. Jack Popplewell was a very popular writer in those days. And I loved going. I absolutely adored it. I mean I adored it the moment I started going.

How old were you?

Nine, ten. Around there. And then my mother sent me to a little drama school. The star alumna was Julie Christie. They had a picture of Julie in a miniskirt, which I remembered very, very clearly pinned up. I can remember her skirt. It was candy striped. We all noticed Julie in the town streets when she was at school. She was a rather memorable figure at the school at fourteen years old.

Why did your mother send you to that school in the first place?

My mother had been an amateur actress in plays in Scotland, and she had a certificate in elocution. She used to put me in for elocution prizes. She taught Scottish accents, which is very difficult. Scottish accents are very, very difficult. So she was the person people got sent to if maybe somebody in the rep had to have a Scottish accent, they'd come and see my mother.

What made you want to tell stories?

Well, I was sort of educated out of that really by going to university. I think because I was studying literature, I never thought I'd make it. Essentially your critical faculty is being developed, and it is, I suppose, directly opposite to your creative faculty, and it's almost impossible to imagine yourself as both. Ted Hughes is very good on this. About Cambridge University, he said, "I did manage to escape from under the wire in spite of the bullets and the guards." But he also sort of says, "I would never have dared write in Cambridge." When I was at university it was profoundly anticreative. You were being taught literature, but you were being taught that all but the greatest literature was a waste of time. An approved list of books which were essentially Shakespeare. Milton was sometimes allowed, sometimes not. Maybe Pope.

Who represented modern literature?

D. H. Lawrence was admired as representing everything that the modern novel could possibly be or do. It was a whole incredibly strong philosophy about English literature being at the center of the humanizing of society. So: only great writers. For instance, when I wanted to study people like Auden, I was told it was unacceptable, that I couldn't study him. This was at Cambridge! When I said in my last year I was going to write about Oscar Wilde, I was told, "Well, you can do it, but you'll make yourself completely ridiculous." And it was very puritanical, the teaching. So that's not the atmosphere in which you are encouraged to be creative.

Was there a sense you wanted to do this?

No.

So when did it come on you that it was plays rather than novels?

I wanted to work in the film industry, but there wasn't a British film industry then as now. It lived a little while, while it was trendy in the late sixties, with some American investment. A friend and I started this company called Portable Theatre, which was a sort of idealistic fringe group, very much a part of the sixties theater movement, except we literally were the only people who used words. All the other theaters of that movement were physical theater or, you know, video, dance and mime and puppets. Physical theater techniques. We were the only fringe group that was still doing Kafka and Strindberg. An avant-garde diet but literary. The revolutionary thing about it was that we took it everywhere. We took it to army camps or prisons or schools. We took it to any space. That was all part of the sixties. We were doing in theater what everyone was doing in music, essentially. But I was the director. I wasn't a writer.

How did you finance this?

Well, it was incredibly cheap.

You didn't need what you need now.

We wrote to Volkswagen, and they gave us a van. We wrote to Olympia, and they gave us a typewriter. There were ten shares each night at the gate, and everyone took one-tenth, and three-tenths was left over to run the company, because seven people were involved. But in those days it was possible to live off that. Not glamorously, but you could live. Now such a thing is impossible. We went as students to see Peter Brook. Why he saw us, I have no idea, we just wrote to him and said we'd like to meet him. We said we were going to start a theater. He said, "Don't start a theater, because if you start a theater, you'll then be doing things the wrong way around. First you must know what your work is. Then when you've found out what your work is, you will then maybe want to build a building to put that work in or you may not." He said, "I've seen so many people who are prisoners of buildings. Do it the other way around. And anyway the work you think you want to do won't be the work you end up doing." He said, "Everyone who comes down from university says I'm going to do Kleist and Webster and rediscover the *Duchess of Malfi . . .*" and he went through this list. He said, "Those are all the plays I thought I wanted to do. And then of course you discover you don't want to do those plays because you respond to something else once you get going." He was dead right. We started doing Kafka and Strindberg, and then Howard Brenton soon walked into our lives, and it became completely different. We then started doing hot, violent contemporary writing that was very politicized and sort of what we used to call "short nasty little plays" designed to upset people.

Is that when you started writing?

I started writing simply because somebody failed to deliver a play. If I hadn't written a play, we wouldn't have had a play to rehearse. So I started writing on a Wednesday, and we started rehearsal on the play on the following Monday, in order for there to be a play to do.

This is the true story of how you began as a writer?

I'd never written before. And then I discovered—which I had no fore-knowledge of, I remember it very clearly, I remember thinking—"Oh, I can write dialogue. I didn't know I had this gift." It was like having a musical gift that I didn't know I had. Or riding a bicycle. And when actors looked at the page, they kind of go, "Oh, yeah, that looks proper." And so just that basic facility without which really you can't be a playwright. I mean, it's always argued that Eugene O'Neill can't write dialogue, but I think O'Neill's dialogue is completely wonderful. I mean, people say his dialogue is very clunky, but I don't think it is. Actors can say it and make it wonderful. Especially the great ones. I don't know. I recently saw his first play, *Beyond the Horizon.* Well, I think it's as great as anything he wrote in his maturity. It's a great play. He can write dialogue the moment he starts writing. That's the thing you have to have as a playwright. Now, being able to write dialogue is not the same as being able to write a play. Not at all. On the contrary. I was actually misled by my facility with dialogue to write badly. I wrote badly because I didn't realize a play wasn't just a lot of people telling jokes.

This must be why actors write plays, because they know what dialogue is.

But that doesn't help you.

It's a start.

So I discovered I had this gift. I was twenty-one or -two. Then a West End producer commissioned me to write a play. So I was in this funny split state of being both on the fringe completely as part of the radical alternative theater movement of the day, and the same time the most successful West End producer was asking me to write a satirical comedy for the commercial theater. So I was very split, which I've remained for the whole of my life. I've moved in and out of mainstream and alternative.

Did you write the satirical comedy?

I wrote a play called *Slag.* So I was established then as a satirist, and people thought that was my gift because I was a very caustic, disapproving young man. Therefore everyone thought I should write satire and hip satire. It was my natural tone of voice at the time. Of course, I would now say that was adolescent insecurity. I didn't find my voice in my first few plays. I found a completely original voice, whether it's mine or not, in *Knuckle*. And then when I wrote *Knuckle,* my agent—he had been the person who discovered me—said, "You're trying to write a serious play. It's a complete waste of time. You shouldn't waste yourself on this. You're a satirist. What are you doing? It doesn't work." And *Knuckle* was an original conceit. It was as if a Raymond Chandler American-style thriller had been reset in the English home counties, so it was a massively complicated conceit to sustain for two and a half hours, just technically a very difficult piece of writing. And so I knew it was really important, this play, so I left that agent. And then everything went against the play. It was the first play of mine to be presented straight at the West End. It was the debut of Kate Nelligan. And it was the first rabidly anticapitalist play in commercial theater, and it was presented during the three-day week when because of the industrial strike in Britain, Edward Heath had ordered the electricity to be off for two days, but people were working three days, so it wasn't an easy time to premiere a play.

How long did it run?

It ran for four months through the incredible generosity of my producer Michael Codron, who kept it going with wind whistling through the stalls. It was the beginning of the thing whereby my work would be acclaimed as the most important work of the period and attacked as a complete waste of time. And so the violence of the reaction to the play, as much as my own sense of how important it was, that I'd finally found my voice, sort of shaped my destiny. In other words, when that happened, I kind of went, "Oh, I see." Because for years I pretended I wasn't a playwright because I was directing people like Howard Brenton, Trevor Griffiths, Snoo Wilson, all of whom had a very strong vocational sense which I didn't have. So I'd kind of go, "I'm not really a playwright, I'm just compensating for the fact that the British theater is so trivial and isn't about anything, so I'll cover subjects that nobody else can be bothered to write about, and I don't pretend to be a playwright." But then, suddenly, when I faced incredible adversity, then I wanted to be a *great* playwright.

And that's even worse than not wanting to be a playwright. The minute you're hooked, you want to be a great playwright, and of course that gets you into all sorts of trouble.

You made a comment when we told you we would be interviewing thirteen great playwrights. You said, "Are there thirteen great playwrights?" The comment just stopped us. We can't get that out of our minds.

I really think you should call your book *Thirteen Good Playwrights*. One of the extraordinary things about the period I lived through in the British theater is that you can name sixty people who have written a really good play. There are sixty. We really have sixty dramatists who have written a really good play. But if you go to the other end and say, name a playwright in that same period who has written ten good plays . . .

America's even harder. The support for the playwright is very difficult to get for the first one; the second one is even harder. If the second isn't as good as the first, the third isn't going to get done.

We talked about your writing starting with your ease with dialogue and then finding your voice in Knuckle. *What kind of playwrights influenced what you did? Or was it just living in the theater?*

I'm mystified by the question of influence. In other words, I never know what to say when people say, "Who influenced you?" For my generation, Brecht was the playwright you had to deal with. But I dealt with him by just ignoring him, and I only really started really dealing with him when I did adaptations of him in the nineties. By that time I was confident enough in my own work not to be threatened by him. But all young socialist playwrights in England obviously were terrified or overwhelmed by the example of Brecht. But the Brechtian ideal—that you would be as capable in the arts of the theater as a playwright, you'd be a director and maybe even an actor and do all the things in the theater and not just write—obviously that's something I aspire to. I thought it was good for my writing that I was involved in the theater as a director.

Can we talk about your actual process and what you do on a daily basis?

I work every day. I don't work weekends, but I work every day. If I don't, I get ill. I really get incredibly jumpy if I don't.

Do you have to produce something?

No, but I have to think. If I'm writing something, then the chances are I'll spend most of my time thinking. I find the dialogue incredibly easy. I just find the whole business of actually writing the stuff easy, so to speak. Once your head is in the right place and you know what it is you're trying to express in the scene, then the actual business of writing it is a pure pleasure. But mostly what you're trying to do is wrestle with what the idea is and where it's coming from, which is completely mysterious. The mistake about political writing is to imagine that those of us who wish to write about social or political things are in any more control of the mysterious artistic process than people who put it down automatically.

Do you read about the subject that you're writing about?

It depends what kind of play I'm writing. Lately I've become—in a derogatory way—called a short-order cook for the British theater. If they want a play on a subject, they come to me, because they know that I'll write about the diplomatic process leading up to the war in Iraq. Or if you need a play about the denationalization of the British railway system—go to David Hare. When the financial crisis came along, the National Theatre said we need to do a play about the financial crisis, get David Hare. He'll do those. I didn't want to do a play about the financial crisis; I said I really don't want to. Nick Hytner just blackmailed me and said, "The National Theatre has to have a play about the financial crisis on its stage this year, or how can it call itself the National Theatre." Very good question.

In America, nobody would write it because it wouldn't get done.

It would get done, but what it would not get done—this is where you talk about Joe Papp—it would not get done in the mainstream. Isn't that right? So, you know, a lot of people came from Europe to the *Power of*

Yes, which is the play I wrote about the financial system, and said, "I cannot believe I'm sitting in a thousand-seat theater watching a play about the events going on outside the building at this time and that it's in a form that everyone understands and accepts." One goes, "Oh, it's the play about the financial crisis," and they take it for granted that it will be there. Do you see? It'll be that play. Oh, it's the play that explains what the financial crisis is about. They understand that. They also say that in any other country that kind of play would be done in the fringe theater down the road in a thirty-seat theater. There was a hilarious thing that Wally Shawn said about *Stuff Happens.* And actually it was also said in the *Journal of Higher Education* here. Somebody wrote in a review of *Stuff Happens,* "This is an excellent school play. It's got parts for people of all different backgrounds, it's got parts for men and women, it really should be put in every high school in America because actually it's also a great way of learning what's happened. It's a perfect high school play." I thought it was the most flattering description of a play I've ever read. I thought, "Yup." And in England it's been done as a school play. To me that's very, very exciting. Schoolboys wrote to me and said we're putting it on as our school play. That's wonderful.

It's exciting that young people are doing it instead of Agatha Christie or Our Town.

The thing of being the person people go to for these plays is a mixed blessing in the sense that I felt during the last ten years that things were happening at such a rate that you had to be the social secretary. Like Balzac, you had to be the person who just said this is what's going on so that it's there as a sort of record: this is what happened in this extraordinary decade. Because it has been a fairly extraordinary decade. Bookended by two astonishing events, and with a walloping great event in the middle, so somebody's got to record what's going on.

Do you do research?

Oh, yes. I have someone working for me, and we read and then I meet dozens and dozens of people. With *Stuff Happens,* there were a lot people who had been, as it were, close to the center of the events. They're happy to talk off the record to playwrights if it's not attributable. They're happier to talk to playwrights than they are to journalists because what they told me will be hidden deep away.

Do you ever make up things?

Oh, yes. *Stuff Happens* is two-thirds invented because everything that happened that was significant in the diplomatic process happened behind closed doors. If you take the most famous event, which is in Crawford, Texas, at the moment at which Bush and Blair go for a walk and dream up the scheme. They wouldn't take anyone with them. They deliberately went into the woods so that no one could listen to them. So nobody knows what they said on that walk. So it's all guesswork. But a lot of people who were involved with the events have told me my guesswork is very close.

There's a nice fact about Fidel Castro in Map of the World—*that as a young man he was an extra in an Esther Williams movie.*

I've forgotten that.

It was so hilarious and so perfect, I wondered if you collected those sorts of interesting little tidbits. Or is it made up?

No, it's not made up. There is an ethical problem with this kind of work, and I take it very seriously.

What is the problem?

If you set real people onstage, then you have an ethical debt to them. When I've done documentary theater, *Via Dolorosa*, for instance, when I was representing those thirty-three people about Israel/Palestine, most of them I sent a copy and said, "Look, I'm gonna have you say this. Are you happy?"

Well, these are your friends.

No. Anybody I met, except the settlers. Because I knew the settlers would be infuriated. So I changed their names. But everything I said was completely accurate, it was scrupulously accurate. In fact, when the settlers came to see the play, they were predictably absolutely furious. They said, "We're not furious with you, we're furious with the audience." I said, "Have I misrepresented you?" They said, "No, it's completely what we said to you, but it's one thing to say it in a settlement where everyone agrees with us, but if you present this on the New York stage, when no one agrees with us or no one who goes to the theater agrees with us, then we're being held up to ridicule."

When they first talked to you, they didn't imagine the situation.

No, because they live in a bubble. Curiosity has been my driving force. I just go into these places. You know if you have a group of people sitting around dinner and someone says that Rabin organized his own assassination, that he wasn't actually killed by a lone gunman but that actually he had a Christ complex and he wanted to be killed right and that he organized that he should be killed—and everyone at the dinner, ten and twelve people, sits and nods and says, "Well, everyone knows that . . ." Well, obviously you go, "Oh, I stumbled on something rather interesting." All peer groups have extraordinary beliefs, and anyone who observed us around this table would go, "Oh my God, isn't it weird what they believe?"

When you're at the table, do you participate? Draw them out?

I'm just always taken aback by what people say. I just find everyone very, very interesting. I sort of bless the fact that I had a classic provincial upbringing. You notice this in writers—if you're brought up in a very boring place, then not being in that boring place is always fun. If I go out into the world and write about it—even the bankers, though I didn't terribly enjoy the bankers' company—but if you go out and talk to American politicians, or when I did the railways, it was riveting. The people who run the railways were riveting people to talk to. So I have a reportorial gene.

And a personal quality that allows people to know you like them and want to hear from them.

I won't traduce them. I won't misrepresent them, and I won't hold them up to ridicule or betray them.

The other plays, the plays for which you are not social secretary—plays like Amy's View *or* My Zinc Bed—*how do they start for you?*

The private plays. By and large, with a visual image usually. It's very important to me that it's like a painting. I like what happens when you go to the theater and you look and you go, "This is going to be good." There's some visual thing that makes you go, "This smells great." You know that feeling. You look at the set . . . *Plenty*, for example . . . the high windows, the light, a single woman with a coat, a naked man on the bed, she's rolling a cigarette . . . I'd go, "Wow, I'd love to see that play!" Because it's such a strong visual hook. Those essential things have got to be an enjoyable milieu, so you go, "It's going to be worth a couple hours in the theater." Whereas if you go to an awful set, and it looks like an office . . .

Were you able to see Ivo van Hove's production of The Little Foxes?

No. Is it very good?

It's very good.

It's with Elizabeth Marvel. Well, she's the best. She's an incredible actor.

Do you ever write for particular actors?

No. Recently I've been asked to write for an actor, a really good actor. And I can't do it.

Is there any play of yours you wrote with someone in mind?

No. Often when I'm halfway through it becomes clear to me who it should be. I think with *Pravda* . . . but that was slightly different because

I was writing with Howard Brenton. But when we'd written one act, we sent it to Tony Hopkins, who was at that period in his life when he was sitting by a pool in Hollywood. I didn't know Tony Hopkins. I'd never met him, but we sent him the first act, and he just said, "Well, if the second act is as good as the first, I'm in." So in the second act, we really relished the fact that we knew we were writing for Tony.

With Amy's View, *did you know it would be Judi Dench?*

No. Judi turned it down. She couldn't understand it. It wasn't my idea to cast Judi. And Richard Eyre, who was then sort of working with Judi a lot, said that when Judi was given it, she said, "I don't understand why you think this is me at all, I don't see anything I can play here. Mind you, those are usually the plays in which I'm happiest finally." So it wasn't her idea. She had a horrible rehearsal period and spent the whole rehearsal period saying she didn't understand the play and was going to be vile in it. I remember a lot of crying. I remember coming to rehearsal and Judi being in tears and saying, "I can't do this. I don't know who she is, I can't play it." It was horrible.

Was there a breakthrough moment?

Yes. It's extraordinary. When those things happen, it's so exciting. Judi's husband, Michael, didn't like the play, and that really upset her and that made life very difficult for her. Because going home, enjoying the kind of success she was enjoying in that play and the feeling of exhilaration the play gave her—it was the same time she won an Oscar and all that stuff—Michael really didn't like the play. So that was difficult.

One of the things I found so interesting was the next to last scene. When Dominic gives her a box of money, it seems like that's going to resolve the play with Dominic not feeling guilty, and she's going to not be poor, and though that would've been an ending, it would have been a lesser one. And then you do this thing with the water, and art triumphs in the end. It's a very thrilling play.

That's if you love the theater. There's the water and that's the killer. A number of people have observed that to be. They say, "I'm absolutely fine.

I'm going to watch this play, but I'm not going to let it touch me. I'm not going to sit crying about this." And when the jug of water is poured over the poor boy's head, the audience always goes to pieces, because that's the unbearable bit.

How'd you come up with that scene?

I've watched actors in the wings do that extraordinary thing when they have to go onstage wet. It's always moved me so much to watch actors in the wings. They do that thing, taking their shoes off and standing in a basin, and the stage manager comes on and pours water all over them so they can go on and go, "I've just come in from the rain." It's just so touching, isn't it?

Well, you made it huge and touching.

It's also a gesture of a religious thing, and that's always there in my stuff. I was recently asked by the Terence Rattigan estate . . . they have his play *The Browning Version,* a very good play. When it's performed, it's always preceded by a terrible play that he wrote called *Harlequinade,* and because it's his hundredth anniversary, they asked me if I could write a play, a curtain raiser, forty-five minutes, to go with *The Browning Version.* I said, "Yeah, I'd love to." It's a very interesting thing of knowing I was only going to write forty-five minutes, although I think it's ended up an hour. But it literally has written itself. I haven't interceded in the process at all. I would wake up in the middle of the night, and my wife would say, "What are you doing?" And I would say, "I am writing tomorrow's scenes." It just came to me. And that is what you pray for—that there's absolutely no editorial process at all. There's about eight lines that I wrote and haven't used, but otherwise everything I've written, I've used. When that happens—and I've talked to a couple other playwrights—it happens once every twenty-five years. I can remember it on *Racing Demon,* I can remember it just going like that. But then, *Racing Demon* needed fixing once I'd been through that process. But this play doesn't need fixing. It's done and it's come I have no idea where from. It just wrote itself. When that happens, it's so incredible. The trouble is you don't want to go back to the old struggle. Because now people are saying to me, "Can't it be longer?" Or "Can't you write a second play?" And you go, "Well, I don't want to go back to the old struggle when this has come from heaven."

What are you calling it?

It's called *South Downs* because that's the part of England it's set in. It's set at a public school about private education. It's about my education, my youth. It's about fourteen-year-old boys, for which, as you know, only real fourteen-year-old boys can play. Not sixteen-year-old boys. I've already started. I'm not having sixteen-year-old boys pretending to be fourteen-year-old boys. They're completely different. So what I'm really saying is that you can go from a play which is pure craft and will to a play where will is not involved at all. All writers I believe move between those two.

What play almost broke you to write or was really a struggle?

A Map of the World. What happened was *Plenty* was not well-received in England. Very badly received critically. I stomped off to America in high dudgeon and lived here for a year. I was really in self-imposed exile, in fury. It was incredibly upsetting. Terrible, terrible time in my life. It was a terrible time because I really did feel, with *Plenty,* I'd written a good play, and if they didn't want a good play . . . I was just insane with anger and despair. I completely couldn't write. Thatcherism arrived at the same moment. So after having spent ten years in this leftish theater movement, suddenly history was turning right. I was completely lost. The Adelaide Festival people asked me to write a play for Australia. I thought, well I've got a year. I'm blocked. I can't write, but I will promise them a play in a year's time. And I will just force myself to write something, and if it's terrible, it will be twelve thousand miles away—on the other side of the world—and nobody will see it. So it's fine. But unfortunately at the first preview, I walked into this theater in Adelaide, and there was Michael Billington from *The Guardian* and Michael Coveney from the *Financial Times,* and I go, "I see now there's nowhere on earth I can hide." This is a grave problem. It becomes a grave problem once you become a known playwright. You can't do anything. I can't experiment. This is a big loss to me. I would love the freedom to be able to experiment, but I'm not allowed to experiment.

When you finish writing something, what is the next step for you? Is there a workshop process that you can just do?

In *South Downs* at the moment we're all puzzling: is this a good raiser to *The Browning Version,* or is this an hour-long play about fourteen-year-old boys? Where does such a play belong? What is it? How do you do it? Literally, how do you organize to do it? Where does it belong? Where will it be understood? The audience has to understand what it is they're at. And a great director will tell the audience what kind of play it is they're watching and how to understand it, how to access it. A great director gives you access. With *The Vertical Hour,* it was originally going to be done off-Broadway at the New York Theatre Workshop. Elizabeth Marvel in fact was interested to play. We thought much better to do it off-Broadway. Then Julianne Moore wanted to play it. So immediately we had to do it on Broadway. Then it goes on Broadway, and people go, "Oh, is it a Broadway play?" No, it isn't a Broadway play, you know, and so then you are trying to interpret how to get what it is you've done best seen. I struggle with this a lot. But that's only the last fifteen years. I think a lot of trouble I got into with *Knuckle,* for example, was because it was presented at the West End. In fact, one critic, Irving Wardle, later wrote a letter to Peggy Ramsay, my agent, in which he said, "I was so discombobulated by the hypocrisy as I thought of it—of an anticapitalist play being presented in the capitalist theater—that I couldn't see the play itself, and it's one of my great regrets that I couldn't see the play." So you know, context sends out signals, doesn't it, whereby things are either understood or not understood.

When you're done with a script, when you think it's reached a point where you can't do anything anymore, is there somebody you show it to before you release it into the world?

Nicole, my wife.

What kind of thing might she say?

Well, for instance, with this *South Downs,* she said, "Well, I was enjoying it so much . . . why does it just stop?" I said, "Well, I was asked to write a fifty-minute play." She wanted it to go on two hours. "I love these people, and I want to spend two hours with them." So that's both helpful and interesting.

It seems that you used to direct so much of your own work, and that's changed, hasn't it?

I don't anymore. The period in which I directed my own work was because I felt that the tendency of all directors, however skillful, was to make your work like other people's. There was an absolutely wonderful moment in *The Knife* when Nick Bicat, the composer, tries to explain to the viola player how to play a melody, and she could not play this bloody melody. And she was going, "Uhh," and he was going, "Nuhh," and Nick just said, "It's a bit like Puccini," and she went, "Ooh, it's like Puccini," and at once she played the melody absolutely perfectly right. And I think if you're a young writer, the director goes, "What is this like?" They don't go, "What is this?" They go, "It reminds me slightly of . . ." I mean, I personally have issues with the production of Frances Ya-Chu Cowhig's play. I felt the director made it more like another person's play instead of Frances's play. It wasn't really what Frances was getting at, which was much more confrontational and agitprop, because people don't do agit-prop anymore—it's out of fashion. So I felt after *Knuckle*, which was a perfectly good production, I'm not complaining about the production, but I felt the tendency had been to smooth it out so it seemed like . . . 1975. I said I wanted to do my own work so that it would sound like the way it sounded in my head. If there was a loss of quality, so be it, but it would mean that it sounded exactly the way I wanted it. And at the same time, I found this great interpreter of my work, Kate Nelligan, who I felt completely heard my music. She was like the perfect instrumentalist for my music, so it was very exciting to be working with her, because I really had found a great interpreter. So all at once everyone now went, "Oh, that's what a David Hare play sounds like." Then you can let better directors take over, because they know the model to which they are working in. And so now everybody knows what a David Hare play sounds like. While I was establishing my own work, *I* had to establish it. Now I'm not establishing my own work, and I love working with more talented directors.

There is a David Hare play, but then there is a variation of a David Hare play. You don't worry about it being generic anymore—that it won't be, "Oh, well, this is a David Hare play," rather than the exploration of—

I think it's almost impossible to get the plays written about intelligently after a certain while because of expectations. The laziest way of writing about movies is to use the auteur theory. You just say, "Oh, well, Fellini in these touches that we saw in his last film, now we see these touches in . . ." That's the laziest way in writing a film review. To say, "Oh, this is a classic David Fincher movie. He takes up the themes of . . ." But when you do that, you don't actually address what the thing itself is or is about, because we're not visual artists, we're moral artists, and moral art is very hard to write about. And it's particularly hard if the way you judge it is on aesthetic not moral grounds. So I would say all my influences are of the outside world. The people who write best about my work are people who themselves are interested in the world outside the theater, not just theater.

I'm very interested in the detail in your stage directions, because in America, playwrights are taught that if you have to put something in the stage directions, then you haven't written the line correctly. The line should do it all. And sometimes it does seem like you have only one stage direction: "She arches an eyebrow." Some of them really help to understand the play since you write what happens between the lines: "She pauses a moment then speaks with great finality as if finishing a coda." I know what it means as a reader, but does it help the actor?

My stuff is very difficult for actors. I have this rather Nazi-sounding theory, which is called "beyond discipline, freedom." I believe that my stuff—and I know this from bitter experience—only works if you get it down like a musical score. Once you have it down, you're free. But you cannot do it the other way around. You cannot, as it were, method act your way into my work. If you try to method act your way into it, meaning search the inner emotion and then just let the stuff that you're saying fall out of your mouth while you're emoting, it will never work. You have to learn it like a musical score. Once you have the score down, you will be completely free, but if you won't learn that score, you never will be. Every actor I've watched who tries to do it the other way around comes to grief. Every actor I know who has turned up on the first day of rehearsal knowing the entire text has given a great performance of my work because they've spent the four weeks totally secure in the music, and then off they go into the emotional exploration. Two of the greatest performers of my work are Bill Nighy in *The Vertical Hour* and Tony Hopkins in *Pravda*. They both knew the whole script on the first day of rehearsal and off they go.

In the course of this, has an actor asked, because they had a problem with the line, would you change it?

Oh yeah, all the time. Constantly. I'll give you an absolutely classic example . . . which was a wonderful thing that Michael Gambon said about *Skylight*. He said, "You don't get me out of the play." And I said, "I don't know what you mean." He said, "Well, I play all evening and then I leave. And I know every evening I'm going to go back and be depressed in the dressing room because you don't really get me out." And I said, "Say no more. I'll get you out." So that in a way the character leaves the experience behind, goes up out of the play. Whereas I was sending him down out of the play. And then I came with some lines, and he said, "That was exactly what I needed. Now I'll enjoy performing it. But if you'd left me the way you left me, you'd have left me hanging." And that was an actor just saying, "I don't want to spend two hours onstage and then feel miserable for the night."

What do you do with an actor who is recalcitrant or reluctant to try anything? How do you get through to him?

That's the director's job. Most directors are essentially members of the audience. If you take the most intelligent, best-taste member of the audience, all they're basically saying to actors is, "I can tell you as a highly intelligent, sophisticated member of the audience, if you do that, they'll all think that, and the effect of doing that will be that." In other words, they sit there on behalf of the audience and say, "From the outside it looks to me as if by doing that . . ." Some of them will have blindingly good taste, and they produce fantastically good productions that way. And some great directors work that way. They work on behalf of the audience saying as the person in the audience with the best taste, "I will now shape this so that everything in the play comes across." The number of directors who can actually help an actor in trouble . . . Zoë Wanamaker once said to me there are three directors in England who can help an actor in trouble. And I think it isn't many more here.

You're not going to name them?

No. A director can tell you what the problem is. But the directors who can actually help the actor are few. And panic of course enters the rehearsal room. When I did *The Secret Rapture* here, panic entered the rehearsal room, and I remember stopping a rehearsal one afternoon and just said, "We're all in panic, let's just stop." Because once panic enters, you can't get rid of it. Once it's there, nobody can work, because panic itself makes work impossible . . . So that's around the time I gave up directing. I gave up directing after directing *The Knife* and *Secret Rapture* because I felt with *The Knife,* I absolutely failed—I felt it was entirely my fault. We had something completely wonderful, something completely enchanting in workshop, which completely failed to communicate onstage, and I had failed to mediate and tell the audience what kind of thing they were watching. It was halfway a Broadway musical because Joe Papp was saying to me, "We'll get this to Broadway." So I was halfway between Broadway and the avant-garde. They didn't know what it was. I had failed. Stephen Daldry I regard in my lifetime as the greatest genius at that act of mediation between the play and the audience. You watch *Billy Elliot,* and he explains to the audience what it is. The number of people who said to Stephen, "No one will understand this! It's from Newcastle, all these people speaking in thick accents. It's about an experience we don't have here. We don't have miners." All this. And Stephen has this genius for putting something across to the audience so that they know. The minute a Daldry production starts, they know where they are and what it is, and that's what he does. And just to finish, when now twenty years later, *Spring Awakening* and these radical rock musicals are acclaimed, we did it all twenty years ago, didn't we? *The Knife* was the most radical rock musical ever. All the sexual stuff, people said it was a revelation with *Spring Awakening.* We did it all twenty years ago. But it was my failure.

You were talking on the BBC about the power of nightmares, which you said pass some of the most traditional tests of art. For starters, nobody could miss the fact it was created by one exceptional imagination. How does that operate in theater when it's collaborative? How do you exert that one point of view?

The tradition of the British theater is that the writer is at the center of it. There's all this dissatisfaction about this at the moment. We live in a period where people are trying to attack what they call literary theater, and so all modish stuff at the moment is done by groups who don't believe in the writer as the fountain of everything in the theater. But I belong to that tradition that believes in the primacy of the writer, and by and large in my lifetime there are exceptions, but by and large the greatest work has been in that tradition. What I'm trying to do is essentially to treat political and social material but bring to it all the traditional virtues of humanist theater based on the individual and the exploration of the individual. I do feel very lonely doing that. I feel I'm the only person doing that. I get lonely doing it as the years go by. And no better understood. I don't think people understand that that's what I'm doing. They immediately say, "Oh, it's a political play, therefore it's journalism." It's different. They really don't understand.

I know you've always had this contentious relationship with critics. Do you still read reviews?

I really don't, but it comes through the ether. I'm not talking about critics. I'm talking about influence, really, and feeling. There's a wonderful quote by Wordsworth, where he writes to a woman he knows, and he says a great artist not only creates the work, but he refashions the taste by which the work is understood. It's a fantastic quote. Take Harold Pinter. In 1957 nobody understood a word he wrote; now everybody can understand it, so one of the things Harold did is change the taste so you can understand his play fifty years later. I feel I've totally failed to change the taste. I feel forty years later, people are no nearer to understanding what I do than they did in the beginning. So I'm also entirely without influence. Nobody's influenced by me. The theater doesn't feel different because of what I've done. That high you get when you actually are hitting the time and it's really, really exciting that you've appeared to demonstrate that uniquely exciting theater is about the lives of the people sitting in the audience, and they've come in off the streets and there it is, what they're going through. Those are the great evenings of theater in my life. You think you've made the case for that and that it's finally established, and then you turn around and theater is the same old rubbish that it was forty years ago. The majority of theater is. And that is depressing because you have to reargue it every single time. I have to reargue it and that is exhausting. I'm exhausted by it.

Everyone acknowledges that what you've done is to paint the last half of the twentieth century in England as no one did. The personal lives and social issues, and that is universally acknowledged. Have you written a novel? Do you feel any pull in that direction?

None at all. It doesn't interest me as a form. I think you have far greater novelists in America than we have. And here it seems to chime with the way of life. Philip Roth said, "I knew to become a novelist because there was company I could keep. I was going to be writing in the same time as Saul Bellow and John Updike and all the rest of them. If I were British, I'd be a playwright. Because I'd like some company." It's a great observation, isn't it?

Everybody's talking today about Jonathan Franzen's novel Freedom. *He was on the cover of* Time *magazine.*

Well, it means my screenplay of his novel *The Corrections* may finally get made. I've written twenty-three drafts.

Did someone commission it?

Oh, yeah. It's been years. I admire the hell out of the book. I think it does what the British theater does, which is to tell you what's going on, what's happening in the society at the time. It's the record, isn't it?

It seems easier for a novel to get attention here than a play. There isn't a tradition of theatergoers here.

I think there's a confusion here about whether the theater is literature or entertainment, and that snobbery existed in England when I started. The

literary pages didn't talk about theater when I started. It was high literature, and the book pages would not be about playwrights. Playwrights,
we belonged with the jugglers and tumblers, the folk who blow into town
and entertain you. That's now blown away because the whole English
tradition of high literature is finished. But here, there is the confusion.
A critic in the *New York Times* is quoted as saying, "If the play has a title
with the word Guantanamo in it, I don't want to go and see it." And I
thought that if that same critic wrote that in the book pages of the *New
York Times*, the book editor would say, "I don't think this is a person who
should be working on the book pages, because they're not really interested in serious writing." So for theater here, the problem is the fight you
have to establish that it has an artistic validity.

*With a play, shouldn't it be judged on seeing the production and reading the
script?*

Pinter wrote resilient plays. They can be performed badly and still work.
Osborne's *Look Back in Anger*, however badly you do, it's indestructible.
My plays are not indestructible. They rely on good productions. They
have to be well done to work, or else there doesn't seem to be any point
to them at all.

They read well.

But they're difficult to *do* well. Whereas the wonderful thing about certain writers is it sort of doesn't matter. I mean, I didn't see *Enron* on
Broadway, but the play is a very, very good play. It really is a good play
but you know, by the time all the fiddle-faddle has gone on, whether that
helps a play or hinders a play, I don't know.

*A Map of the World is very detailed, very cinematic. You never thought to
do it as a film?*

Well, actually, a very strange thing happened to me in Knightsbridge
the other day. I thought it was a tramp who was asking for money. He
was yelling, "David! David!" He said, "You're David Hare, aren't you?"
I said, "Yes." I thought, "Oh my God." I was terrified, I'm going to be
assassinated. He said, "I've always wanted to say this to you: *A Map of the*

World should be a film." I said, "I'll bear it in mind." "It'll make a really good film, that play."

But then in Stuff Happens, *there was very little of that descriptive stage direction.*

Incidentally, I think it was criminal when it wasn't televised. No question. But I think descriptive stage direction was a phase I went through. And I think it was to do with the perfectionism in my mind, and I think probably not a good thing. I think I reached a point it was only a little toy theater in my mind. I was lucky enough to work with Irene Worth, who had been directed by Bernard Shaw. She was in a Bernard Shaw play, she knew Shaw, she had the best line any actor ever had. I said something like, "Do you find it odd with the author in the rehearsal room." She said, "Oh, no, Bernard Shaw was always in the rehearsal room, Noël was always in the rehearsal room, T. S. Eliot was always in the rehearsal room." I said, "OK, I'll join the queue." She said, "Shaw was more like a stage manager than a director, he simply moved the actor." I've directed *Heartbreak House,* and if you try to move the door not to the side of stage where he wants it, the play simply doesn't work. It's complete chaos. You have to literally do it in this little toy theater that he has in his mind. And I do think my plays did get overly prescriptive, and I think I have tried to open up. For instance with *The Power of Yes,* I just said I'm far too busy writing this in the time you've given me to write it to worry about how it's going to be staged. I just threw it at the director.

Who was the director?

Angus Jackson. He did a beautiful production. Gorgeous production. It looked like a Bill Viola projection is what it looked like. It was gorgeous. I left it to him. I said these are the scenes. He came back to me occasionally and said, "Can you do this? Can you do that? Change this, change that?"

Did you sit in on rehearsal?

Yes, I did sit in on rehearsal, but I left him to conceive the production entirely. It was Bob Crowley designing it, who I've worked with so many times. I was completely secure. Bob would look after me, so to speak.

Via Dolorosa *was a monologue. Why did you do that?*

Because when I came back from the occupied territory in Israel, I'd been sent to write a play about the Mandate period, and I found my time there so extraordinary I just wanted to tell everybody about it. So I said to Stephen Daldry, "I'm sorry, but it's gonna have to be a monologue, because that part of the world is not the way people think it is, and I've just got to tell them. And if I dramatize, falsity will arise. North London Jewish actors do not in any way resemble Israelis. Who's going to play the Palestinian? The one Pakistani actor we can find? Oh, there's an Egyptian actor that's not bad. And I see it. What, are they going to stand at different checkpoints? You know. Fake guns. Falsity will pour out of such a play. It will not resemble the reality. I can describe the reality. The problem is I'm going to have to do it myself."

Was it a big decision?

Oh, yeah. I said to Stephen, "You've got to teach me to act," because I'd never acted. And so he taught me to act. And a lot of time I felt he was sending me off. I said, "Are you actually preparing me to this? Do I really have to do all that? Are you planning that at the first preview I will just be mocked out of London for my absurdity?" Acting felt so horrible to me. I had a great moral problem with it. He said, "Every time you see Jerusalem, you must be deeply moved." I said, "But I'm not deeply moved." He said, "But you've got to pretend to be deeply moved," and I would say, "I find it really objectionable to be deeply moved when I'm not." He said, "It's called acting." I said, "All I can tell you about acting is that it feels horrible. Pretending to have a feeling you don't have feels horrible to me."

You couldn't find some imaginative moment to make you feel?

I used to go, "I'm now going to be deeply moved by Jerusalem. How does that look?" Stephen would say, "Fine. You're convincing me." I'd say, "Well, I'm not convincing myself." I was mystified by people who were convinced by my acting because it felt so hideous to me. There was a wonderful moment when Paul Newman came with Joanne Woodward. Paul Newman said to me, "You know what you remind me of? There's always a three-year-old at the party who wants to perform. You remind me of that three-year-old that gets up and says, 'I'm going to sing a song for you now.' He said it's kind of like acting, but it isn't really acting." I thought Newman put it perfectly. I didn't mind.

Did you learn anything that would help you direct an actor?

Definitely. Mostly the little things. When an actor had previously said to me, "I don't want the menu card to be there, I want it to be here," secretly, I'd be thinking this actor is so off himself. But actually when you do it, it becomes incredibly important whether the menu card is there or here. And you go, "I'm really unhappy with that menu card there, could it possibly be . . ." and now as an actor, I've done it. I understand completely what it is that makes it all comfortable. "Oh, I feel comfortable now the menu card's there." I totally get that.

Did you get acting offers?

Yes. I got lots of offers.

You turned them all down?

I did. I felt I shouldn't take work from proper actors. One of the things I turned down, Richard Jenkins played brilliantly. And I thought it would have been so stupid if I'd done it. I was offered a whole lot of parts. But then when they asked me to write a Bond movie, I said, "I don't want to write a Bond movie, but I'd be very interested in appearing in a Bond movie." But then they didn't take me seriously.

In terms of your success . . . has it influenced at all the way you write? How does it work at all in your life or your work?

The great thing about writing is that you're no further on today than you were. You have to start again every day. It's been very good for me as a way of life. In other words, I think that being at the mercy of the gift I am not able to exactly control was better for me than if I had gone into a profession where you could achieve things by will. I haven't minded being at the mercy of something which came and went. I've always accepted that you'd have good times and bad times when the gift was working for you, but it has felt like a gift, something over which I have no control, unlike directing or unlike all the practical arts in the theater.

When you come to the end of something you're writing, do you have the next thing in mind? Or do you work on more than one project when you sit down?

I can only work on one thing at a time. Other writers who work on fifteen things at the same time completely mystify me. When I'm on something, it becomes my whole life. There's a wonderful phrase from Richard Eyre, who directed a lot of my work. He says that I work out what the production is working up to a first night. The fax machine is on. Every morning he's getting pages and pages and pages: "I think I should change this," or "I'm not happy with that or change that" . . . or "You should do this." He said, "When the first night comes, you never hear another word except it's like dust you just hear coming down behind walls." And that's it. I just drive toward that and I never look at it again, or I never read them again. I really haven't read my plays. You drive them to a certain point and then . . .

Do you go see them again?

I've got to next year. There's going to be a festival of my work in Sheffield, so I'm going to have to see some plays I haven't seen in a long time, but I'm bullshitting the directors when they ask what did you mean in this scene. I don't remember. I haven't read them, so I don't know. I think there is one thing I wanted to say, which is that when you're working on something, you reach a tipping point, usually half or two-thirds of the way through, where it feels that it's always there, and your job is to uncover it. The feeling is that it already exists, and you've just got to move the sand off it, and if you move the sand off it, you'll find it buried under the sand. Because the idea has the destiny, and it's prewritten. All you have to do is sit very patiently, and you will find the way to the end. And it will be right. Once you've thrown it in the air, then it'll fall down in a certain arc, and that's a lovely feeling, it's a fabulous feeling. This will write itself now because you've got it up in the air, and the coming down will look after itself.

When does it happen?

Once you've got past halfway, and you feel the idea's going to get there, you just sit waiting for it to uncover itself correctly, and that's one of the pleasures of playwriting. It's a fabulous feeling.

Did you ever think of writing Plenty *as a screenplay first?*

I'd always been trying to make the stage have the freedom of film. People who say, oh, I write films for the stage, I don't really. I do want that freedom, and I find the life in the theater very exciting. I loved it in *Angels in America*. I love that kind of writing, you're with something for a bit then you collide with something next to it and you move to somewhere else. It's misunderstood. When it's done badly, it just seems bitty. And people think epic writing is just a lot of short scenes, but it isn't; it's deliberately abutting one thing with another and getting a change of color and tone by going from one to another, which Tony Kushner completely understands. When it's done well, it's so exhilarating. But it needs emotional continuity that is actually tying all those scenes together, but writers who don't understand that just write like television. Short scene, short scene, short scene.

How do you help the actor do that, since it's not a long scene they can build up to?

You have to explain. You have got to come in on a certain musical note that is the answer to the previous scene. And they find that frustrating at first. You say, "If you don't come in on that note, the music won't work." And that's what you were on about earlier, my plays are prescriptive about that. You've got to hit that, and if you hit that, you'll be fine.

When we interviewed Meryl Streep and asked how does an actor do these short little scenes without the continuity of a play, how do you keep it up? And she said it was just like doing short scenes in acting class.

But she has a fantastic sense, almost more than any actor I've worked with, of the architecture of the part. She's the master of, "Oh, I can hold off for a long time and now I get it." She understands because she spent her whole life doing it. The two films I've worked on with her she's been absolutely clear: this is the bit where I have to reveal what it is I'm feeling, and this is where I go somewhere else. Help me do this, I need this or I need that. And when you say do I change things, well you're crazy not to change for her, particularly on a movie. You're watching her do something, you'll go, she's inspiring. So you go, oh, well, if you can do that, I'll give you this, so you're working off of that. She's very high level.

You've written extraordinary roles for women. What is it about a female that has you give them the fullest arc, the fullest roles, the people who go through the most change that influence the world?

I don't know the answer to this question. The play that I've just written has made me think differently about this. So I'm nervous of saying what I think I know—that because I am not a woman I find the business of imagining what it's like to be a woman initially very exciting. Because I'm not an autobiographical writer in a classic way, I don't write about the problems of a playwright in Hampstead. Although I am a playwright with problems in Hampstead, the act of imagining what you cannot be is the beginning of the excitement of art to me. So gender is the most obvious leap for me. Just as Chinese peasants were in *Fanshen* or settlers in Israel. I get stimulated by the act of imagination. But also I am, in my life, romantic about women, so that it means that it's been exciting to me to imagine women's arc.

Would it have been true twenty years ago? After Plenty?

Oh, I would have had a whole lot of political bullshit about how feminism was the great political movement of my time, and you know there was this incredible resource of great actresses who were not being used, and it's meant that I've had incredible actresses in my work. Every great actor who is a woman is underused. Except Meryl. Every great actor who is a woman is underused. That's just a fact of the actress's life. So you have this incredible pleasant time because everyone is so grateful, whereas the men are never grateful because the men are all spoiled.

There's a line in Zoo Story *that I thought applied to this. Albee writes, "Sometimes you have to go a long distance out of the way in order to come back a short distance correctly."*

You mean writing about women?

Or any of the settlers in Israel. To imagine going very far away in order to tell a truth.

Yes. It's exciting. It's stimulating. You don't really want to write about yourself. Or I don't want to write about myself. I want to write about other people. I'm much more curious about other people than I am about myself. I'm bored stiff by myself because I've lived with my own thoughts for so long. They bore me stiff. I wouldn't wish to put them on the stage. I found it very frustrating writing about banking because there weren't any women in banking. There simply were no women. We eventually had twenty-four actors onstage and one woman. We could not get women in the story because they aren't part of the story.

They are part of the story in America.

There are more in America. And a guy who ran one of the biggest banks in England said we are just the most reactionary businessmen.

Just to talk about Plenty *a bit. It wasn't told chronologically. Have you done that again?*

Yeah. Rory Dempster, who lit *Plenty* originally, said, "Oh, I never bother to read the first scene of David's plays. It's always the last." It's true. I can't remember, I got terribly excited about the idea of the flashback, and the hilarious thing was that when I wrote it, Harold Pinter came running into the theater in panic, into Peter Hall's office, and said, "I hear David's written a play that goes backwards." He was writing *Betrayal* at the time. He was in total panic. I said, "Mine doesn't actually go backwards. It starts at the end and ends at the beginning, but otherwise the scenes are written in the right order." He went, "Oh, thank God." What I felt in those days was the arc of somebody's life. Of course, now I would regard that as completely ridiculous, because she's only forty-two, and there's a lot more life. But to me it seemed the arc of a whole life because I was such a fathead who disregarded human life after forty. *Plenty* was the play to which my life led and from which my life led away. It remains that. Nothing I've ever done has had that centrality in my life. It was what I wanted to do, and there it was exactly as I wanted it.

The critics didn't love it.

They didn't know. Peter Hall was really great to me. He was fantastic. We had a really disastrous reception. Peter Hall just said to me that the board said to him, he had to take it off, and he said if we cannot put on work that we believe in, in spite of the fact the critics don't believe in it, there is no point in the National Theatre. And so he said, "I'm going to put it on Fridays and Saturdays, which are good theater nights. And I'll just play it twice a week." We did Friday, Saturday matinees and Saturday evenings. Got a good audience and then word of mouth. And after about three months, it was full, and it was entirely by word of mouth, it was entirely the audience, and then it began to get standing ovations, which in England you never got. It established itself. And that meant that I've never been dependent on the critics, and the critics know I can get an audience without them. Which has been both a good thing and bad thing. In other words, they've resented that they have no power. The audience will come to my work and have come to my work many, many times in spite of the critics, and so that's been a great thing, but it's been a curse and a blessing.

You've also had a life as a playwright on this side of the Atlantic, which is rather rare.

A producer here was talking to me the other day that they fear that the life I have led, that Tom Stoppard has led, not only producing a play every eighteen months or two years, whatever it may be, or writing a play being performed, moving to film when we wanted to, or moving to television when we wanted to—that that kind of life in the performing arts is not going to be possible. And I know young writers who say to me, "I don't see how we are going to be able to do this." I know Polly Stenham feels it. I know Lucy Prebble feels it, who I think are the very brilliant young English writers. They feel, "We cannot do what your generation did. It won't be possible." And here almost nobody's done it.

David Mamet's done it.

Mamet's moved between the three media, and he's regularly staged a play. But that model of a playwright—Arthur Miller or behind Miller was Inge—are now not so well remembered. We're particularly now threatened by government cuts. A conservative government which is starting the whole business again about subsidy to the arts. Discussions we thought were long dead. A number of us have been saying to each other how lucky we were to have been at a time where we could do our work. The failings of our work are entirely our failings. I personally feel near the end that everything I've failed to do is entirely my own fault. I've been given every possible opportunity. I've never ever felt that it was through lack of opportunity that I failed. I feel it's entirely my own fault. And so that's an incredible thing to be able to say. I've always had producers, I've always had actors, I've always had directors, I've never had a problem getting a play on. If it's gone wrong, it's because there's something wrong with the play, so that's a remarkable thing to be able to say.

Was there something wrong with the play or did you feel you were not being understood?

There's a wonderful wonderful, wonderful letter from Chekhov to his nephew. Chekhov's nephew wanted to take up playwriting, do you know this? And he wrote this letter to his uncle, saying, "I'm not understood." I wouldn't send a letter to Chekhov saying I'm not understood. I think that was a brave thing to do. And Chekhov said, "A writer can never complain about that. If you're not understood, make yourself understood. Or you may not want to be understood. I've written some plays knowing in advance that they won't be understood." I think he meant *The Seagull.* I think he meant when he wrote *The Seagull,* he knew nobody would understand it. But he wanted it at that level that he wanted it at. He said, "A writer can never say he doesn't feel understood. It's a writer's job to be understood."

Do you think the audience is always right?

No, because I've seen too many different kinds of audience. But you're crazy not to listen to the audience. You're crazy not to take note. I mean when *Plenty* was revived with Cate Blanchett, in London, the scene in which she goes to a young man and asks him to inseminate her to have a baby caused so much offense, and the people were walking out, young men were conspicuously getting their mobile phones out, it was very depressing. And Cate Blanchett used to say to me, "I can't believe how much I scared people and how terrified they were."

You've always been very outspoken about critics. What would you advise young writers about dealing with critics?

Finally, they're what you've got to deal with.

Do you think they held your outspokenness against you in subsequent plays?

I don't want to discuss that. You must do what you want. There isn't a correct way to proceed, is there? I mean, I personally found Harold Pinter's sense of grievance ridiculous. In other words, toward the end of his life, Harold was still complaining about what was written about him. And you sort of wanted to say, "Well, you've won the Nobel Prize. You're also the only playwright I know whose life has ended well." Tennessee obviously . . . that was a terrible end. Tennessee was really in despair. If Tennessee saw how he was received now and treated, it's just a joke. Every time I read of another revival, I just go, well . . . Tennessee's only subject of conversation was his neglect, how nobody liked his work. How unpopular he was. He just went on and on and on how the world hated him and passed him by. That's how he died. John Osborne died like that. He said to me, "It made no difference. It would've been better if I'd never lived." It has been pointed out that most playwrights end badly. Moliere. You can go through the list. Arthur Miller lived long enough to see himself come back in fashion, though never in New York. Never really.

There was a pretty great production of Death of a Salesman *maybe ten years ago.*

Arthur lived long enough, but he saw the cycle of fashion really turn against him and back toward him. So it seemed more ridiculous that Harold—more or less the only playwright I know who has gone out with general applauding. I used to think, "Do you have any idea how lucky you are?"

NILO CRUZ

It was raining hard the morning we interviewed Nilo Cruz. He arrived at Barry's apartment wearing a leather jacket, carrying a tiny umbrella and a small paper bag, the contents of which he kept secret, and a hat which he kept on during the interview. Nilo lives in Miami, and we happened to catch him on one of the few days he was in New York to attend a New Dramatists luncheon. He's tanned and handsome, with a small mustache and goatee. During the interview he often addressed each of us directly, reaching across the table to make a point. His body, as much as his words, conveyed the passion he feels for his work.

In preparation, as we do with all the playwrights, we reacquaint ourselves with your work. We feel like we're rediscovering them.

Thank you . . . Everything seems to be *Anna in the Tropics* and that's it. It's like I never wrote anything before that or after that.

We think your plays are very different from those of any other writer whom we talked to. Your plays just seem romantic in the best way. The language was lyrical without being "poetic." Is that a Latin sense, or is that you, Nilo Cruz?

I think it's both. I think it's a Latin sensibility. But I'm also very much inspired by the music that comes from my country, especially the romantic boleros. Not that when I sit to write a play I listen to boleros. But I think it's part of my DNA, it's part of my upbringing. I grew up in a house where this is the kind of music my parents used to listen to. This is the kind of music I would even hear in my neighborhood. I think that sort of romanticism is part of the culture.

Is it the music of the middle class? Is it high music? Is it popular music?

I think that it is the music of the people. It is the equivalent of fados in Portugal—the equivalent would be ballads in this country. So in Cuba we have boleros, which are songs of the heart. I'm interested in—for lack of a better word—in love and expressing that through my plays. I love love stories. I think it's important to see a good love story.

But they're very hard to write without being sentimental or wrapping things up in some kind of neat way that makes people go, "Aww." Whereas A Bicycle Country *is very romantic and it's even joyful, but it's not happy.*

No, it's not happy.

And others. The Color of Desire.

That's brand new. I'm still even exploring that. It's interesting because I'm doing a translation of *The Color of Desire* right now into the Spanish language. What's so curious about doing the translation is that it's allowing me to enter the play again and to even edit the play a little bit. So when I'm looking at the scenes and looking at the dialogue, thinking, "Is this really what this character is saying at the moment? Do I need this line?" I've been able to edit a few things from the play through the process of translation.

Did you always write directly in English when you wrote? How did that start?

It's a curious thing with me. I do write in English because I did educate myself in this country, even though I was ten years old when I came here.

Did you know any English?

I did not, no. I don't know if you've noticed, but I still have an accent. It's not major, it's not very pronounced, but I do have . . .

You came here at ten. So in Cuba, your influences were the bolero, the music? Did you go to plays?

I did go see a couple plays when I was in Cuba. But more than anything it was cabaret. Even at that age, what happens is that there's an age difference between—I'm the youngest in my family. My two sisters were teenagers when I was nine, eight years old. So they were going out with their boyfriends. And the family sometimes would go to a retreat, a beach retreat, resort. And cabaret is very big in Cuba, as we all know, from the fifties. So one of my first experiences with the performing arts was through cabaret. All the family had gone to this resort; no one wanted to stay home with me, including my grandmother. So basically, my father knew the owner of the restaurant, and he says, "You know what, we'll take him tonight. He's eight, he's nine, he can see one of these shows." They snuck me in through the kitchen, and, basically, I came into the restaurant, they put me underneath the table. Then when the show started, you know, I kind of lifted the tablecloth and started to see this show. By that time, the waiter had seen me and said, "Oh, he can stay." So basically, in terms of the performing arts, the first thing that I saw was, you know, burlesque comedic sketches. Plus a lot of flesh, but no stripping and really wonderful, electrifying Cuban music. It really made an impression on me. The show also has sketches and comedians. Then, of course, there were some boleros that were being sung. That was my introduction to the performing arts. Of course, when I came home after seeing this—experiencing this—I wanted to re-create what I had seen on the stage with all my friends in the neighborhood. So that was sort of my way into the world of theater. And also my sister was dating a musician, so I was a chaperone in the family, and I used to sort of go out with her . . . I grew up in a world of music.

What is it about Cuban music that is so from the heart? I haven't been to Cuba, but I've been to Mexico, and Mexican music doesn't seem like that. It seems a little harder, a little more dramatic.

It's probably because it's a mixture of the Spanish with the African, especially because a large immigration that came to Cuba was from the south of Spain where you have flamenco. Flamenco is music of the heart. It's influenced by northern Africa, all this lament. So basically, you mix that with the drumming of the Africans that came to Cuba, and you have Cuban music.

So how did you get here?

The States or New York?

Let's say the States first.

Well, my father had tried to leave the country in the early sixties. We were pro-Castro at the beginning, when Castro came into power. Then my family got disenchanted with the regime, and my father tried leaving the country. He got caught leaving the country illegally, and he was imprisoned for two years. So basically I didn't get to know my father for the first two years of my life. When he was out of prison, he was sort of a marked man. They knew that he was against the system. My family made the decision that they still wanted to leave the country. It took us eight years to leave the country. It wasn't just because my father was disenchanted with the regime—my father was also afraid that I would turn military age and then maybe be transferred to another country like Russia or Czechoslovakia, because that was what was happening. My family was trying as much as they could to leave the country, whether it was through Spain—and we had relatives in Spain, we also had relatives in the United States. You need to have somebody to claim you to come to this country or to Spain. But we came to Miami legally—on an airplane, not on a raft.

Did you become a little American boy?

Did I become a little American boy? Well, the phenomenon is that Miami, by that time, there were a lot of Cubans in exile. So when I went to elementary school, of course, I first started with the ESL classes full of Hispanic kids. But even as a child, I realized I had to get out of ESL. I really wanted to integrate, I wanted to be American. I wanted to be with the American kids because—I don't know—it seemed the right thing to do. When I was in school, I made sure that every time I needed to use the restroom that I told my teacher, "I need to go to the restroom," in English instead of Spanish. So she knew, "Oh, this kid is learning, so we better transfer him to another class." I knew that when I was transferred to another class, then I would pick up the language in a better way, much faster than being with Hispanic kids.

When did you start to think of yourself as a writer? Or when did you start to write things?

I did start, even at that early age, even at ten years old, I did start writing poems. I wanted to be close to books at that early age. As a matter of fact, I volunteered to work at the library to be close to books, to discover authors. I thought that would be the way to do it, shelving books.

Were there books in your home? Were your parents readers?

In Cuba, yes. But in the United States—you remember, you leave the country with nothing. You can't take anything with you. By the time my parents came to the United States, they were living the life of an exile, which is all about work and trying to make a living.

Did they speak English?

No, they did not. And they actually never learned to speak English. Just basic language. Because they stayed living in Little Havana. My father worked at a shoe store, and my mother worked at a purse factory. So basically the employees of the factory spoke Spanish, and if you needed to speak to someone that was non-Spanish speaking, you would have somebody to translate for you. And you imagine, you spend hours working, it's hard to go home and pick up a book.

Do your parents figure in your plays?

Ah, yes. There's a play of mine called *A Park in Our House*, in which there are aspects of my family in that play, especially my mother.

So you started to write poems, you were ten. When you first came here.

Mm-hmm.

Did that move into any other form?

Ah . . . I was intrigued by theater. I remember when I was in junior high school, I remember reading Shakespeare and loving Shakespeare. I think it was the first time I made a connection with my classes. Taking math classes, what do I need math for? But when we started reading Shakespeare, there was something about that language, which just did something for me. Even before that, I had discovered a poem by Emily Dickinson at the library at the school. I was completely taken by her work, especially this poem.

Which poem was that?

Oh, I do not remember. It was a borrowed book from the library, and I don't remember what it was . . . You know prior to that, we have a wonderful poet and a politician in Cuba in the 1800s, who was an emissary, who lived actually here in New York, but he translated Emerson and Walt Whitman. So he really was an emissary for North American literature . . . José Martí. We in Cuba, of course, growing up in school, we knew some of his children's stories, some of his poems. So he was one that was also inspirational as a kid.

Did you think of it as something that you could do?

Not until much later, when I discovered the Emily Dickinson poem. That's what I said: "Ah, this is what I want to do. I want to write. I want to write like this."

How old were you?

I think I was in elementary school. I must have been eleven years old.

So how did you . . .

How did I make my way to the theater?

Yes, that's the question.

Well, I did take some theater classes when I was in high school. But I wasn't serious about it. It wasn't until much later when I was, say, in my early twenties, and I was working in a hospital. I sort of had this epiphany to go to the theater. I said, "I must go to the theater this evening." I didn't know what I was going to see.

Were you in Miami?

I was in Miami. During that time, we had the Coconut Grove Playhouse, which no longer exists, unfortunately. I thought, "I'm just going to go to the theater, I'm going to buy myself a ticket and I'm going to go see a play." I did go see a play. I saw *The Dresser* that evening, and I loved the production, I loved the piece. I was so inspired by that piece that I said, "I must start taking theater classes." I didn't know in what capacity I was going to be part of the theater, whether I was going to be an actor, a writer, or a director. But I knew I wanted to take theater classes. And, of course, when I started the classes with this teacher, which is really interesting because she was teaching a noncredited class because she really wanted students in her classroom that were committed to the art form, not someone who just wanted the credit. I started taking classes with her. This was at Miami Dade College. In class, instead of bringing in a scene from Lorca or Chekhov, I would write my own scenes, and I would direct them. I would use the students in class, and then that's when the professor said, "You're a writer. You need to continue writing."

Was it a revelation when she said that?

It was. Actually, she said that not only was I a writer, but that I should be a director. She gave me the opportunity to direct, and I directed a play by Reinaldo Arenas, the Cuban writer. *Before Night Falls.* It was actually the world premiere of his piece in Miami. It went really well, it was very much liked by the community.

In Spanish?

In Spanish, yeah. Because her theater class was in Spanish. I started really doing Hispanic theater in Miami. This professor of mine really wanted to honor the Spanish language and honor Spanish.

So was that a choice of yours to go from The Dresser *to take theater classes in Spanish?*

Well, I knew of her. I knew she was an excellent teacher through a friend of mine who was an actor taking her class. I actually had visited her class once before, but I thought it was a very difficult class, and I wasn't prepared for it. But now I felt it was the right time for me to be part of her class. So we did theater in Spanish.

If you knew of a teacher who ran a theater class in English, would that have interested you, or did the Spanish?

It was the teacher. There was something about her. She was magical . . . Teresa María Rojas. She was magical. But by that time, I was infected by theater. I wanted to be part of the theater world. I started taking credited classes with another professor of mine who was very good too, Patricia Gross, at the same school. She started to form a theater company called South and Alternative Theater. She brought María Irene Fornés to do a workshop in Miami. By that time, this professor of mine, Patricia, asked me to direct a play for her company. I directed my teacher in *Mud*. It had really good reviews. She invited María Irene to come see the production and to do a workshop. I took a workshop with Irene, and Irene liked very much what I had written in class, and at that time she was running INTAR Lab on Fifty-Second. She asked me if I wanted to be part of her lab. But I had to make my decision right away because the lab was starting on Monday, and I had met Irene on Friday. And I had to move to New York immediately. I didn't even have money to move to New York. Thank God I had a friend in New York. I called her up and asked her if I could crash in her living room, and she said yes. I got some money, I had a little bit of money, I think I probably asked my parents for some money, and I came to New York, and I started to study with María Irene Fornés. I was twenty-eight by that time.

Did she ask that you start writing in English?

No, but everybody was writing in English in her classroom. To be honest with you, before I came to New York, I had also really wanted to move into North American theater. I really felt it was important.

For the same reason that you made your teacher aware that you spoke English?

Absolutely. I knew that if I just stayed doing Hispanic theater in Miami that I would be limited to just one particular kind of audience. I just wanted to do—I was interested in North American theater too. María Irene Fornés was very important to me because María Irene Fornés is Cuban. She came to this country in the forties or something, late forties or fifties. And I thought, "If there is this woman who is Cuban and is writing in English and is well known, especially here in New York, off-Broadway, I can possibly do this too." So she was an inspiration. But her language, what she was doing with style and everything, was really inspirational for me. So when she gave me the opportunity, gosh, immediately, I said, "I have to do this." I basically quit everything and came to New York to study with her.

Did you make any money?

Let me tell you, yes. The experience of having worked at a hospital was very helpful, because when I moved here, I worked for someone. I was like a nurse for a woman who was quadriplegic. So I was sort of like a physical therapist, nurse. And so I helped her in the house, I helped her. But INTAR had funds from the Lila Wallace Foundation, so we got paid to also write. So I got a little bit of money from INTAR and a little bit of money working for this lady. That's basically how I survived the city.

So now you're in New York, you're writing in English, now you're with all the other playwrights.

All the playwrights that really want to write about Latino characters, but in the English language. All the other people around me, Caridad Svich, Migdalia Cruz. Many of us. It was incredible.

How long was this?

Three years.

Did you get any plays done during that time?

No, I did not. I wrote a play called *Not Yet Forgotten.* I don't even know where it is, I don't even know if it exists anymore. Then I wrote a play called *Graffiti,* and then I wrote another piece, which was not even about Latinos. It took place in Italy. I was really inspired by Italy. I had gone to Italy before coming to New York. Then when I was studying with Irene, Paula Vogel asked Irene if she had any participants in the lab who wanted to go back to school. I told Irene that I did want to go back to school, that I wanted to continue to take writing classes, that I wanted to take more directing classes, etc. So Irene suggested for me to apply to Brown University, to meet with Paula. I met with Paula and I got accepted to Brown.

Did you do a full-year thing at Brown?

Two years. I only concentrated on playwriting. I took other classes, the-ater history classes, that sort of thing, but it was a lot. Being in the work-shop as a graduate student was a lot of work.

When you write, do you just feel informed by the history of your people? Does that always fill your mind?

Yes, in many ways . . .

Do you start from there?

I do go back there quite often, whether it's my childhood in Cuba or whether it's my upbringing in Miami. But I'm also inspired by other things. For instance, I wrote a play called *Night Train to Bolina,* which takes place in Central America. I was heavily inspired by an autobiogra-phy that I had read of Rigoberta Menchú, who is from Guatemala, and she won the Nobel Prize for peace. I was very inspired by her life. I didn't write a piece about her life but wrote about the struggles of children in

Latin America and the guerilla warfare of the eighties. It's not set in any specific country, just somewhere in Latin America. So, yes, I draw from my life, but I'm also inspired by things that come my way.

So Lorca . . .

Is definitely an inspiration because I discovered Lorca when I was studying with Teresa María Rojas in Miami. I was inspired by Lorca's work. I actually did a couple of exercises that had to do with Lorca's work . . .

Well, it seemed very daring, really, to bring him onstage as a character and have him speak and have this famous poet speak in Beauty of the Father.

It was brave . . . I was very inspired. I did a translation with Karin Coonrod that was commissioned by the Public Theater. We did a translation of Lorca's *The House of Bernarda Alba.* Of course, I really started to immerse myself, not just in *Bernarda Alba,* but in his other plays and also his life. When I started to do research about his death and how he was killed, I thought, "I have to write about this." And also because a friend of mine, a Spanish friend of mine who lived in Miami and was a student at the school with Teresa María Rojas, said to me that when she was in Spain, they didn't teach Lorca. During Franco's regime. I thought to myself, "Oh, Lord. I have to write . . ." Mind you, by that time, Franco was out of power. But still, I felt like I had to write about it. That's when I decided to write *Lorca in a Green Dress.* Then I went to Spain. You know, I went to Spain to write *Lorca in a Green Dress* through a Lippman Award, which you get through New Dramatists. So I went to Spain and stayed with my friend Maria. You know what's interesting when I went to Spain, I had started to write *Lorca in a Green Dress.* Then out of the blue, my Spanish friend I was telling you about, who told me Lorca was not taught in school, out of the blue, I hadn't spoken to her in years, she calls me up and says, "I'm not living in San Sebastian, northern Spain, I'm living in Grenada, in the south. Why don't you come to visit me?" I said, "I just got money to go to Spain, I would love to go visit you!" And there I finished writing *Lorca in a Green Dress* and got inspired. I wasn't finished with *Lorca* yet, and it was really curious, because I got in touch with this biographer Ed Gibson, and he said, "Wasn't writing about Lorca, wasn't he like a magnet?" He's written about Dalí, he's written about Buñuel, but he said, "But Lorca. There's something about him. I couldn't let go of him." I said, "That's happening to me!"

So you have your inspiration, you have something in mind, and you go to your desk. What happens there? Do you have a schedule?

I write every day. I try to write in the morning. And usually, I don't write an outline of my plays. I never understood outlines, to be honest with you. I don't understand writing it down, you don't even know what you're going to write about. It doesn't make any sense to me. But I start with characters, more than anything. For instance, when I was writing the piece *Night Train to Bolena,* I was interested in the children. I started to write, just try to imagine children in Latin America, and thought of my own life too, as a child. That's how I started to create the characters.

You hear them? Are they speaking in English or Spanish?

No. It's a really fast translation. They feel in Spanish, they think in Spanish, but they speak in English.

That's connected in you.

It's connected in me. Because I live in two cultures. I came very young to this country, but when I speak, I speak very much like a Cuban person, but I was educated in this country more than anything.

So you start with scattered characters, and how does it become a play?

Well, I write a series of scenes. Then I look at all the scenes, and then I start sculpting the play. To me, writing is like sketching. You don't enter the canvas immediately—you do a series of sketches. Picasso did hundreds of sketches before he started *Guernica.* So I do the same thing, just to find out about my characters. Some of those scenes make it to the play, some of them don't. So it is a process of search, doing a little bit of research about their lives through actually writing scenes and finding out about them. Again, some of them make it to the play and some of them don't.

Is there a moment when you go, "Ah, now I see where this is going"?

Yes, absolutely. Through the process.

Do you see the end?

Not until much later. Sometimes the end has come early, and I have an idea what the end is. But I also try to trick myself not to go there until I arrive at that moment.

So you never have an end and think, "How do I get there?"

No.

So it's very organic?

It's very organic. It's really the long way. It's almost like Red Riding Hood.

You write until you have a draft, then what do you do? Leave it for a while? Have somebody else read it?

I don't have people read my work. I have actors read my work. Because I need to listen to it before I get feedback from other people. Certainly, I get feedback from producers at the theater.

But before you bring it to a theater . . .

No, I don't. There's a lot of writers that do that, but I've never done that. I don't show my work to another writer or someone whom I respect . . .

So the first time you hear it, it's actors.

For instance, when I was in graduate school, it was with playwrights who'd read it out loud and I would hear it. Of course, you would get feedback immediately. But when I'm on my own as a writer, I just come up with a draft. Then I bring a couple of writers, whether it's New Dramatists or at a theater, The Public Theater, and I do a reading to hear it. Of course, I get feedback from producers, that's sort of thing.

So what might you hear when they read it to you? What are you listening for?

Well, I'm listening to the rhythms of the piece more than anything. How the dialogue is operating. If the rhythm is dynamic. Or if the scenes have the same tempo, and then I need to do something about that. First of all of the rhythms, then, of course, I'm listening to storyline. I think that's what I do. It's one thing when I sit around the table with a group of actors, it's something else when I hear the actual reading, which I think is good because then I have a little more separation, and then I can sort of see . . . Because when you're around the table, you're almost like in the play. But when you have a little more space, and it's actually being presented, you have a little more space, you can see, you can be a little more objective.

What kind of notes do you get from these readings?

I have gotten feedback from producers and dramaturgs about my play. I take into consideration the notes, some of them, what I feel works, other things I just put them aside.

You feel secure with that? You don't feel vulnerable? Because some writers have a hard time with it, and they just kind of try to please everybody. Do you feel, "Oh, that's not right, but this is"?

Absolutely. Also, for instance, with a piece like *Lorca in a Green Dress,* it's a very complex play because it's sort of surreal. If you think of dramaturgy in North America, which is so realistic and so literal sometimes, sometimes what theaters—especially dramaturgs—ask for is more information, which sometimes can really weigh down a play. There's only so much information a play can have. If you start putting in so much information, it becomes something completely different, it doesn't sing. So then, yes, you get information for an audience that maybe doesn't know about the circumstances about someone like Lorca, but the play does. So, yes, you're serving this person, but at the same time, you're not serving the art form. I feel like as a writer, you have to take commentaries with a grain of salt.

Do you find it difficult to find people who can enter your play and talk about it?

I have a really, really difficult time with dramaturgy sometimes in this country, because I write about other cultures. I write about a culture that is very difficult, it is very foreign to a North American. A lot of people don't know about what's happening. I don't mean to underestimate an American audience, nor American producers or people in the theater. But usually my plays take place in other countries, like in Spain or in Latin America, some of them here too. But, for instance, *Anna in the Tropics*, nobody knew about Tampa, Florida, and the cigar industry there. So I had to have a certain amount of exposition in the play, but I couldn't overwhelm the piece. As it is, the play has a lot of exposition. You know, even sometimes, I have to make choices as an artist, as a writer. I think maybe my plays could've been a little more experimental if I wasn't writing about other cultures. But as it is, it's unfamiliar territory. Imagine if I made it more experimental. It would be completely unfamiliar territory. So I had to make choices sometimes. Yes, I can be experimental with form, but not too much. It's already unfamiliar material.

In the early days, you brought your plays to the Public. Where else?

Well, you know where I really started—I started with the Magic Theater in San Francisco. I started through the Bay Area Festival. That's where my plays were first read and then got picked up by the Magic Theater. Then Morgan Jenness came to the Bay Area Festival at the Magic Theater, saw my work, then came to The Public Theater and told George and Rosemarie about me. And that's why I came to New York.

Now who do you show your work to? Or do you work on commission? Or both?

Listen, I was very lucky. When I got out of graduate school, I went to the Bay Area Festival. It was very helpful, when you spend two or three days with a group of actors and a director and you can really explore the material and see how the play is operating. You can go back and do a little bit of rewriting: "This is not working, well, here, let me do a little bit of re-writing before the rehearsal tomorrow." So that was very helpful for me. I really do like working with actors and a director. Or sometimes I direct the play with actors, just to hear it, just to see how the play is operating. That's helpful for me to then go into the second phase.

So Bay Area was very helpful for you, to work without the big stakes of a New York opening. Can you still do that? Has that changed?

Yes, I still do that. It's very helpful for me. You know, it's nerve-wracking because you feel extremely vulnerable. It's a new piece, you don't even know how it really operates on the stage. So then I go to readings of my play, especially when I invite an audience, which is very helpful too because you can feel the presence of the audience in the room and whether the audience really has made a connection with the play, which is very helpful for me also as a writer.

Do you do that more in Miami now?

No, I haven't found a place in Miami that does that kind of work. Un-fortunately, Miami is lacking in terms of script development. Not a bad thing, not a good thing because I find that the rest of America is over-developing plays.

You still come here to New York?

I come here. And I'm lucky. For instance, with *The Color of Desire*, I did a reading at the Manhattan Theatre Club, I did a reading of The Public Theater, I did a reading at O'Neill. That play has taken me a couple years to write, fifteen drafts. Every time I do a reading, every time I do a presentation, I learn more and more about the piece.

So is it that you learn, "Oh, that doesn't work, take out that line because the rhythm is wrong," or is it that you see an opening into something that needs to come out more?

That too. I realize that I perhaps need to write another scene or I perhaps need to expand a little bit more a section of the piece.

Or do you go into it, hoping this is it?

You're always hoping this is it, and you don't have to do any more work. I'm always hoping, but that's not the case.

So in rehearsal when you're not directing, what kind of director do you like working with?

I'll tell you something that I . . . I've sort of been a little disappointed in directors in this country. I mean, there're great directors here. But I don't really like—I'm really after a theater that doesn't just deal with the actual texts that I brought in. But really with a director that really deals with images too, that takes the play to another level. Because a play can only do so much through dialogue. We have to remember that theater takes place in the third dimension, and we have to take into consideration the visual aspect of the play. I found a few directors here and there, but I really want a director that just goes between the words and really brings also an image. Because I really think images are important for the theater. Because I do write images.

Have you found a difference in London?

In some ways.

Because the designer seems more important in London. They get second billing . . .

In some ways. You know, I just did a play in Paris, and I worked with a director who was very visual. Very pared down, but very visual . . . I think it's a combination of creating an atmosphere—because my plays are very atmospheric—but you really have to create images. For instance, right now, I'm about to direct one of my plays, *Night Train to Bolena,* and I'm thinking, it's a very particular play because the beginning of the piece, it only starts with two characters, then I add other characters. And I thought, "Wow, if I were to direct this play, what if I start this piece with some of these other characters and try to create a visual narrative for them, even though there is no written language?" The audience might be wondering, "Who are these people? They haven't even spoken yet, but I see them." And try to create a narrative, a past history only visually. In between the scenes. Or at the beginning of the play too.

Would you feel free to let a director do that, even though you hadn't necessarily been thinking that way?

That's a really good commentary, Rosemarie, because I tell you, I think at the beginning, when I just finish a play, I'm still so caught up with being a playwright, wearing the playwright's cap, and with the specific world, that these ideas don't come to mind yet. We're not allowed to direct our own plays in this country, and I think it's really unfortunate.

I think maybe you should direct your own plays because they come from a different culture than most directors in America are familiar with. And you were brought up directing. But you also know the dangers of directing your own work.

Absolutely. And I agree. And there's dangers to that too. I realize there's dangers. But listen, every director is always directing around the play. If you have an actor who really doesn't get the character well enough, you have to direct the play around that character. You have to make choices with that actor. If you have an actor that really doesn't get the role and has certain visions of the role, sometimes you have to direct around that actor. I was directing *Anna in the Tropics* in Spain, and I'm the writer, and I was the director of the piece, and I was working with a very important actress, and we didn't meet eye to eye on a particular role. And she said, "No, I don't see it that way."

And what did you say?

I had to respect it.

Was there no way you could . . .

I tried to direct her a certain way, where she would meet me halfway, and she did meet me halfway, but . . .

Was she right at all?

It was an interpretation of the piece.

That you didn't agree with?

I didn't disagree with it. It's one way of looking at the role. I might be contradicting myself, but not really. Because theater is about interpretation and what an actor and what a director brings to a piece too. So this was one interpretation of the role, you know. It was not my ideal role, but you've gotta be open to that. I'm open to it every time I work with a director and a group of actors. I have to be open to that interpretation. I'm not one of those hysterical playwrights that come and say, "This is not what I intended to do." It's one rendition of the piece.

I noticed this particularly when I saw Beauty of the Father *at the Manhattan Theatre Club—that the play was taking place in Spain and the people were Spanish and speaking English with Spanish accents. Does this often happen to your plays?*

That was a directorial choice. Michael Greif felt that he always wanted to be reminding the audience that this was not America, that the passion of these people, that this kind of behavior is not a behavior that you see in this country. This kind of love that these people feel for each other, according to Michael, you would never see in this country. This is a particular group of people that have nothing to do with the United States. And he always wanted the actors to use an accent to remind people that this was not happening here. Now I tell you what I like. It's not an accent. I like inflections. For the actors to use certain inflections that capture the flavor. If you notice, I have a slight accent, but really my inflections are Latin more than anything. So I like that instead of an accent.

Did you say that to him?

I did say that to him, but he felt that it was important to have an accent.

Were they Spain Spanish accents?

Well, the problem was we had one actor who really didn't know, the accent was completely wrong. He was not even a Hispanic actor, he was an English actor, and he just couldn't get the accent right. You could really tell. It's very hard to get . . . without falling into a stereotype . . . I did have problems with that production.

So if a situation like you had with this actress in Spain happens in a rehearsal period in New York, and you're not the director, how do you manage to work with a director?

Well, the good thing about theater in this country, one of the good things, is that the playwright—I mean, we are playwright-oriented theater in this country, unlike Latin America. Latin America is more director-oriented. But here in this country, we do have a say, especially in the beginning, when the play is being discussed around the table. We talk about the play, and the actors listen, and there have been cases, like you're saying, you disagree on something . . . I mean, actors don't usually tell you what they're going to do, they do it. Of course, you try to speak with the director and say, "Is there any way you can bring this actor to do something different?" You try as much as you can, but then, you also have to be open to interpretation . . .

Have you ever written for a particular actor?

Yes, I wrote for an actor at the Asolo Theatre. It was a commission in Sarasota, Florida, for the Ringling International Arts Festival. I wrote for an English actor there who's really brilliant with language, and I thought that I should write a role for him. It was spectacular. It's my new play called *Hurricane*. It's really interesting because it's a mix . . . He's European. The actress who played the wife was African American, and the boy was Latino. It was really great. And I thought, "Oh, God, this is the future of theater, especially in this country." I thought it was really good for me. It was a departure for my work. I've been writing more about Latino characters, and here I was writing about a European man, and the wife could be Latino or African American, but I loved the way that it was . . . I changed the title, it's called *Aperecio and the Hurricane*.

Do you ever try to protect yourself as a playwright? When you go to publish and say, "Oh, this should be pronounced like this or the type of actor you cast should be like this"? Some playwrights do that when they go to publication. Like a guide for future productions.

I've had a few notes here and there. I don't overwhelm my plays with notes, because it's not the right thing to do. If I feel something is really important, I might just write a little note.

I've noticed you do one thing, which is you will write a line and then the next line doesn't follow it on the same line. It follows it underneath.

Like a poem.

It suggests a slight shift or a slight . . .

Not really. I think it's easier on the eye . . . I actually cut my sentences a lot too. I'm very aware of the actor, giving them too many words—just a mouthful of words—it's difficult sometimes for an actor. So I'm kind of aware of breaking sometimes the line, the sentence with a comma where maybe there wouldn't be a comma there. Just to give a breathing space for the actor, just to be aware of that.

During rehearsals, do you work with designers?

I have in the past. But I really think I want to do more of that. Because I've seen productions of my plays ruined by the set design. As a matter of fact, I recently did a play that I was very unhappy with the set designer. I really think that the set design really bogged down the production.

What do you do? Do you just say, "No, no, I really can't even look at this, it's terrible"? Or do you realize too late?

The real professional theaters, you know, have a dialogue with you and with the director. You come in before and you discuss the set with the designer. Like a place like The Public Theater, absolutely. You sit down and you talk.

Do you have veto power? Do you say no?

I've never done that, but, I think, yes, you can. Absolutely.

Were you consulted at any time? Did the director say to you, "This is going to be the design"?

I was consulted at one point, but it was not a mock-up. It was like a really rough draft, and I had no idea what was going on. It was one of those computer kind of drafts, and it was kind of an idea of what was being done. I really love mock-ups, you know, a model, because you really have a sense of the space and how it functions in the third dimension.

What about critics? How do you relate to them? Do you listen to them? Do you read them? Did you ever learn from anything a critic ever said?

It's something that I'm always torn with, the critics. You know, obviously, I've had bad—the production of *Dancing on Her Knees* . . . that play was completely destroyed by the critics. All the critics hated it. It was completely destroyed. It was only Ben Brantley that said something about, "This is an important voice in the theater." But what I find is it's very confusing when one critic tells you one thing and one tells you something completely different. Unless all the critics agree on parts of the play that just didn't work. I have stopped reading reviews, to be honest with you. Because I find writing is all about courage. You must have courage when you start writing a play and you cannot have the voice—you must write things out. You cannot have the voice of a critic telling you, "That didn't work in that play, you cannot make it work in another play." It's all about experimenting. Every time you do a production, it's an experimentation. Every time you write a play, it's about experimentation. I just don't want that voice lingering in the back of my mind when I sit down in my room to write a play. So what I do is I call my agent and say to her, "Tell me if the review is positive or negative." And there's been times too when I'm sort of intrigued what they had to say, but the problem is that voice stays with me for a long time, especially if it's a bad review. You know, it's a slap in the face. It's almost like someone telling you your child is not normal, you had a miscarriage. The voice stays with you. Listen, more than anything, I want to celebrate what's there, the fact, you know, the accomplishment of getting a group of people, getting a theater. It takes a lot of work to get a play mounted. The effort from the actors, the theater, the money that goes into it. In the end, I just want to celebrate what's there. I want to stay with that feeling inside of me.

When you won the Pulitzer Prize, has that influenced your career, your work habits, anything? In a good way, in a bad way? You started saying that every- one knows Anna in the Tropics *and no one . . .*

I think that the Pulitzer Prize is definitely a blessing, but it's also a curse. Because I think that it is a blessing because the work gets more exposure, especially that particular play and then other works of yours too. And then it's a curse because people anticipate that you will write another play like *Anna in the Tropics*. I think it's really wrong because, you know, I think, as a writer, I'm in a process and I'm somewhere in that process, and I need to continue to develop. I'm not interested in repeating *Anna in the Tropics. Anna in the Tropics* is what it is, but every time I write a play, I find that what I have to do is learn the rules of that new play and what are those rules and what is that world about. It's not that I come in and I project a set of rules to the play. No, I have to learn what are those rules. And I think being open to it and not repeating formulas and what worked in one piece and what didn't work. You know what I'm saying? I'm not interested in formulas. I think that's the problem with Holly- wood. When I'm seeing a Hollywood film, I'm so aware of the formula, of the cliché. OK, this worked in another film, therefore, it's going to work in this one. And I think it's very dangerous territory, and, therefore, I don't want to repeat myself in the same way.

Did you get Hollywood offers?

Yes. At the beginning, yes. I had to have to a conversation with Peregrine Whittlesey, my agent, and I said, "You know, I struggled for many years, as you well know, when I used to live at New Dramatists, to get to where I'm at and to do the work that I want to do for all of sudden, to do something that is not related to my sensibility as a writer . . ." Yeah, we were getting offers—things that had nothing to do with me, that didn't interest me.

Were they just, "Oh, well, he's the Hispanic writer"?

Yeah. To write a film about basketball. I don't even like sports.

Do you see yourself as having strengths that really guide you and weaknesses that you have to struggle against?

Yeah. I mean, I don't want to repeat myself. Even though that . . . If you read some of my plays, if you read the body of my work, you can see that these are my plays. I think I have a certain kind of style. I think at the same time, I'm aware that there's certain things that I did as a playwright in certain plays, and again I try not to repeat myself, even though I have a certain kind of sensibility, and I tend to gravitate toward certain things, you know.

So that's your strength?

No, well, it's my weakness too. It's both.

The pull toward perhaps repeating yourself?

Yeah. It's both my weakness and my strength. How to learn not to repeat myself in the same way. Yet, it's your oeuvre, it's part of you.

Do you believe, as some people say, that a writer has one story and just tells it over and over again in different ways?

I don't think so. I'm interested in human behavior, so I might explore the subject matter in certain ways that maybe other writers wouldn't. For instance, my last play, *The Color of Desire*, is about obsession, and I chose to write it in a poetic way. Maybe another writer would have written it in a more realistic way. So even though it's a subject matter that I had never written about before . . .

When you look at your writing, in terms of an evolution, form and theme or in style, is there anything in which you can see an arc?

I'm very intrigued by this new play I've written. I'm interested in multiculturalism in my work. That's something I had not written about before. So it's a departure for me. Because I think the world is that way. I don't want to write about just one group of people but explore the others and what they have in common with each other. That's a change. That's my arc.

I know that we talked a little bit about how your characters think and feel in Spanish but speak English.

I sometimes incorporate Spanish into my work.

Do you find yourself frustrated when you write the dialogue in English instead? Or is it something you're so used to doing?

I'm so used to doing it. But sometimes, for instance, now with this new piece, I'm enjoying so much doing the translation into the Spanish language. It's a different way of falling in love with the piece all over again.

I mean, sometimes, you just can't say it in English.

For instance, I'm trying to capture some of the rhythms. I originally tried to capture the Spanish rhythms into the English language. But when I write it in Spanish, I have to think of the syntax of Spanish, which is very different.

Why don't you write a play in Spanish?

Why don't I write a play in Spanish? I am. I'm writing an opera at the moment in Spanish. I'm writing an opera about Frida Kahlo in Spanish. Right now it's through a Carnegie Mellon Foundation grant. We have a residency at Whittier College. I'm working with a composer named Gabriela Lena Frank, who's Peruvian. So that opera I'm writing it in Spanish, but I'm also translating it into English language. So I'm back and forth. Again, the whole thing, there's something about the English that informs the Spanish and the Spanish informs the English.

You're your own editor.

I am my own editor, which I would love to do that. I just wish I had more time. Just to go back to these plays and do that kind of work, I just don't have enough time. Also, at the end of the day, you just say, "Enough, I need to go into new territory."

Do you get to look at the Spanish translations?

Well, I tell you, for *Anna in the Tropics*, because I was so busy when *Anna in the Tropics* got the award, that immediately there was a producer in Spain that wanted to do the piece in Spain. And he did a translation of the piece, but it was Castilian Spanish, which is very different from the Caribbean Spanish in Cuba. So I had to go back, I had to look at his translation and make it into Cuban Spanish.

How did it work for the Spanish actors?

They were fine. Some of them couldn't really capture the Cuban accent, so they did it in kind of neutral Spanish.

Do you find that you experience a lot of xenophobia working as a playwright?

Yes, all the time. Especially in my last play. Especially from one critic, it was complete xenophobia.

How do you work with that? I mean, you talked a little bit about working with dramaturgs. Do you think about, how is an American audience going to perceive this?

I feel like I have to be a walking encyclopedia—I constantly have to be explaining myself—especially when I do table work or when I'm talking to a dramaturg about, you know, the culture, but also what I'm trying to do as a writer in this particular play. You know, you have to protect yourself too.

But you don't want to write a play about the situation. I mean, a writer might. You know, a Hispanic writer might write a play about how xenophobic the culture is. But that doesn't sound like you.

You know, the problem with that is I'm not a victim kind of writer. You know what I'm saying? That would be a choice. That's not me. I'm all about celebration, not about victimization. There are other people that do like—and it's great that they do that. I'm not that kind of writer.

Are there any Spanish dramaturgs coming up in the world? Are they trained?

Yes, there is a really good one. He's from Spain. He is Juan Mayorga. *Way to Heaven* is the name of the play. It's been done here in New York, at Repertorio Español. He's really a wonderful, wonderful writer, Spanish writer.

I was asking about dramaturgs. Is there a Cuban or a Mexican dramaturg who could work in this world . . .

It doesn't exist in Latin America. It only exists here and in France, in England. I agree.

There are some people who think dramaturgs shouldn't exist at all.

But I like dramaturgs. There's a couple of dramaturgs that I've had problems with in the past. But, for instance, I dedicated my play *Anna in the Tropics* to a dramaturg. Janice Paran from the McCarter Theatre. She was very good, and I dedicated my play to her, so imagine the impression that this woman made on me. I know that there are all these terrifying stories from playwrights working with dramaturgs and all this stuff. You know, you have to listen, and then you also have to, "OK, I agree with this, I don't agree with this." Just go and do your own thing. You might get frustrated sometimes. For instance, I was working and I had done a translation of a classic from Spanish to English, and I was being asked to fill in blanks of certain things. I said, "Wait a minute. We're talking about a classic. You don't do that with Shakespeare. You don't add information. You don't do that with Shakespeare. Why would you do this with . . . ? Because it's different culture?" And they said, "No, we don't know this way of being in this country." Anyway, I was shocked.

Do you feel sometimes as a playwright, when you're writing about a group that you're a part of, a responsibility to represent that group?

Yes, to a certain degree. But I don't like that . . . you know, I can't be the voice of the people.

But you're expected to be?

Yeah, I think there's certain expectations, but I don't want that cross to bear at all.

TONY KUSHNER

We were all set to meet at Tony Kushner's office way uptown, but the evening before, his assistant informed us that construction was being done in the building, and though the noise was intermittent, it was very loud. We moved the venue to Barry's apartment, not too far from Tony's office. It was raining the next day, as it had been for days. Tony called from the street, saying he'd be right there, he was just hailing a cab. He arrived a little late: no cabs and a sluggish subway system because of the rain. He was dressed all in black, with two black leather bags slung over his shoulders, and passed on having his jacket hung up. There was the usual arranging of recording devices—two digitals and a cell phone—and we gathered at a round table, armed with coffee (Tony takes his light with real sugar). Tony talked a bit about his early years growing up in Lake Charles, Louisiana, surrounded by classical music; his mother was a bassoonist, his father a clarinetist and conductor.

Do you remember your earliest interest in the theater?

I remember I was very young, and my mother was in a play, and she played a character who was carried across a threshold by her lover. This made a big impression on me, and I don't know exactly what the connection was, but I went on a school trip to a farm and got ill, and because of that I had to be carried around by my handsome uncle, and I imagined I was my mother's character in the play. My grandmother was interested in serious theater, and she and several others split off from the Little Theatre to do *Death of a Salesman,* because the people at the Little Theatre thought it was a dirty play. The theater they founded was called Artists Civic Theatre & Studio, ACTS, and is still in existence in Lake Charles today, incidentally. My mother was Linda Loman in that production, and I remember that she slapped someone onstage, which excited me no end.

Did that lead to you wanting to work in the theater?

I did do some acting when I was very young. I was in the Scottish play playing Macduff's son. I think I was six. And every night when I was killed, the audience would laugh, and that was the end of my acting career. But I wasn't interested in being around the theater. At the time I was deeply closeted, and the theater seemed to be all "theater queens." Also my father had very high standards. To him the theater was very serious business, not frivolous. My father was very well read and had an incredible memory for verse. He paid me and my sister a dollar for each poem we memorized. I have all of the poems from *Alice's Adventures in Wonderland* memorized, but I can't get anyone to listen, not even my niece!

It must have been strange to be Jewish in Lake Charles, Louisiana.

There were other Jewish families in Lake Charles, but not many, and I certainly knew what anti-Semitism was. But I was taught that anti-Semitism was not my problem, but the problem of the anti-Semite, and to be proud of myself and my cultural history. And my parents were committed to social justice. My mother's commitment was deeply emotional and passionate. When I came out to my parents, I think in 1982, I used that same argument, that it didn't matter if a million people hated you, you had to be proud of yourself. I also went to an integrated public school when busing was still happening. My takeaway from that was that social engineering works, for better or for worse. Interestingly enough, the born again coach of the debate team who was otherwise very conservative was a huge proponent of integration.

Where did you go to school?
I did my undergraduate work at Columbia University in medieval studies. After I graduated, I worked in a bookstore for a year, and I happened

to read an issue of the *Yale Drama Review* about Ronnie Davis and the San Francisco Mime Troupe and their work with Carl Weber, who had worked with Brecht at the Berliner Ensemble, so when I found out that Carl Weber taught at NYU, I decided to apply to their graduate program. I applied as a directing student and unfortunately didn't get in, but in my interview with Weber, he seemed to like me and suggested that I reapply. Which I did, and the second time I got in.

Why directing and not playwriting?

It was a period when the most interesting theater artists, the ones I was interested in, anyway, were writer/directors, like Joe Chaikin, Richard Foreman, Robert Wilson, María Irene Fornés. I was particularly drawn to her writing. Also I just didn't feel confident enough to try writing. I wasn't ready. I wasn't confident I'd be good. I also had an intuition that I didn't need to sit in playwriting classes for three years. The conservatory program was appealing to me. I could be in on rehearsals. I needed to know what actors did, what directors did, how to get a play on its feet. I did have some classes in playwriting with Jean-Claude van Itallie, and he gave us some exercises that made writing less scary for me.

Were there other significant influences?

One of the most important influences in my life was Nora Dunfee, who tried to get me thrown out of the program at NYU because I did a feminist theater piece with five actresses in which they soaked tampons in water and threw them against the wall, where they promptly exploded. Nora thought I should be expelled from the program, but we buried the hatchet, and I was forced to take her text analysis class, which was revelatory. She emphasized specificity in the text. You would start to say a line, and she would stop you and ask you what that word meant. And then you'd start again and she'd stop you again and ask you what the next word meant. I began to realize that lines themselves could be active, that someone doesn't have to get up and stab someone with a knife, but that each line can forward the motion of a play. Lines actually do something in their own right and ideally help a character get what they want. This is one of the problems when actors and directors do my work. There are times when it appears the characters have gotten what they want from a scene, but they continue to talk. Logically, the scene should end when there is some form of resolution, so if they continue talking, either the playwright hasn't done his job, or the characters still want something. Directors and actors fall into the trap of just sitting around and talking when the characters are actually trying to get something from one another.

Are you conscious of writing lines in order to achieve this "active" status?

Mostly I let myself write, going on digressions and such, and then I go back to review. Generally, my subconscious does the heavy lifting and takes care of such things, though there are times when I find the need to make the lines active. There's a scene on the steps of the courthouse from *Angels in America* with Louis and Joe which I call a "penny drop" moment, which is the moment when everything coheres due to the specificity of the text and what the words are doing. An audience is in fact one entity, a collective with individual pieces, this beast waiting in the dark that reacts as one to the events onstage. Sometimes it has a divided opinion and is fighting with itself about what it is watching, and this "penny drop" moment is when everything coheres. Not all plays have them, which makes them difficult for critics to review, because those moments are generally what a critic is looking for.

When you see a different production of one of your plays, does it tell you something that you didn't know you had written?

Oh, yeah! Oh, absolutely! I realized the day we sat down, the first day we sat down to read *Angels* with this current company, with Bill Heck reading Joe, I suddenly heard as I had never heard before, that—you know, we read both parts in one day and—Bill was so amazing in the *Millennium* part, and then his character stops talking, and I realized, "Oh, he just doesn't have anything to say in *Perestroika*." I had just stopped, for various reasons over the years, stopped writing Joe in that play. And what was interesting to me, you know, because the unconscious has such an enormously important role in all of this, is that I had left little places all through the play where there were . . . I mean, I didn't have to write, I didn't have to restructure anything to finish him as a character. All the places were there, they were just these little moments that didn't work, that I'd never liked, and when I went back I sort of made a little map of those places. In every single one of them there was room for Joe to say a little bit more or *something*. And then as I had him talk more, it became clear that this was also what was wrong with Louis in *Perestroika*, that Louis—because he didn't have anyone to talk to—wasn't responding. And I'd really never worked out what the two of them were doing with one another in *Perestroika*, why they needed . . . I mean, I think I had maybe made some sense of why Joe needed Louis, but I'd never really—except for knowing that Louis can't be alone, ever—worked out why Louis needed Joe. I mean, it was there in embryo, but the thing that—

But it took Bill Heck to—

Well that was what started it.

What I'd always heard was that Stephen Spinella was who you had in mind when you wrote Prior.

I wrote Prior Walter for Stephen.

Does that mean that you wrote it around the personality of Stephen or that you knew Stephen could do it?

On opening night of IHG, I was talking to Stephen and I said, "You realize that I literally learned how to write on you." Stephen was Nora Dunfee's teaching assistant at NYU and one of her prize pupils. I also think Stephen just has a brain that . . . it's impossible for Stephen to talk without being specific with language. He's like the platonic ideal in that regard and Linda Emond, I think, is the female platonic—they're both actors who just . . . they know—partly consciously and then, really importantly, partly unconsciously—when they talk, they love language and they get it. They get that it's—that language is an enormously important part of stage action. Carl Weber, my directing teacher, did a production of *The White Devil*, and Stephen played the villain, whatever his name is, and it was one of the first things I saw when I started at NYU. Stephen was a third-year student when I was a first-year student, and I saw him doing this scene and, "Oh, that actor is unbelievable, I mean that guy is terrifyingly good." And so I immediately made friends with him. You know, the first time I actually feel like I ever wrote, as an adult, a piece for an actor . . . I did this play called *Age of Assassins,* which was about anarchist assassinations at the turn of the century. It was all collage material. I thought of it as a directing project. I did it in the summer with my little theater company between my first and second year at NYU, and Stephen was in it. It covered the five anarchist assassinations between like 1897 and 1906. They killed the prime minister of Spain, the president of France, the president of the United States, the king of Italy, and the empress of Austria. It was a five-act play, and each one was involved in one of those assassinations. The only one that I felt compelled to write anything for was this lunatic who killed the empress of Austria, which was the only assassination that really . . . well, it was sort of a stretch to say that it had any political meaning. The guy was basically a celebrity stalker who stabbed her with a nail file on a pleasure boat on Lake Constance, and she bled to death into her black clothing—which she wore because her son had shot himself at Mayerling—and she couldn't feel the pain of the knife going in because her corsets were so tight that she was always in excruciating pain. And that guy, that assassin, his name was Luigi Lucheni, who I realized was a lunatic. There was nothing from the historical record that I could use, so I had to write something, and it was scary to do it, but I wrote a little speech for him for Stephen and then wrote another piece in a project I did in my second year called *La femme de la bohème,* where Stephen played a dead archbishop, and the first really good thing I think I wrote was his monologue. He was amazing in it, and it was just scary and terrifying, and I thought, "Oh, this is good, this writing is good." And then my thesis project at NYU was this musical that I wrote called *The Heavenly Theatre* about an actual incident that happened in 1580 in France when a troupe of actors were murdered by a local judge during a plague in Romont during the carnival time, and the part of the judge I wrote for Stephen. And then I wrote the character of Baz in *A Bright Room Called Day* for Stephen, which was the first gay character that I wrote, and I wrote the part of Dr. Brown, the lead in *Hydriotaphia*—which is, I think, the play where I taught myself how to write jokes—for Stephen, and then Prior Walter. So he's been central. I said to him on opening night, and I mean it, "You'd be nothing without me, and I'd be nothing without you."

But has he now set kind of a mark for you for an actor to play Prior?

Well, I mean, I'll never hear that part without hearing Stephen. I mean, it's indisseverable.

What about when you collaborate, like when you work with Maurice Sendak or the musical Caroline, *or when you did the screenplay for* Munich? *Does your whole work process change when you have a collaborator?*

Oh, yeah, yeah. I mean, I really love doing that. Working on *Brundibár* with Maurice was absolute . . . I couldn't believe how lucky I was to get to watch him begin a book and work all the way through it. Maurice is, I think, a very great artist. I mean, I think, you know, a genius, which is a word that I very rarely use and . . .

What's the process? I mean, does he—

Oh, he suffers through it. The thing about him is he takes it—which is true of anybody who's great at anything—he takes it very, very seriously, and he thinks about it very, very deeply, and it's his art. I mean, he's a brilliant man and a man with immense erudition and sophistication, whose role models are Verdi and Shakespeare and Blake. I mean, he loves children's books, and he knows everything there is to know about children's literature and illustration, but his gods are, you know, Mozart and Shakespeare, and he, I think, strives in his work—I mean, it's complicated because you're working within a medium that is, you know, immensely important. Graham Greene said, when you get down to it, the most important books are the books that kids are reading, because those are the ones that have the biggest impact. I mean, I think, it's, you know, inarguable that *Where the Wild Things Are* is one of the essential books of the twentieth century.

And how is it when you work with other collaborators?

I'm working with Stephen Spielberg right now, in fact. I have to send in a rewrite. We're about to start filming my Lincoln screenplay, which I've spent the last six years working on. We start filming in October, so—

Let's talk about the theater first.

I will say that the collaborator . . . probably the easiest and happiest collaboration in my life—the closest is with Jeanine Tesori. *Caroline* was an absolutely sublime experience for me. I'm madly in love with her. We've just finished our second thing, a little opera about Eugene O'Neill that's opening at Glimmerglass this summer, which is a wonder. Her music is just . . . she knows when you're going to cry. It's like Puccini. She is a director. I don't know what she'd be like if she tried to direct, but one of the great things about *Caroline* is every time I go and see a new production of it, I don't really have to worry, because if you just follow the score, there isn't a moment that doesn't work. I mean, some of it came from conversations with me, but a lot of it was stuff she discovered on her own. She is a genuine theater composer. She knows what it means to write music for drama as opposed to music. I don't know if she would say this about her other collaborators—and I hate them all—but we work together really beautifully. And I have enough music—I don't even read music because of issues with my parents, but I've grown up around music, I go to the opera all the time, I know music, so I have a fairly complicated and sophisticated sense of it—so I know enough to chip in usefully with her. And she isn't a writer, but she has an incredibly intense response to text, specifics—I mean, Nora would love her specificity.

So is that what you also appreciate in a director, specificity?

Directors are . . . it is a vexed, complicated issue, and I don't have any—

Is that in any way because you have trained as a director?

It's interesting how few director-playwright combinations, no matter how successful, last very long. You know, Kazan and Williams and Miller—I mean, well, with Miller there were obviously political reasons that got in the way. Or you think of Woodruff's production of *Buried Child,* and that's completely sublime: you have a very great playwright and a very great director, and then, of course, people blame Joe Papp for tearing them apart. But you know, I've always wondered if that was true. I just think . . . I think it's hard and I think that one of the reasons it's hard, I think that the real problem—I mean, a lot of times I find playwrights who stick with the same director over and over again are doing so at their own peril. I don't want to name names—but most working American playwrights go from one person to the other to the other to the other, and it's very hard. Suzan-Lori Parks, who I consider to be one of the genuine greats, worked so spectacularly with Richard Foreman on *Venus* and then so spectacularly with George Wolfe on *Topdog/Underdog,* and I know nothing about whether or not they'll ever repeat that. I think it's always a fraught relationship, and I think part of the thing that makes it fraught, and probably the main thing, is time. I think it's probably the biggest casualty of the insanely short rehearsal periods that we have. I mean, we don't rehearse anything long enough, not even remotely long enough, and it's impossible for anything to happen as it should. I mean when people show up at first or second previews, I want to smack them. It's like, "What are you doing here, you're paying to watch a rehearsal!" And if it's a new play, you're paying to watch a rehearsal of a play that's not finished yet or, at least, certainly in my case it's not, and in most people's cases it's not. I always wait until last week of the run to see a play, because then it's the best shot that you have at seeing—you know, not if it's *The Fantasticks* and it's like ninety-five years later, but, you know, you go close to the end of a six- or seven-week run, and then you're gonna actually see the actors having really had, if it's well directed and if it's a good play—the actors will have grown into their parts.

Isn't that a reason to work with a director again, so there's a certain shorthand that lets you get down to work faster?

Yes. Yes. But it's the issue of authority, in both senses of the word—I mean power and also authorship. I mean, directing is really close to writing. It requires an investment in the material almost as complete as the playwright's. You don't have to imagine it out of nothing, that's the difference. But on the other hand, you don't have the luxury that a play-wright has of doing it in the privacy of his or her room and throwing it in the trashcan if you're fucking up and starting over and taking as many weeks or months or years as you need to get it right. They have to do it in public, and that's a hideously difficult thing. You have to get up and turn this thing into a stage event with an audience of colleagues, but they're still an audience watching you every step of the way, and you have to produce it, and you have to design it. I mean, you have to do all those things. I sometimes write plays where I see the set in my head. I never try to describe it, but sometimes I really know what it's supposed to look like. More often than not I don't. I sort of blank out on that. When I taught playwriting, it was always an irritation to me when playwrights would start to write and it was about the set, you know, the set will do this magical thing and then this . . . it's like no, no, no, no, no. That's not your job, that's cheating. But directors really have to take this thing on paper and infuse it with real blood and do this incredibly difficult thing of both guiding actors and not turning them into meat puppets. The British and the Germans, God knows, are completely unconcerned about that. They just say, "You move here, you move like this." But apart from Robert Wilson and maybe Foreman, maybe Elizabeth LeCompte, I don't know. I mean, LeCompte is interesting, she never lets go of it. I mean, she works and works like Deborah Warner. It's a constant rehearsal, and they never allow it to become something that they're not a part of. But American directors have to keep the actor on some kind of reasonable course that makes sense while at the same time doing what a playwright like me wants, which is specificity, specificity, specificity—without making the actor feel afraid that every time they open their mouths they're doing the wrong thing.

Do you go to rehearsals?

I do but, you know, it's always the Heisenberg problem. I mean, if you don't go to rehearsals on a daily basis, then you show up and they're all scared to death and they stop acting. They don't want to show anything 'cause you're sitting there with your little pad, and I take lots of notes. Probably partly that I was trained as a director is both a blessing and a curse. I know how to direct a scene, and I've been around actors enough, and I love what actors do enough, so that I think I'm pretty good at knowing what an actor does and how to talk to actors. I'm not somebody who says stupid things to them and scares them, right? But you show up, and they haven't shown you your stuff, and all but the bravest are gonna get self-protective, especially if it's like second or third week of the run. So you always hear, "Oh, it was so much better yesterday, you fucked it up by being here." The reason I call it the Heisenberg principle is because you change the thing that you're observing by observing it.

What about in rehearsal, though . . .

The way that I've always said it should work is I think that the playwright should have three or four weeks with the actors around the table. The first week is all about terror, right? The first week of rehearsal is all about nobody knows what they're doing, everybody is mortified, nobody's really figured out anything, and everybody's in this state of panic. So it's all about sort of calming everybody down and getting everybody acquainted with everybody else, and then you start the work. But the way that that week is used is primarily with some dramaturg showing up with a ring binder with 900 pages of research about what Chekhov ate for breakfast and what Bohemia was actually like and what they wore in *Lear,* and in prehistoric Britain the druids were—

Too much information, huh?

It's terrible information. It's useless information. By all means, go and do some research, and it'll help you and it'll help you quicken yourself, but if it's not in the play, the play sucks. If everything you need to know is not in that script, you've got a bad script. If there are lines in the script that you need help understanding . . . if you go and look at *Intelligent Homosexual's Guide,* you're probably gonna need to read some Marx if you're playing one of those family members, 'cause they're all very conversant in Marx, and you want to feel not like a fake, so you should do that. But everything that you need, that I want an audience to know, is in the goddamn play. I don't need an 800-page program insert: "This is a teaching opportunity to tell you exactly who Roy Cohn was and where he really died and what he really died of."

Can't you control that in terms of the first week of rehearsal?

Well, you do, but what you are aware of is that you have to immediately go against a machinery. I mean, *I* do. I think it's OK to say this: I shocked Jim Houghton by saying at the first read-through of *Angels* . . . well, the board and the entire staff has been invited to watch. I'm the twentieth Signature playwright, and I was apparently the first one he said who's ever said, "No fucking way." You can't do that to these actors. They've never said these words before, they've never come out of their mouths in front of anybody other than their boyfriends or girlfriends or husbands or wives. Zoe Kazan is going to be talking to Bill Heck for the first time as Harper and Joe. I don't think it's in any way fair that she should have an audience. They're actors. Actors are trained, no matter what you say to them, when the audience comes in, it's a different animal, and this is our first day of rehearsal, and it's the first time they're gonna hear it. It's the first time I get to hear them do it. I want to hear them do it where the only person they're worried about is me and the director, Michael Greif, nobody else. I said to Houghton, "There will be no one in the room except you and Beth Whitaker, your associate producer, and if I want to invite a couple of friends, if you want to invite a friend, but otherwise, no." Young playwrights who go into these new play development things . . . I mean, when I was teaching and more connected to young playwrights it made me so angry. You take a play that somebody's barely finished, and you give them like half a day of rehearsal with some cast that they probably had no say in assembling, with great actors and not-so-great actors. That night it's in front of an audience, and then the most horrifying thing of all, the playwright has to get up afterward and listen to what the audience thought, and it is so brutal. Brecht says the reason there were so many great playwrights in the Elizabethan and Jacobean era is because he said they treated the plays—masterpieces—like old Kleenex. You know, they would do *Much Ado About Nothing* or *As You Like It* and then throw it away and say what else have you got?

Isn't that a little reckless?

That recklessness is a big part of—you don't want to be too precious—but on the other hand, you know, it's why I hate playwriting programs. It's like, you've got your work years—you're twenty-five, twenty-six years old. How many plays, first of all, are you really gonna write? Shakespeare, who's infinitely better than everybody, wrote thirty-eight of them, or whatever it is. Shaw wrote thirty-nine, and most of them aren't all that good, though the good ones are unbelievably great, but most playwrights write about eight or nine, ten or fifteen, you know. In the Spanish Golden Age, dramatists wrote 600 . . . and Aeschylus—but that's a different time. Now we don't write plays in such numbers, and you go to a graduate playwriting program, and you've got people who are immensely talented in their late twenties and early thirties. Brecht wrote *Baal* when he was twenty-one. I mean, you know, playwriting is not something that you mostly start when you're fifty or sixty, and most playwrights' reputations are made around their second or third play so . . . get busy. You know? Tennessee Williams's first play, that anybody really saw, not *The Battle of Angels,* you know, *The Glass Menagerie.* You've got work to do, and it's not homework. It's so counterintuitive to me that you would take a scene in a play that you're working on and go into a room full of other playwrights and say to them who are your fellow students and your competitors and the teacher, who's a playwright, and say, "Here's what I'm working on," and then listen to nine other people say, "Oh, I would do this," and, "I don't know why you're doing that."

Do they do that?

Oh, they do . . . oh, yes.

Because in an acting class you would never do it. You would only try to say something if that would help.

Well, you might be trying to help, and honey, you know in acting classes very often, horrible things get said. You know, "You're too fat." I mean, ask Camryn Manheim. But the thing is that as an actor, that's where your work is gonna take place. You don't do Hamlet in your bedroom and then bring it to the rehearsal. You learn how to do Hamlet in rehearsal in front of the person playing Claudius who is thinking, "I'm not so old, I could do this a lot fucking a lot better than this jerk and why am I playing Claudius, I should be doing Hamlet—I never got a chance to show them my Hamlet! Which I did in, you know, the Buttfuck Theatre in Selma, Alabama, twenty-five years ago, and boy, it was great, but you didn't get to . . ." I mean, actors have to have that kind of weird combination of vulnerability and rhinoceros hide, but a playwright . . . when you write a play, you have to dismantle yourself psychologically . . . but actors are sort of permanently dismantled. It's why they're so difficult, but playwrights have to dismantle and then reassemble themselves. There's a time in my writing process when I'm not there anymore. I mean, when you're really in it, you have to be very careful crossing the street, because it's the time that you get hit by a bus. I mean, you atomize yourself. You sort of open things that usually you don't have open, so that stuff that's inside of you that ordinarily does not get out will get out. I find the idea, and maybe it's just me, but I find the idea of an enormous amount of input in the middle of that . . .

Can you show your work to someone during that period?

I will, if I'm stuck. When I finished the first sixty pages of *Millennium*, and it was sixty pages and I hadn't gotten past, you know, a tenth of what was on my outline, I sent it to Oskar Eustis, because he was the producer as well as the director, and I said, "OK, I don't know what I'm doing." And I sent it to Joyce Ketay, because she was my agent, and I trust her, and I wanted to say, "Does this suck? I'm really enjoying this, but is it—?"

Do you still do that, in terms of those two?

I do, I do, I do very largely. Yeah, and I now work with a former assistant of mine, Antonia Grilikhes-Lasky, who works as my assistant and went to Columbia Film School. She graduated yesterday with her master's in film. I brought her in when I was stuck about three years ago on *Lincoln*, and I had to finish this immense first draft, and it was the hardest thing I've ever written, and I just needed somebody to sit there. I work very well talking things out with people. I need to say things out loud to somebody. I usually do that with Oskar, but Oskar's running the fucking Public Theater, and you know, I certainly talked a lot to Steven Spielberg, but I was in a place where I needed a babysitter, somebody who was just gonna sit there and say, "OK, now do the next scene." And I adore her, she's a wonderful person, so I brought her in for that and discovered all of a sudden in talking to her . . . I mean I knew she was very smart . . . that she's actually a magnificent dramaturg. So I've hired her back, not as an assistant, but as a kind of dramaturg. I also gave it to Oskar to read, act by act. It was a 500-hundred page first draft, so it was a lot to read. Oskar read it in about two and a half hours, which is one of the scary things about Oskar. I mean, literally. When I started *Intelligent Homosexual's Guide*, which I wrote in rehearsal at the Guthrie, a feat of which I'm proud and also ashamed at the same time. I mean, I literally wrote the first scene of the play on the second day of rehearsal. And I finished it by the end of tech. The first time anyone had ever heard the whole play from start to finish—and it's a three-hour-forty-five-minute, eleven-characters play—was the first preview. And the first preview was the most put-together thing of any play of mine ever. I mean, it was a perfect first preview. There wasn't a line dropped. The set . . . Mark Wendland designed without ever having read a word. I didn't even have a plot, I just said, "I know I need a brownstone, I've been reading a lot of Arthur Miller, 'cause I'm editing Arthur's plays for Library of America, so I think it's gonna have something to do with Arthur Miller. It's a kind of a . . . my take on a postwar, you know, big family, Arthur Miller–type play, but it's also *Long Day's Journey,* and it may have something to do with Chekhov, and I don't know what it is that I'm sure of. I want to stay in this one room, but I maybe want to go elsewhere in the brownstone, and if I get really bored, I want to go into Manhattan, so I have to be able to do that." And Mark sort of sat there imperturbably and then came up with a set that sort of magically is . . . it is the play. I don't know how he did that, but it's the play.

What did he come up with?

This matrix of abstract spaces with that one central, absolutely beautiful—like, whoever it would have been did those sets for Miller, *The Price* or something. And, you know, Michael Greif—who is heroic in terms of his ability to keep a cast of rather complicated actors from murdering the playwright while the playwright is slowly stumbling his way through—I mean, Michael just kept everybody and never broke a sweat. I mean, I'm sure it was hell on him.

Is that something you would continue to look for in a director?

When Joe Dowling asked me to do this three-play season, this festival at the Guthrie, it was right when I was beginning work on *Lincoln,* and it was gonna be for 2009. It was like 2005 or 2006 or something, and I said, "Oh, well, of course I can do that." He wanted to do *Caroline,* and he wanted to do these five one-acts, called *Tiny Kushner,* in the studio space, and then he said we want a new play for the proscenium. And I thought, "Well, you know, I should write a new play now. It's been a while since *Homebody/Kabul* and *Caroline,* and I'm ready, and I'll finish *Lincoln* this year, and then I'll be ready to do it." And I finished *Lincoln.* I mean, I got it down to what I consider to be kind of the beginning of this draft of it from, I think, a really good 500-page first draft, but to something you could film, as a feature film, in February of 2009. I worked on nothing but that, that entire time.

Are you in a position where you can direct something of your own?

I'm curious about directing something of my own. I think I'd probably really do a bad job because . . . I forget who it was—I hope it wasn't John Simon; let's say it was John Lahr. I think it *was* Lahr, who said that the weight—he may have said the dead weight—of Beckett's authority, in those German productions that he directed and filmed, is a clear reason why playwrights mostly shouldn't direct their own plays. I mean, it's not always true. Richard Nelson is a fantastic director of his own work. I mean, really wonderful. *The Dead* and *Goodnight Children Everywhere.* And of course there was María Irene Fornés, who directed her own plays more sublimely than anyone that *I've* seen since. But that's rare. I think it's hard. I just feel myself with *The Illusion* right now; it just really matters to me that they get every fucking word and that they invest, or it can get kind of lifeless. I've developed a fun thing that I do with Tony Taccone now, when he directs my stuff—he did *Tiny Kushner.* We have a very nice relationship in that I can really put my oar in and just talk the actors to death saying, "This moment, this moment"—and really map out the text. And then he gets it up on its feet and makes it lively or something. He's very funny. And that's been fun. I've done three shows with him now. We did *Brundibár* when it came to The New Victory. It's only half an hour long.

With your big major works, you're writing while you'd be directing . . .

Well, certainly not on *Intelligent Homosexual's Guide,* I couldn't even come to the rehearsal room. Well, there are older plays that I think about. I directed Ellen McLaughlin's play *Helen* with Donna Murphy and Phylicia Rashad and Marian Seldes and Johanna Day and Denis O'Hare.

How was that? Was that a good experiment?

It was very, very hard. Ellen and I had a hard time, but also I found myself sitting there talking with Susan Hilferty about what kind of wig Donna would be wearing and spandex and why Phylicia Rashad's dress, which was made of silver chainmail, kept stretching out and getting longer; we had to keep taking it up 'cause it was so heavy. And I was thinking, "I'm gonna scream. I don't wanna do this, I just don't want to do it." I don't think that I'm great with designers. I think that I'm OK, but it doesn't excite me. I don't have a confidence about it. I've said this many times, but when I was trying to figure out who would direct *Angels* on Broadway—before I saw *Jelly's Last Jam*—I went to George's apartment and just saw the way he had decorated it and pretty much made up my mind then and there. I thought, "OK, this guy is visual, he's an immensely brilliant man. His visual sense is jaw dropping." I mean, the apartment was like—he didn't have any money at that point, and it was gorgeous. And then I went and saw *Jelly,* and that cinched it. This is somebody who has an incredibly powerful visual eye, and I don't really have that.

So that's also something you really value in a director?

I'd like to try and develop a model of working with directors where it's a kind of codirection, which is sort of what I think Taccone and I have developed, where it's really OK that I'm there all the time talking. What I really like is to be able to be there for, as I said, about three weeks, really work through the play exhaustively with the actors, with the director. And then they would need another two, three weeks to forget everything I had said or discard the parts that weren't useful to them or go in other directions, and then I think several more weeks to rehearse it.

The system doesn't seem to support that, unfortunately.

We have certain drawbacks in this country. We have a tortured relationship to our own language. It still belongs to the British in some hideous way. We have yet to understand the ways in which the creole mixture, the mongrel mixture that American English is, works onstage. We've made really interesting forays into that, but it's essential—if we want to really grow as a theater culture—to start to address this.

But you can command a series of workshops, and start work on it for four weeks in January, do your thing, whatever, come again in May, and put that together.

That can work. And I realize that the fact that I can do that is a privilege of being who I am.

And people wanting to work with you and spend the time with you.

And arguably somebody on my level should need it less than somebody who's young and starting out.

Not necessarily.

Well, but I mean learning. I know some young playwrights who are writing immensely complicated texts . . . people like Rinne Groff or Chris Shinn, Adam Bock—young writers out there who are doing astonishing things. Kia Corthron is not a young writer, she's been around, but Kia's texts are really difficult, they're demanding. Suzan-Lori's stuff is immensely challenging. I mean, she's done very well for herself. I mean, she's gotten the right people all along. But I don't know, I mean, it worries me.

It's worrisome. It's definitely serious.

One thing that I've learned with the rewrites on *Perestroika*—even if you think you're not changing the text to suit a cast, you are. And we send these young writers with their brand new plays out to Cleveland or, you know, someplace where there are some good actors, but not great actors, and they're gonna—it's like a musician, a composer, who's gonna hear his symphony played by somebody who's good but not great, and boy is that gonna change things. If you have a playwright's instinct, you should have an instinct to make it work in front of an audience. You don't want to give somebody a monologue where they have to set their kishkes on fire in front of the audience, if they're just not going to do that. They'll be embarrassed, you'll be embarrassed, it'll make you look like a bad writer, it'll probably make them look like a bad actor, and why put an audience through that. And so you start to try and adjust it to what they can do, and it's hard, 'cause there are really three cities in the United States where you have any shot at all at getting a great pool of actors—New York, Chicago, Los Angeles. But Los Angeles is very tricky because everything that you do there is about movies. Every play you do there is about movies. Every actor who's there is there because of movies, and who's gonna come and see them in this play, because of the movies, and your audience is, I hate to say, really deeply not a theater audience. I mean, you go to Minneapolis, you find great actors there, but in Los Angeles it's like doing summer stock at some really beautiful, idyllic location, at the beach, or in Martha's Vineyard, and you realize nobody will focus because everyone wants to be out on the beach. I mean, they'll really try, but half of their energy is going into not being on the beach.

But sometimes they're so hungry—

Sometime they are, but it is not an audience that's particularly interested in anything dark or complicated. You go to Minneapolis and you see the audience that the Guthrie created—and of course he picked well, he picked the right—that *bürgerpflicht* German, you know, "We are not here to be entertained, we are here to work for knowledge that art will give us." I mean, it's so *Biedermeier,* but it's fantastic. Those audiences are unbelievable. At the first preview of *Intelligent Homosexual's Guide,* I had to go to a fundraiser at some rich person's house the next day, and the play was like ninety-five hours long, and it was beautifully staged and everything, but, you know, the play was a mess, and these people came up and asked these questions—like they had picked little details from act 2, scene 5, when everybody's talking on top of everybody else—they were asking these incredibly smart questions. They're like a British audience, except they actually think it's OK to laugh. And I've seen great things at the Guthrie and not so great things at the Guthrie. And whatever it is—it's sixteen degrees below zero outside, and they are there in those seats, and they are working and it's phenomenal.

Do you find the same kind of response in Chicago?

Chicago has a really smart, good theater audience and New York as well, and New York also has, you know, the best actors. One of the great joys of this season, for me, has been the actors. I mean, look at who the *replacement* cast of *Angels in America* was. I had Adam Driver and Michael Urie and, you know, Keira Keeley—I mean, it was ridiculous, it's ridiculous, the number of phenomenal people in this city who can act.

You've been answering our questions without us even asking them.

I will say one other thing about directing and acting. I really, really, really think that everybody who trains as a director and as an actor needs to read Freud, seriously, really needs to understand psychoanalysis, psychoanalytic theory, and they really, really, really need to have done some work in literary theory, in theories of interpretation. This is why I hate undergraduate drama majors, because they don't go and study literature with the best scholars available to them. They go to "Shakespeare for Drama Majors," where they get up and they act out scenes, but they don't go and study with a great Shakespearian scholar. And whatever happens with us, as a theater culture, it would be so great to believe that every answer is in the text and you have to go back to the text and you always have to ask yourself, "Is what I'm doing supported, genuinely supported, by the text? A radical new interpretation is great, but is it in the text? Is there evidence for it in the text? What is the text telling me at this moment that I don't know the answer to?" A director has to have the nerve to say, "I don't know the answer to that. Let's go back to the table and look at the text. This isn't working, let's go back and look at the text. Let's figure it out. Why is there a semicolon here?" One of my most exciting moments as a playwright was going to one of the first read-throughs of *Angels* at ACT in San Francisco, and Mark Wing-Davey was directing it, and Ben Shenkman and Julia Gibson were reading it for the first time, and Mark said, "Stop. Wait, go back and read that again; it's a semi-colon, not a period. Would you please do that?" And the actor, whoever it was, said, "But, you know, are we gonna have to do it—really, we're gonna have—" There was like a panic in the room like, "Oh my God, he's gonna make us do the punctuation." And Mark said, "No, I'm not going to make you do the punctuation, but the first time we do it, do the punctuation—hear what he was thinking when he wrote it, and see what that does. You may have other ideas later on, but first learn *that*." And I was like, "Ooh my God! Because there is nothing there at the beginning but the text. It's your originary, it's your constitution, it's your document, it's your bible, it's the floor, and even if it's not a very good play, it's the product of someone's conscious and unconscious mind, and so most likely, the answers are in it, if you're clever about understanding it. And if you start to believe that you can't trust it and you have to not ask certain questions or just make up stuff, if you give an answer that's a fake answer to an actor and the actor starts to build on that, what you've done is rewrite the play, and the actor will start to go off in another direction, and soon the play is in one place and the actor is in another, and then the other actors who are maybe a little bit closer to the play are trying to have interaction with this person who's out in cloud-cuckoo-land, and the whole thing starts to come apart. You have to ask hard questions. You have to say, "Well, is this person, is Harper psychotic? What are the clues in the script that she's not? I mean, there's a psychotic person in the script who's actually called psychotic. Does Harper sound like the psychotic person? Is she in any way, shape, or form a dissociative person? Is she crazy?" And the answer is no, but in so many productions of this play where people make it, "Oh, she's nuts," and then they go off on that, and it just leaves the play behind. So I think everybody in theater should be in psychoanalysis, because I think it will teach you to read text very, very, very carefully and with the assumption, the great Freudian assump-tion, that there is no accident. Nothing is accidental, nothing—which is another way of saying nothing is meaningless, and so everything you do is telling a story. Everything you do has meaning and needs to be parsed and interpreted, and if people would do that, I think we would have bet-ter productions.

So are you hopeful about the theater here?

I flew to Amsterdam recently to see the revival of Ivo van Hove's production of *Angels* at the Toneelgroep, because it had been this huge hit the year before, and they brought it back, and I hadn't seen it, and Ivo is a director I adore—I think he's just astonishing. And I heard that the production is amazing, and Jim Nicola told me that I had to see it, and I couldn't see it 'cause I was working on *Lincoln*. So when I finished it, I got on a plane and I flew to Amsterdam, and it wasn't clear at that point who was gonna play *Lincoln* or that the film would ever get made, and it had been five years of my life, and I wouldn't trade a minute of any of them, but I thought, "OK, I may have just flushed five years of my writing life down the toilet, and what am I doing?" And I went and I saw Ivo's production, which was done on a completely bare stage; there was not a stick of furniture. If you sat in his production, you just sat on the floor.

I wish I could have seen it.

It was five and a half hours long. They edited it fairly severely, they did both parts. The only thing on the set was a big, like, coffin-shaped thing with an old record player on it, a little like a sixties turntable, and a stack of Bowie records. And when the actors went into a monologue if they felt like they wanted—I don't know, I'm sure this was planned—but they would go over and put like a record on the thing and then start talking. And everybody was in one costume. So the woman playing Hannah played the Rabbi as Hannah and you were just expected to do the math. And the angel was cast, ignoring my instructions, they cast a man, this sort of hot guy in a nurse's costume, who played the nurse, the bag lady—I think they may have cut the bag lady scene—but all those parts that the angel does, and then the angel. And the arrival, at the end of *Millennium*, of the angel . . . the guy playing Prior is on the ground and a Bowie record is playing, and he's doing all this screaming about the lights, and of course nothing's happening, there's some video stuff in the background, but it was just a brick of the theater, this old, nineteenth-century theater. The guy playing the angel just walked out and held out his hands, and Prior took his hands, and the angel just spun him around, really, really fast and then let go, and he shot across the stage on his butt.

And then the angel walked—there's this Bowie record playing—walked up and grabbed him again. And he spun him around again and let go, and he did it like six times. I don't even know how to explain it, but by the end the whole theater was sobbing. It was playful and violent at the same time. Prior wasn't resisting, he was sort of . . . I can barely talk about it without crying. I mean, I don't even know where that came from. And the guy playing Roy, who won all these awards, it's the first time I realized that this is a play about AIDS, but it's also really a play about illness. And by the end of the play, the only costume change is he wore a diaper. And there was a moment where he's walking after the Negro night nurse scene, the scene where he and Belize share these sort of dreams. He took his IV pole, and he starts walking across the stage and he farted. I don't know how he did it—this long, horrible sound, and it was so humiliating and hideous. It really was a play about watching a body die. It was astonishing.

Does that kind of invention happen in the American theater?

About three days later, I ran to CSC and saw Austin Pendleton's production of *Uncle Vanya* with Denis O'Hare and Maggie Gyllenhaal and Peter Sarsgaard and Mamie Gummer, which I thought was like one of the great Chekhov productions I'd ever seen. Of course, all the critics got it completely wrong and didn't like it. They preferred that British thing. Everybody was talking on top of everybody else. The set was designed so if you sat in one place you couldn't see the other. You saw Astrof and Yelena kissing, and Vanya's standing on the other side of the wall with his little flowers for her. Half the audience could see Vanya, but they couldn't see them kissing, but they could see something's wrong. And the other half could see them kissing but couldn't see Vanya, but the audience could watch each other. It was one of those moments in the theater where you just think, "Oh, I mean, yum." But it felt to me, like especially with Ivo's production, like I was being given a message by the end. It's like with all the difficulties of film production and writing for a great film director and everything, the message was, "Come back to the theater—look what you can do with absolutely nothing at all, and look at what you can make."

PLAYWRIGHT BIOGRAPHIES

NILO CRUZ

Plays: *Anna in the Tropics, Beauty of the Father, A Bicycle Country, Dancing on Her Knees, Hortensia and the Museum of Dreams, Lorca in a Green Dress, Night Train to Bolina, A Park in Our House, Two Sisters and a Piano*

Grants and Awards: Pulitzer Prize (2003), American Theatre Critics, Steinberg New Play Award: *Anna in the Tropics;* TCG Artist in Residence Grant; Barrie Stavis Award; Kennedy Center Fund for New American Plays; Alton Jones Award; AT&T Award; Helen Merrill Distinguished Playwriting Award; PEN/Laura Pels Mid-Career Playwriting Award

CHRISTOPHER DURANG

Plays: *The Actor's Nightmare, Adrift in Macao, Baby with the Bathwater, Betty's Summer Vacation, Beyond Therapy, 'dentity Crisis, Durang/Durang* (collection of one-act parodies), *A History of the American Film, The Idiots Karamazov, Laughing Wild, The Marriage of Bette and Boo, Miss Witherspoon, Mrs. Bob Cratchit's Wild Christmas Binge, The Nature and Purpose of the Universe, Sister Mary Ignatius Explains It All for You, Titanic, The Vietnamization of New Jersey, Why Torture Is Wrong and the People Who Love Them*

Grants and Awards: Obie: *Sister Mary Ignatius Explains It All for You, The Marriage of Bette and Boo, Betty's Summer Vacation*; nomination Best Book of a Musical: *A History of the American Film;* Guggenheim, Rockefeller Grants, CBS Playwriting Fellowship, Lecomte du Nouy Foundation Grant, Kenyon Festival Theatre Playwriting Prize; Pulitzer Prize finalist: *Miss Witherspoon*

DAVID GREENSPAN

Plays: *2 Samuel 11, The Argument, The Closet Piece, Coraline: The Musical, Dead Mother or Shirley Not in Vain, Dog in a Dancing School, Five Frozen*

Embryos, Go Back to Where You Are, The Home Show Pieces, Jack, The Myopia, The Old Comedy, She Stoops to Comedy, and numerous monologues

Grants and Awards: Guggenheim, Jerome Foundation, Joyce Mertz-Gilmore Foundation, Charles Revson Foundation; McKnight Fellowship, CalArts Alpert Award, Lucille Lortel Award Foundation Fellowship

JOHN GUARE

Plays: *Atlantic City* (screenplay), *Bosoms and Neglect, Chaucer in Rome, Cop-Out, A Few Stout Individuals, Four Baboons Adoring the Sun, A Free Man of Color, Gardenia, The House of Blue Leaves, Lake Hollywood, Landscape of the Body, Lydie Breeze, Marco Polo Sings a Solo, Moon Over Miami, Muzeeka, Rich and Famous, Six Degrees of Separation, Two Gentlemen of Verona* (musical), *Women and Water;* revised book for *Kiss Me, Kate* and *Sweet Smell of Success* (musical)

Grants and Awards: Obie: *Muzeeka, Six Degrees of Separation;* New York Drama Critics' Circle Award: *The House of Blue Leaves, Six Degrees of Separation, Two Gentlemen of Verona;* Tony Award: *The House of Blue Leaves, Two Gentlemen of Verona;* Drama Desk Award Outstanding Lyrics: *Two Gentlemen of Verona;* Olivier Award and finalist for Pulitzer Prize: *Six Degrees of Separation;* Member American Academy of Arts and Letters and received Award of Merit; Member Theatre Hall of Fame; New York State Governor Arts Award, PEN/Laura Pels Foundation Award

DAVID HARE

Plays: *The Absence of War, Amy's View, The Bay at Nice, The Blue Room, Brassneck* (with Howard Brenton), *The Breath of Life, Fanshen, Gethsemane, The Great Exhibition, The Judas Kiss, Knuckle, A Map of the World, Murmuring Judges, My Zinc Bed, The Permanent Way, Plenty, The Power of Yes, Pravda* (with Howard Brenton), *Racing Demon, The Secret Rapture, Skylight, Slag, Stuff Happens, Teeth 'n' Smiles, The Vertical Hour, Via Dolorosa, Wrecked Eggs*

Film and TV Scripts: *The Corrections* (adapted from the novel by Michael Cunningham), *Damage, Dreams of Leaving, The Hours, Licking Hitler, Murder in Samarkand, The Reader* (screenplay adapted from the novel by Bernard Schlink), *Strapless, Wetherby*

Awards: BAFTA Award: *Licking Hitler, The Hours, The Reader;* New York Drama Critics' Circle Award for Best Foreign Play: *Plenty;* Berlin Film Festival Golden Bear: *Wetherby;* Laurence Olivier Award and London Theatre Critics Award: *Racing Demon;* Evening Standard Award: *Pravda* and *Racing Demon;* Drama Desk Award: *Via Dolorosa;* Golden Globe and Oscar nomination: *The Hours* and *The Reader;* London Critics Circle Award, British Screenwriter of the Year: *The Hours;* Writers Guild of America Award: *The Hours*

DAVID HENRY HWANG

Plays: *Bondage, Chinglish, The Dance and the Railroad, Family Devotions, FOB, Golden Child, The House of Sleeping Beauties, M. Butterfly, Rich Relations, The Sound of a Voice, Trying to Find Chinatown, Yellow Face;* adaptations: *Aida, Flower Drum Song;* opera: *1000 Airplanes on the Roof, The Fly*

Grants and Awards: Obie: *FOB, Golden Child, Yellow Face;* Pulitzer Prize finalist: *The Dance and the Railroad, M. Butterfly, Yellow Face;* Tony, Drama Desk, John Gassner, Outer Critics Circle Award: *M. Butterfly;* Tony nomination: *Golden Child, Flower Drum Song;* Guggenheim, Rockefeller, New York State Council on the Arts, Pew Charitable Trust, National Endowment for the Arts Grants; New York Foundation for the Arts Award; East West Players christened its new main stage the David Henry Hwang Theater.

TONY KUSHNER

Plays: *Angels in America: A Gay Fantasia on National Themes (Part One, Millennium Approaches; Part Two, Perestroika); A Bright Room Called Day; Brundibár* (opera with Maurice Sendak); *Caroline, or Change* (musical); *Henry Box Brown, or The Mirror of Slavery; Homebody/Kabul; Hydriotaphia; The Intelligent Homosexual's Guide to Capitalism and Socialism with a Key to* *the Scriptures; Munich* (screenplay); *Reverse Transcription: Six Playwrights Bury a Seventh, A Ten-Minute Play That's Nearly Twenty Minutes Long; Slavs! Thinking about the Longstanding Problems of Virtue and Happiness; Tiny Kushner: 5 Shorter Plays;* adaptations: *A Dybbuk, or Between Two Worlds; The Good Person of Szechuan; The Illusion; Mother Courage and Her Children; Stella*

Grants and Awards: Tony, Drama Desk: *Millennium Approaches* and *Perestroika;* Pulitzer Prize (1993): *Millennium Approaches;* Drama Desk and Tony nominations: *Caroline, or Change;* Golden Globe, Oscar: *Munich;* First Steinberg Distinguished Playwright Award, Evening Standard, Obie, New York Drama Critics' Circle Award, Glickman Award, American Academy of Arts and Letters Award, Whiting Writers Fellowship, Lila Wallace/Reader Digest Fellowship

LYNN NOTTAGE

Plays: *By the Way, Meet Vera Stark; Crumbs from the Table of Joy; Fabulation, or the Re-Education of Undine; Intimate Apparel; Las Meninas; Mud, River, Stone; Poof; Por'knockers; Ruined*

Grants and Awards: Pulitzer Prize (2009), Obie: *Ruined;* Fellowships: Manhattan Theatre Club, New Dramatists, New York Foundation for the Arts, Playwrights Horizons, Amblin/Dreamworks, National Endowment for the Arts, Guggenheim; Steinberg Distinguished Playwright Award; MacArthur Foundation Fellowship

SUZAN-LORI PARKS

Plays: *365 Days/365 Plays, The America Play, Betting on the Dust Commander, The Book of Grace, The Death of the Last Black Man in the Whole Entire World, Devotees in the Garden of Love, Father Comes Home from the Wars (Parts 1, 8, & 9), Fucking A, Getting Mother's Body* (novel), *Imperceptible Mutabilities in the Third Kingdom, In the Blood, The Sinner's Place, Topdog/Underdog, Venus;* screenplays: *Girl 6, Their Eyes Were Watching God*

Grants and Awards: Pulitzer Prize (2002): *Topdog/Underdog;* Obie: *Imperceptible Mutabilities in the Third Kingdom, Venus;* Whiting Writers'

Award, Lila Wallace Reader's Digest Award, Guggenheim Award; Tony and Drama Desk nominations for *Topdog/Underdog;* Pulitzer Prize finalist for *In the Blood;* MacArthur Foundation Fellowship

SARAH RUHL

Plays: *The Clean House, Dead Man's Cell Phone, Demeter in the City, Eurydice, In the Next Room (or The Vibrator Play), Late: A Cowboy Song, Melancholy Play, Passion Play, Stage Kiss, Virtual Meditations;* adaptations: *Lady with the Lap Dog, Orlando*

GRANTS AND AWARDS: Susan Smith Blackburn Prize and Pulitzer Prize finalist: *The Clean House;* Tony nomination and Pulitzer Prize finalist: *In the Next Room;* Helen Merrill Emerging Playwright Award; Glickman Award; MacArthur Foundation Fellowship

WALLACE SHAWN

Plays: *Aunt Dan and Lemon, The Designated Mourner, Essays* (nonfiction), *The Fever, Grasses of a Thousand Colors, The Hospital Play, The Hotel Play, Marie and Bruce, My Dinner with Andre* (screenplay), *Our Late Night, A Thought in Three Parts;* translations/adaptations: *The Mandrake, The Threepenny Opera*

Grants and Awards: Obie: *Our Late Night, Aunt Dan and Lemon, The Fever;* Boston Society of Film Critics Best Screenplay: *My Dinner with Andre;* American Academy of Arts and Letters Award, Guggenheim, PEN/Laura Pels Foundation Drama Award

PAULA VOGEL

Plays: *And Baby Makes Seven, Apple Brown Betty, The Baltimore Waltz, Bertha in Blue, A Civil War Christmas, Desdemona: A Play About a Handkerchief, Hot 'n' Throbbing, How I Learned to Drive, The Long Christmas Ride Home, Meg, The Mineola Twins, The Oldest Profession, Swan Song of Sir Henry*

Grants and Awards: Obie, Eliot Norton, Edwin Booth Award: *The Baltimore Waltz;* American Academy of Arts and Letters Award; Pulitzer

Prize (1998), Susan Smith Blackburn, New York Drama Critics' Circle, Obie, Drama Desk, Lucille Lortel Award, Outer Critics Circle, Hull-Warriner Award: *How I Learned To Drive*; American Academy of Arts and Letters; PEN/Laura Pels Award, Guggenheim, Fund for New American Plays, AT&T New Play Award, two National Endowment for the Arts Fellowships; in 2003 the Kennedy Center American College Theatre Festival established the Paula Vogel Playwriting Award.

DOUG WRIGHT

Plays: *The Creditors* (adaption), *Dinosaurs, I Am My Own Wife, Interrogating the Nude, Quills, The Stonewater Rapture, Watbanaland;* musicals: *Buzzsaw Berkeley, Grey Gardens, The Little Mermaid*

Grants and Awards: Kesselring Prize, Obie: *Quills;* Pulitzer Prize (2004), Tony, Toleranzpreis Europa: *I Am My Own Wife;* Charles MacArthur Fellowship at the O'Neill Center, HBO Fellowship, Alfred Hodder Fellowship, United States Artists Fellow